Face Value

To Ted, Jr. —
With best wishes,

Cary Carson.

2 · 2017

Face Value

>>>><<<<

The Consumer Revolution
and the Colonizing of America

CARY CARSON

University of Virginia Press
Charlottesville and London

University of Virginia Press
© 2017 by the Rector and Visitors of the University of Virginia
All rights reserved
Printed in the United States of America on acid-free paper

First published 2017

ISBN 978-0-8139-3936-0 (cloth)
ISBN 978-0-8139-3937-7 (paper)
ISBN 978-0-8139-3938-4 (ebook)

9 8 7 6 5 4 3 2 1

Library of Congress Cataloging-in-Publication Data is available from the Library of Congress.

Cover art: *Portrait of Elizabeth Boush*, by John Durand, Norfolk, Virginia, 1769, oil on canvas. (The Colonial Williamsburg Foundation, Museum Purchase, accession #1982-271)

To the memory of
Barbara Gilbert Carson
My teacher too

Nowhere in the world has shared culture been a more imperative require-ment than in America. More than 300 million people live here, and they had descended over the course of a very few generations from a huge number of disparate cultures, with different histories, ways of behavior, worldviews and experiential backgrounds. All of them, sooner or later, had been required to relinquish their old culture and enter the new one. That must be why the most striking thing about the United States [today is] its sameness.

—Karl Ove Knausgaard, "My Saga, Part 2,"
New York Times Magazine, March 11, 2015

Contents

Illustrations

Preface

This book marks the second coming of this essay. It debuted more than twenty years ago in a collection of papers that was presented first at a U.S. Capitol Historical Society symposium in Washington, D.C.[1] After that meeting, Ronald Hoffman, the conference organizer, encouraged the authors to revise and expand their talks for publication. I am afraid that I took liberties with Hoffman's invitation and later his forbearance. Having much more I wanted to say and a daytime job that left too few hours to write an entire book, I jumped at the chance to piggyback a novella-sized treatise on top of an otherwise respectable collection of conference proceedings. My chapter tipped the scales at 215 printed pages! Whether that burden fatally weighed down the volume is hard to say. But the collected essays, entitled *Of Consuming Interests,* soon went out of print and dropped out of sight.

 Curiously that was not the end of it, however much deserved. As the years went by, I occasionally heard rumors that my contribution, "Why Demand?," was alive and well and leading an underground life as a bootleg facsimile that popped up here and there on college syllabi. Along the way it acquired a reputation. It became what one colleague termed a cult classic. The cultists were mostly teachers and students of architectural and decorative arts history and American and material culture studies. Eventually even they could no longer find secondhand copies to Xerox and scan. It was then that teachers and colleagues began urging me to consider updating the material and reprinting the oversized essay as a stand-alone publication. To humor them and, as I will explain in a moment, to try again to reach an audience that had largely missed the original publication, I approached the University of Virginia Press, the original publisher, by then under new management. The encouragement I received led to the comeback book that follows.

Out of print is not reason enough to reprint. Scholarship moves on. So has the scholarship that stands behind this revision. Historians, archaeologists, architectural historians, curators, and students of material culture have added depth and breadth to subjects that I could only touch on or guess at twenty years ago. I have adjusted my retelling of the story accordingly and cited these newer works in the endnotes.

Otherwise the organization of the book remains much as before for good reason. However much the original essay has enjoyed classroom use in the years since its initial publication, back then I was writing for another audience altogether. I consider myself to be a straight-ahead historian of early modern America, notwithstanding the special skills I have had to learn as an architectural historian and a student of decorative arts to do my work. Consequently my chapter in *Of Consuming Interests* was deliberately pitched to two issues vigorously debated by mainstream economic and cultural historians, then and still today. The origins of demand for the manufactured goods that eventually it took an Industrial Revolution to supply was one. The other had to do with the rise and spread of gentry culture in the seventeenth and eighteenth centuries. I had hoped that the interpretive argument I published in my expanded conference paper would contribute to the historical discourse in both areas. I was disappointed. In reality the essay attracted little notice. The reason was partly because my argument was buried in a collection of essays that caught the eye of few economic historians (Jan de Vries being a notable exception) or because it failed to come to the attention of cultural historians who continued to write about the history of the consumer revolution itself. Partly too the essay simply disappeared when the book went out of print.

Although here it is now resurrected, expanded, updated, and repackaged between its own two covers, the essay is still essentially an argument, a hypothesis to test, a case to be made. It is the solution I offer to a thorny historical problem posed by economists—why demand?—and, at the same time, my explanation for the appearance of a remarkably new kind of visual literacy beginning in the seventeenth century. Scholars have continued to write about and debate both topics since I weighed in with my essay. Be that as it may, I have chosen to cite these more recent works in the endnotes rather than discuss them directly in the text if they have not substantially altered the thrust of the argument I presented in the original essay and do again in these pages.

Two newer books have. Two exceptions have earned special notice. The first is Jan de Vries's *The Industrious Revolution: Consumer Behavior and the Household Economy, 1650 to the Present* and the other Timothy Breen's *The Marketplace of Revolution: How Consumer Politics Shaped American Independence.*[2] Both appeared ten or more years after my essay, and both bear directly on the interpretation it advanced. Each prompted me to rethink parts of my argument. The resulting adjustments are called out in this revision, but only insofar as they recast my line of reasoning or enrich its implications. A historian's brief, for that is what this book sets out to be, is not the place to review and substantially critique other works of scholarship, however significant. I am building a case here as lean and mean as I can make it in hopes that this time it will engage the audiences that it was always intended for and thereby contribute to the historical inquiries it missed the first time around.

Readers looking for more general treatments of consumer behavior and the consumer revolution from the seventeenth century onward will find the canons acknowledged and cited in the endnotes to chapter 1. The essay I wrote twenty years ago was raised on a foundation of pioneering books and articles by J. H. Plumb, John Brewer, Jean-Christophe Agnew, Neil McKendrick, Lorna Weatherill, and, for the American colonies, Carole Shammas, Richard Bushman, and Timothy Breen.[3] Since then, still others have written additional broad-brush books on the topic, usually, like me, with an interpretive angle that connects the fact of a consumer revolution to something else that we now see quite differently as a result. Chief among them are these few, starting with Woodruff Smith's *Consumption and the Making of Respectability, 1600–1800.* If consumer culture can be said to have an intellectual history, this dissection of respectability into its components comes close. Smith arrives at a comprehensive understanding of consumer behavior by joining together the several contexts (his word) in which it bred—gentility, luxury, virtue, and masculinity and femininity.

Also not to be overlooked is Linda Levy Peck's *Consuming Splendor: Society and Culture in Seventeenth-Century England,* an account of high-end luxury consumption among Jacobean courtiers and London's merchant princes that becomes a prelude, full of surprises, to Maxime Berg's *Luxury and Pleasure in Eighteenth-Century Britain.* Berg has written a full-blown life history of what she calls the product revolution, her term for the whole remarkable, complicated, and at first very British achievement of inventing, making, marketing, selling, buying, and ultimately using and enjoying the myriad goods and gewgaws that improved the lives of a great many middling Britons in the eighteenth century. For newcomers to the British literature, Berg is now the place to start.

Historians of colonial America have also had more to say on the subject recently. The first part of Timothy Breen's *Marketplace of Revolution,* already mentioned, brings the British story and "An Empire of Goods" to the colonies. It is the fullest account so far of Americans' consumption of imported manufactures up to the moment in the 1760s and 1770s when those goods became chess pieces in a war of nerves with Parliament and British tax collectors, the subject Breen addresses in part two. Kate Haulman's *The Politics of Fashion in Eighteenth-Century America* approaches consumer politics from another angle by reading gender into the imperial crisis and going on to explain how men's and women's sartorial choices continued to stir up republican politics after the War for Independence was won. In *Purchasing Identity in the Atlantic World: Massachusetts Merchants, 1670–1780,* Phyllis Whitman Hunter writes about self-fashioning in a different way. Her protagonists, prominent merchant-capitalist families in Boston and Salem (and by implication entrepreneurs elsewhere), invigorated commerce and transformed the culture of urban life by embracing and flaunting new-model gentility. As I do, she attaches significance to the mobility of widely traveled merchants and their cultivation of gentility. Finally one more title rounds out the reading list of newer works: David Jaffee's *A New Nation of Goods,* a book that shows how a post-Revolutionary generation of village artisan entrepreneurs refashioned and made affordable for a multitude of middle-class consumers goods that previously had been imported or city-made for sale to more affluent buyers. This volume supplies an important missing link between eighteenth-century consumer studies and a vast literature on mass production in Victorian America.[4]

These and other important recent works add depth and interest to a number of topics dealt with in the pages that follow. But because they do not seriously deflect the trajectory of the argument that drives the narrative, I have been content simply to call readers' attention to them in endnote citations wherever they best pertain, with the exception of the books by De Vries and Breen. One of the pleasures of revising the original essay was discovering how rich and connected consumer studies have become in the meantime.

Some of that richness accounts for the most significant new material that this book-length edition now takes into account. Historians have widened their study of consumer behavior in the last two decades to include whole groups of people who were easily overlooked in the first flush of scholarship, when fashion-conscious ladies and gentlemen in Britain and Europe and their counterparts in the colonies were so obviously the central players. We now know that manufactured consumer goods insinuated themselves into the lives of many people on the margins of polite society as well. Accordingly my overall hypothesis is now further supported with this newfound evidence. It draws on work by archaeologists and historians who have explored the hybrid material cultures of African Americans—both enslaved and free—Indians, and many immigrant Europeans who came to British North America still in full possession of time-honored folk customs from homelands all over northern and central Europe. Their acquisition and often their creative adaptation of English-made goods add complications to the way we understand how a visual language of objects communicated with individuals and groups across a broader spectrum of class, gender, race, and culture than was known previously. Those complexities were hidden from view twenty years ago before much of this new research was undertaken.

Recent consumer studies have opened new geographical territories as well. They have enlarged the study area where people's consumption of goods can now be closely observed, analyzed, and thereby made intelligible. The backcountry and the Carolinas are welcome newcomers to the early American literature. Even so, two outside readers who reviewed this manuscript for the press expressed surprise that the action still takes place for the most part in southern New England and the Chesapeake colonies of Maryland and Virginia. Those regions are still home to the best, data-rich, probate inventory studies that give depth to generalizations about consumer behavior across entire communities. A general survey such as this one can only venture confidently where the groundwork has been thoroughly prepared. For the time being, I am satisfied to leave to the next generation of younger historians and archaeologists the task of bushwhacking my thesis into terrae incognitae, testing it there, and making whatever adjustments the new and different evidence warrants.

Abroad, economic historians have gone on to explore living standards in several parts of northern Europe that were unstudied two decades ago. Their work falls outside the scope of mine for the most part, but it has been useful (and so is cited) in drawing a picture of the cultural transformations that accompanied emigrants to North America from far beyond the British Isles.

Eager as I am for this book to engage with working historians, loyal fans of the original essay—the cultists—have been much on my mind as I prepared this revised and expanded edition. *Face Value* is therefore also designed for classroom use. A thin volume to start with, the prominence it gives to a closely reasoned argument about two great transformations in Western society—one economic, the other cultural—invites teachers and students to test my hypothesis against other interpretations of these events. A further aid to teachers are the extensive endnotes, now fully updated. These can serve as roadmaps for newcomers into literatures as specialized as medieval furniture, animism, and the luxury debates and as generalized as European and African diasporas, modernization theory, and the Industrial Revolution itself. Along the way, readers will find mentioned in the notes many topics that deserve further investigation. Some of them would make good research papers, and a few might be expanded and expounded upon in theses and dissertations.

I have included something else specially for teachers and students: photographs and drawings that are not illustrations in the usual sense. The figures in this volume do not simply show readers pictures of things that are otherwise described in the text. I have chosen them, drawn them myself, or engaged a technical illustrator to draw them to my specifications because students of consumer revolution history must not forget that objects and images are sometimes indispensable primary sources of historical evidence in their own right. Researchers miss a bet if they fail to reckon with the very things that consumers consumed. Not always, but often, buildings, landscapes, furnishings, clothing, and other personal possessions hold information about the past that documents pass over in silence.[5]

Some of the figures found in these pages are more akin to pictographs than to conventional illustrations. They are pictorial representations of data, different from but not unlike tables and graphs that transmute quantitative data into something visual. The illustrations here are not simply to be looked at, but studied and deciphered. That said, paintings, drawings, and even photographs seldom speak for themselves. They are interpretations contrived by their creators and further construed by my selection of them here. For that reason, more substantial captions accompany most of the figures. The captions complement the images by inviting readers to look hard at the visual evidence for information that amplifies the text. In so doing, they demonstrate what more can be learned from a knowledgeable examination of objects and images. That lesson too should prove useful to classroom teachers who would convince students that three-dimensional things can and should be taken at more than face value.

That done, we come now to the organization of the book as a whole. As debaters know, a formal argument opens with a proposition, something asserted, something to be parsed and then proved or disproved. Proponents marshal the best evidence they can offer to make their case. Chapters 1 through 6 are presented in this fashion. The first sets out to find an answer to the question *why demand?* by advancing a series of four propositions that can be inferred (or sometimes only hypothesized) from research that bears on the matter at hand, even though in some cases it was undertaken by scholars who were studying something else altogether. The first chapter concludes with a fifth and final proposition that sets out a premise that becomes the brief I argue throughout the rest of the book.

To better understand how the meaning and use of everyday objects changed over several centuries, chapters 2 and 3 set up a contrast between folk consumers (the users of things before my story begins) and men and women who acquired personal possessions beginning in the seventeenth century which answered needs that ordinary people had not felt previously. Chapter 3 begins an analysis that continues in the next. Both dissect one by one the pieces of furniture, images, and tablewares that were newly invented to meet these needs in the second half of the seventeenth century. Conventional treatments of early consumer behavior often illustrate the worldly goods that consumers acquired. Few however ask how their appearance and function enabled users to do whatever it was that those things were expected to do, or, to put it another way, to do what could not be accomplished without them. Eventually students of the history of material life learn to understand that the physical form of things informed fundamentally the functions they served. No matter what symbolic or aesthetic values personal and household objects may have possessed, they were first and foremost tools, stage props, necessary to the socially acceptable performance of people's everyday activities. Those object-rich performances were greatly elaborated as the practice of gentility spread to the four corners of the colonized world before 1700 and ever more rapidly thereafter. Chapters 4 and 5 assemble the props and set in motion the genteel performances that finally demonstrate the *why* of why demand.

Closing arguments are presented in chapter 6. My aim here is to explain Americans' exceptional need for consumer goods in American terms. How did this wide open land of opportunity earn dual reputations as both "the best poor man's country" and a ferociously materialistic society where "pride of wealth" trumped all other values? Here the propositions that opened the book are matched and tempered by two opposing corollaries that round out my defense and finally rest my case.

Chapter 7, the last one, is intended for readers who want to raise the hood and talk car talk. Most will be students of material culture—

those cultists again—who are curious to know how writing social and cultural history that draws heavily on artifacts as evidence is both similar to and different from history writing that relies mostly on quantitative data or written records. The final chapter puts the case I have been making in the rest of the book into company with a long-running historical debate about the transfer and transformation of American culture from its European roots.

Out of that comes one last thing, a prescription for a new and different kind of social history. To tell the truth, I always had an ulterior motive for wanting to republish this essay. The last chapter takes the wraps off my hidden agenda. It gives voice to my conviction that there is a large and important realm of human endeavor that warrants concerted investigation and deserves to be known as *the history of material life*. This book as a whole is offered as an example and, if the last chapter finishes the job, a model. After twenty years, it is a great satisfaction to me to know that my essay has finally come in out of the cold and back into the classroom.

A book so long in the making, even a slender one, needs help to cross the finish line. Friends, colleagues, teachers, and here and there perfect strangers have offered advice, set me straight, and shared their own work with me from the inception of this project as a conference paper to its culmination now as a late-bloomer book. The many Good Samaritans include Peter Albert, Laura Pass Barry, Linda Baumgarten, Michael Bourne, Joanne Bowen, Susan Buck, Nancy Carlisle, Lois Green Carr, Purcell Carson, Edward Chappell, Tara Chicirda, Emma Christopher, Brice Clagget, Juleigh Clarke, Abbott Lowell Cummings, Andrew Edwards, Wies Erkelens, Inge Flester, Peter Follansbee, Jillian Galle, Patricia Gibbs, Harold Gill, Eric Goldstein, Willie Graham, Heather Harvey, Cathy Hellier, Ronald Hoffman, Graham Hood, Carter Hudgins Sr., Robert Hunter, Silas Hurry, Ronald Hurst, Peter Inker, Rhys Isaac, Odai Johnson, Martha Katz-Hyman, Kevin Kelly, Julia King, Jeff Klee, Angelika Kuettner, Jon Kukla, Nancy Kurtz, Kelly Ladd, Hans Lorenz, Carl Lounsbury, Nick Lucchetti, Gloria Main, Ann Smart Martin, Marianne Martin, George Miller, Henry Miller, Tricia Miller, Del Moore, David Muraca, Ivor Noël Hume, Jonathan Owen, Meredith Moody Poole, Emma Lou Powers,

Margaret Pritchard, Joanne Proper, Jonathan Prown, Kym Rice, Timothy Riordan, Linda Rowe, Susan Shames, David Shields, Bly Straube, Robert St. George, Garry Wheeler Stone, Kevin Sweeney, Paul Touart, Robert Trent, Dell Upton, Carolyn Weekley, Camille Wells, Mark Wenger, and Wendy Woloson.

Two lifelong colleagues deserve special thanks. I have discussed many subjects covered in this book for so many years with my friend Lorena Walsh that I can no longer remember or sort out all the contributions she has made to my thinking. Not only has her generosity always been unstinting, her deep knowledge of early American and early modern British history and her keen editorial eye made her my ultimate reader of choice long ago.

If Lorena is my preferred expert of last resort, Fraser Neiman has often been the first to whom I turn for advice. Formally trained in both philosophy and anthropology, time and again he has been a dependable guide as I sought to pick my way through the treacherous and always shifting sands of archaeological method and theory. However much I have deliberately buried my own methodological articles of faith in a few footnotes, I openly acknowledge that no other confidant has so greatly influenced the way I understand how human history works.

I have run up still other debts to those who helped me turn a recycled manuscript into this book. They start with the anonymous outside readers recruited by the press. There were two, a good cop and a bad cop. Both favored publication. Their very different recommendations pushed subsequent revisions in two directions. The enthusiastic reader urged me not to forget the strengths that sustained the original essay during its long exile in the wilderness. Those I preserved and reinforced. The more critical reader's comments challenged me to explain forthrightly how my twenty-year-old interpretation of the consumer revolution tallied with more recent scholarship. This preface and the additions and amendments made to several chapters take account of that too. The book is a better book and I a better historian for the advice I received from both readers.

The editors and designers at the press have been true to the interest they expressed several years ago in republishing the 1994 essay if I were willing to bring it up to date and "re-vision" it, as they like to say. Boyd

Zenner, architecture and environment editor, deftly steered the draft manuscript through the review and approval processes. Later, assistant managing editor Mark Mones fine-tuned the prose much to my liking and advantage. Along the way, design and production manager Martha Farlow came up with a layout plan that somehow made room for easy-to-read illustrations alongside extended captions. On Martha's retirement, a new team, Sylvia Mendoza (design and production manager) and Cecilia Sorochin (senior designer and assistant production manager) brought fresh eyes to the page layouts and a playful wink to the jacket design.

The last acknowledgment, but really the first, foremost, and most endearing tribute, I save for Barbara. She was my classmate in the Winterthur Program where this all began so long ago and, after that, my wife and intellectual companion for forty-seven years. This book is dedicated to her.

Face Value

I

⟫⟫⟫⟫⟫⟫⟩⟨⟨⟨⟨⟨⟨⟨

WHY DEMAND?

Hear tell the familiar story of the Industrial Revolution in England and America. Textbook after textbook intones the standard recitation. Once upon a time in the reign of George III a "string of important inventions in a few industries began a profound alteration of the British economy."[1] Steam engines, flying shuttles, water frames, and power looms, operated by men, women, and children summoned to work by a factory bell, produced prodigious quantities of inexpensive personal and household goods. Machine-made textiles, pottery, ironmongery, and a multitude of other "necessities," "decencies," and affordable "luxuries" were transported over improved roads and along newly built canals to markets in every corner of the realm. There they were snapped up by a rapidly growing population of eager consumers. These were people who waxed healthier, wealthier, and happier than ever before on rising wages, falling death rates, and a diet of roast beef and white bread supplied by model farmers and progressive stockbreeders. Echoing the modern corporate slogan "Better Things for Better Living," orthodox histories long ago endorsed a supply-side explanation for the events that led to industrial and commercial expansion. They presented consumer demand as a universal given, as immutable as mankind's quest for a dry cave and a square meal. Mechanization, the factory system, faster cheaper transportation, and new banking and credit facilities were simply those English-made miracles that finally in the eighteenth century drove down the cost and increased the supply of goods and services that everyone had always wanted and that ordinary people could now afford.

Industrial progress, traditional schoolbooks implied, thrived on freedom and waited on genius. Histories of the United States provided the classic example. Because Old World mercantilists had frowned on colonial manufacturers, Americans first had to win independence, then steal British industrial secrets, to bring the factory system to these shores. Soon thereafter the wheels began to turn and the spindles spin. The rest was textbook history: "A great change in American ways of making things soon reshaped American ways of living." Colonists "had made the things they needed in their own homes and for their own use. Now goods were produced in factories and by machines for sale to anybody willing to pay for them." Projected into the future, these events eventually created "an American Standard of Living." This version of history was even more supply driven than the one in which the Industrial Revolution sated a universal natural appetite for consumer goods. Mass production in the United States not only met existing demand, aggressive merchandisers deliberately created a market of "new consumers needed to buy the masses of goods now produced in the factories."[2]

Either way, the main lines of the cause-and-effect, supply-and-demand argument remained largely uncontested either by historians or economists until recently. Conveniently, their unanimity seemed to be confirmed by the observations of numerous eyewitnesses from the eighteenth century. Listen, for example, to one of many contemporary voices, this one Henry Fielding's, heard not in his fiction, but in the pages of a pamphlet on public policy.[3] "Nothing," he observed, "hath wrought such an Alternation in this Order of People, as the Introduction of Trade." He described the extraordinary consequences: "This hath indeed given a new Face to the whole Nation, hath in a great measure subverted the former State of Affairs, and hath almost totally changed the Manners, Customs, and Habits of the People, more especially of the lower Sort. The Narrowness of their Fortune is changed into Wealth; the Simplicity of their Manners into Craft; their Frugality into Luxury; their Humility into Pride, and their Subjugation into Equality." Prosperity, equality, luxury, and pride—the virtues and vices of modern life, the blessings and blights of mass production and mass marketing.

Two hundred years did little to alter history's verdict. Few doubted that the Industrial Revolution awakened an enormous unquenchable thirst for material goods. It sired the race of getters and spenders that we all have become, we Americans nonpareil. The essential truth of supply-side economics stood unchallenged as the incontrovertible central thesis that explained the genesis of our consumer societies in the industrialized nations of the West.

Incontrovertible except, it turned out, for one little problem, one awkward fact: *Demand came first.*

Henry Fielding was writing in 1751. Already what he called "the former state of affairs" was a memory. Already the manners, customs, habits, and possessions of very ordinary people had "almost totally changed." Nor was his polemic the earliest one of its kind. The downward and outward spread of luxury had been a favorite target of preachers and pamphleteers for going on fifty years. Before Arkwright, before Watt, before Hargreaves, Wedgwood, Boulton, and Kay, almost before even Abraham Darby, people up and down the social order had discovered and were indulging the most extraordinary passion for consumer goods in quantities and varieties that had been unknown, even unimaginable, to their fathers and grandfathers. It was indeed a revolution, but a *consumer* revolution in the beginning. The better-known Industrial Revolution followed in response.

Only recently have historians begun to understand and present this story the right way round. It makes a difference. Putting the consumer revolution first opens the door to a broad retelling of seventeenth- and eighteenth-century British and American history. At a stroke it places a vast body of historical evidence—much of it visual and three-dimensional—in the service of history-writing that too often has ignored art, artifacts, and architecture altogether. Either that, or quarantined them in separate histories of their own. This book draws heavily on these neglected sources and goes on to explore the implications of the new perspectives they open to the past.

The problem of chronology—which came first, supply or demand?—is not significant in its own right. Chicken-or-egg propositions are seldom useful starting points for historical research, and certainly not for students of industrialization. Revisionists who set out along that path will trip up over ample evidence to support the conventional and entirely accurate view that eighteenth-century manufacturers and retailers deliberately created markets for products and services where none had existed previously. I would have little success trying to deny that, once people began thinking and behaving like consumers, they became fair game to swarms of entrepreneurs who quickly spotted markets to exploit and expand.

There is a more important purpose to be served by paying careful attention to the timing of these events. It acknowledges that a dramatic rise in consumer demand after 1690 or so was sustained for decades by workbench artisans using old-fashioned technologies improved in only a few minor ways at best. Putting a demand-driven consumer revolution before power-driven industrialization begs questions that historians have been slow to ask. It shifts their perspective from the means of production to the consumption of the goods produced. It challenges them to reexamine the notion that demand is a constant that has remained strangely impervious to the forces of historical change that alter other aspects of culture.

At first, asking *why demand* requires seeking answers to even more basic questions. What goods did people really acquire? How did they use them? How were people's everyday lives changed by their possession of newfangled artifacts and the things they could do with them? Who shared in the wealth of material possessions? How evenly or unevenly were they distributed, and how did those differences recalibrate the social order? Descriptions of material life eventually send historians in search of explanations. What caused ordinary people at certain times in the past to spend their sometimes meager earnings on expendable goods and services in preference to longer-lasting investments? Why was there demand for some things at one time and different things at others? Why did the pace of consumption quicken so dramatically in the eighteenth century?

Ultimately historians who pursue this line of inquiry end up exploring a set of fundamental relationships in modern society. These are social relationships, to be sure, but with this difference: they require the intercession of inanimate agents—namely, the household goods and personal possessions whose ownership and use first became widespread among northern Europeans and North Americans in the eighteenth century. Artifacts and the activities to which they were instrumental defined group identities and mediated relations between individuals and the social worlds they inhabited. We ourselves take the facilitating role of material things for granted. Competence in understanding and using the "language" of artifacts is learned along with the ability to speak, read, and write. Actually it is a far more general form of literacy than the latter two. Ours has become a very complex material culture; two hundred years ago it was simpler; three hundred years ago very much simpler almost everywhere the world around. Only small groups of affluent courtiers, prelates, merchant princes, and other elites had always led well-furnished lives of luxury.

The consumer revolution changed all that. That is the term historians now give to that great transformation when whole nations learned to use a rich and complicated medium of communications to conduct social relations that were no longer adequately served by parochial repertories of words, gestures, and folk customs alone. Artifacts expanded the vocabulary of an international language that was learned and understood wherever fashion and gentility spread.

For a time the old handcraft industries supplied the needs of the first new consumers. But they could not keep pace, and, as venture capitalists came to see the tremendous potential for growth in home markets in England and in overseas markets in the colonies, the search began for new technologies to increase production and new sales strategies to enlarge those markets. Consumer revolution and Industrial Revolution were mutually necessary and complementary sides to events that textbooks must put back together again—the right way round—before we can appreciate the full significance of one of the great divides in the chronicle of human experience. When one looks back on the whole history of material life, it exaggerates nothing to say that the mass of humanity were only rudimentary tool users before the eighteenth century. A bare hundred years later, by 1800, everyday life for many people in England, northern Europe, and North America was scarcely livable without a cupboard or a chest of drawers full of things they used to deal with virtually everyone they encountered every day—family, friends, neighbors, fellow workers, business associates, servants, slaves, and perfect strangers.

Why? Historians want reasons that explain why material things became so essential to the conduct of social relations starting only two or three centuries ago. They see it as a historical problem, of course, but the issue draws its intellectual vitality from something that concerns a larger body of thoughtful citizens, as good scholarship in history should. Recent trends in our national life have reopened a debate about the celebrated American standard of living and our persistent belief in a beneficent materialism. For a generation now the poor in this country have been getting poorer, absolutely poorer in terms of real disposable per capita income. There have been other periods when the value of wages declined, but the prolonged slump now coincides with an unparalleled glut in new consumer goods and services available to those higher up the economic ladder whose buying power remains constant. The growing disparity between rich and poor, or more accurately and significantly, between rich and middle, puts at risk a basic element in the American Dream, the promise of almost universal access to a shared material culture.[4]

For generations that aspiration helped unite a nation of immigrants into a democracy of fellow consumers.[5] Compared to a world deeply divided between haves and have-nots, Americans are fortunate always to have been a nation of haves and not-yets. That appears to be changing. We therefore need to consider what consequences might follow were the wages of hardworking men and women to deteriorate so far that they and their children gave up all hope of eventually participating in the consumer culture that has served as one of the great equalizing influences in American life. Meaningful solutions are the province of politicians and policy-makers. We look to historians for the hindsight that helps sort out the real issues from the specious ones and, in this case, to learn how it happened that we Americans, more than any people on earth, came to require such an orgy of goods and gadgets just to keep us steady on our daily course.

That history—the rise and spread of a consumer society—is no longer the neglected topic it once was.[6] Yet, given the newness of historians' interest in the subject, it is hardly surprising that studies launched from different academic disciplines are only now arriving at a common destination after traveling along separate intellectual paths. There are, first of all, economic historians who study the wealth of nations and have discovered a notable increase in people's consumption of durable goods around 1700.[7] There are political economists who believe that this shift was reflected in the importance that economic theorists began giving to home markets from the 1690s onward.[8] Literary scholars and intellectual historians note an extraordinary outpouring of eighteenth-century books, pamphlets, and sermons on the subject of luxury and decadence.[9] Art historians see the middle and upper middle classes portrayed in countless paintings and prints that are both product and record of a new affluence and leisured lifestyle.[10] Cultural historians chart the spread of gentility and etiquette-book manners.[11] Pattern books also interest architectural historians, who see more than coincidence in the appearance of numerous inexpensive handbooks popularizing a standardized classical architecture at just the time when vernacular building traditions were losing their hold on the folk imagination.[12]

So it goes among other historical disciplines as well. The history of technology,[13] business history,[14] and even political history[15] have responded to the sense historians have that people's basic attitudes toward themselves as individuals and their place in the social order underwent a fundamental change in the years immediately before and after the turn of the seventeenth century. Among the many consequences, none was more novel or conspicuous than the pleasure that men and women took in their physical well-being and the value they placed on material things.

Something new was in the air. About that historians are sure. *What* it was they find easier to say than *why*. Some have attempted explanations, but the reasons they give tell us less about the origins of demand than about the preconditions that they argue had to be present before consumers could finally fulfill the ambitions that had long been burning holes in their pockets. If anything, arguments based on propitious circumstances only strengthen the simplistic view that these new wants were intrinsic to the human condition, that they awaited only the lifting of demographic, economic, and commercial constraints to achieve some inevitable, natural fulfillment. What has been mostly missing in the literature so far is a serious attempt to explain the mainsprings of demand in terms of the commodities that eighteenth-century consumers consumed. There had always been Joneses to keep up with, even in peasant communities. Social upmanship was nothing new. The real question is why social standing came to be measured not by the number of cows a man owned or his acres of ploughland but by the cut of his coat and the fashionableness of his wife's tea table.

We ourselves are so used to reading status into objects that it takes a conscious effort of imagination to see an older, unfamiliar world through the eyes of a man like William Cobbett. He decried the forces of change that were encouraging plain ordinary farmers to turn themselves into "mock gentlefolks" by furnishing their sturdy, old-fashioned farmhouses with mahogany tables, fine chairs, and woven carpets—"all," he wrote contemptuously, "as bare-faced upstart as any stockjobber in the kingdom can boast of."[16] Who can dismiss his incredulity? If historians would but stop and think about it, the pursuit of fashion is indeed surpassing strange. What reasons can be offered to explain the extraordinary meteoric demand for commodities that finally took an Industrial Revolution to supply?

Historians from several contributing disciplines are busy investigating people's overt behavior as consumers. They are discovering where changing living conditions expanded the boundaries of human experience in the eighteenth century. Their scholarship has developed lines of force that arguably follow deeper realities which, although still hidden from view, begin little by little to define the shape of explanations that one day we will see more clearly. For the time being it is safe only to hazard an answer to the question, *why demand,* by stating it in the form of assumptions and propositions to be tested by research, most of it not yet finished, some of it not yet begun.

The argument I pursue in the pages that follow is therefore organized around five summary propositions and two corollaries that add up to a broad historical interpretation of this central theme in modern life. From them we may also speculate why circumstances peculiar to the American colonies may have favored the ready acceptance and rapid spread of the highly developed materialistic culture that has seemed so characteristic of this country ever since. Because much of the ground that this interpretation covers is still unfamiliar terrain, there are good reasons to arrive at these propositions one at a time by considering those aspects of the subject that historians have already begun to explore.

As so often happens, the first discoveries were largely serendipitous. Beachcombing through records as seemingly dissimilar as probate inventories, storekeepers' accounts, vernacular buildings, and faunal remains from archaeological sites, historians and anthropologists began to see related patterns in both the physical and the documentary evidence. The story they tell goes something like this. Beginning in England as early as the sixteenth century and soon thereafter in its newly settled North American colonies, people gradually became better furnished, better clothed, better fed, and better sheltered than ordinary folk had ever been before. W. G. Hoskins first called attention to the "rebuilding of rural England" some sixty years ago.[17] Subsequent research has adjusted his dates and refined his conclusions, but the idea that medieval peasant houses were almost everywhere rebuilt or extensively remodeled during the two centuries before 1700 is now accepted orthodoxy.[18]

Periods of widespread rebuilding mark the history of early American architecture as well. The earliest was largely completed within two generations by the most affluent settlers in New England. By constrast rebuilding in the Chesapeake colonies was prolonged for almost two centuries.[19] Everywhere the consequences were similar for the occupants of improved dwellings. Where poor, impermanent buildings were replaced by houses built with durable, weather-tight materials, the lives of their inhabitants became warmer, drier, and more comfortable. Innovations in the arrangement of interior space had even more far-reaching effects on domestic life, in small houses as well as large. The building of chimneys, upper floors, and connecting passages partitioned old-fashioned open halls and cavernous multipurpose rooms into warrens of smaller, warmer compartments conducive to social segregation, specialization, and privacy.[20] Built-in ovens put new foods on the dinner table. Glazed windows brought in light and kept out cold. The evolution of the modern house as we know it—one big box containing many smaller boxes inhabited exclusively by humans and no longer shared with farm animals—was largely complete *before* the end of the seventeenth century, *before* the consumer revolution really got underway.

Further improvements followed from a noticeable increase in the use of furniture and household equipment. There is sufficient antiquaries' testimony to document a "great (although not general) amendment in lodging" in Britain going back to the middle of the sixteenth century.[21] But it has been left primarily to historians of early America to explore basic standards of living among ordinary people by making systematic use of probate inventories. By and large they find little evidence of fashion-conscious consumers before the eighteenth century. These still were men and women who acquired and learned to use, often for the first time, tools that we consider essential to everyday life—tables, bedsteads, frying pans, forks, and individualized drinking vessels. Many small planters in seventeenth-century Maryland and Virginia, which scholars have studied most thoroughly, lived all their lives almost completely without furnishings. They slept on mattresses laid on dirt floors, ate pot-boiled stews and hominies prepared in the only available cooking utensil in the house, and sat on boxes and storage chests or just squatted on their haunches for want of stools, chairs, or benches. Middling farmers, who were marginally better off than their poorer neighbors, usually provided themselves first with pans and spits to prepare more varied meals, then with additional sheets and blankets and perhaps a bedstead, and only thereafter with tables and chairs.[22]

Beyond these basic necessities, wealthier householders accumulated more goods of the same kind, plus a few such traditional amenities as candles, extra linen, and silver plate. But their inventories reveal that there were no agreed-upon luxuries that upper-class planters acquired in order to assume a distinctively affluent lifestyle. A traveler to Virginia in 1715 was surprised to find that one of the colony's most prominent gentlemen, "though rich . . . has nothing in or about his house but what is necessary." There were "good beds," but no bed curtains, "and instead of cane chairs," the traveler noted, "he hath stools made of wood."[23]

Inventory studies in the Carolinas, Pennsylvania, and New England paint a sketchy but similar picture of ill-furnished farmer-settlers who eventually were satisfied to achieve a modicum of comfort and convenience.[24] The choice to build inexpensive temporary buildings and furnish them sparingly was an immigrant's and frontiersman's deliberate decision to allocate his limited resources to capital-productive land, labor, and livestock.[25] Homesteading, then and later, meant skimping at first to reap greater rewards afterward. The noteworthy point to observe, therefore, is not the substandard living endured by newcomers to North America and by those who only eked out a livelihood, but the very modest and relatively unsophisticated material life enjoyed by prosperous Americans throughout most of the seventeenth century.[26]

The general picture, which homesteaders' hardships distort, can be corrected by looking carefully at Old World household inventories, as more English and European historians now have.[27] They find somewhat larger houses and more furnishings almost everywhere along the social scale, as one would expect in long-established communities where fewer things had to be purchased new or built from scratch. It is also true that these and other records show a steady increase in domestic amenities over the long term from 1400 to 1700. Likewise, the food ordinary people ate and the beverages they drank were more varied and more nourishing.[28] The clothes they wore became more plentiful, sortable, and warmer.[29] Economic historians tell us that these improvements in people's material lives were buoyed by growing economies in England and across northern Europe long before the technological breakthroughs associated with the Industrial Revolution. Widespread depopulation wrought by the Black Death beginning in 1346 eventually had the effect of boosting wages and lowering rents, and thereby raised living standards for the survivors and their progeny in the decades and centuries that followed. It is now generally believed that rising standards of living surpassed bare-bones subsistence levels in England, the Netherlands, and elsewhere from the fourteenth century onward, but most rapidly after 1650.[30]

While such amendments to everyday living are beginning to form a fuller picture, explanations remain elusive.[31] The one certain lesson to be learned from inventory research is that there was still a decided sameness to people's material lives. Some had more of the same, others less, and accordingly their lives were more or less tolerable. But before the second half of the seventeenth century, most people living in the same locality shared the same material culture despite individual differences in the quantity and value of their household goods and personal possessions. Buildings, furnishings, diet, and clothing, all ever more improved and widely enjoyed, partook thoroughly of local custom. Differences were greatest between regions, not between groups within the same region. A century later the reverse was true. The consumer revolution would make comrades of ladies and gentlemen half a world away while leaving near but unequal neighbors worlds apart.[32]

Saying even that much anticipates later developments in a story that starts with a few simple observations drawn from recent research. They can be summarized this way: *Ordinary people all across England and much of northern Europe had enjoyed a rising standard of living for three or four hundred years prior to the end of the seventeenth century. These were basic improvements to diet, dress, shelter, and furnishings. American colonists aspired to these higher standards as well and used them as benchmarks against which to measure their success in overcoming the hardships of homesteading. Notwithstanding, folkways everywhere were still thoroughly parochial.*

They did not long remain so, not exclusively. The same research that mined these richly descriptive historical and archaeological sources to discover the facts of everyday life in traditional communities has gone on to show that the quality of that life underwent profound and fundamental alterations after the turn of the seventeenth century. To understand the difference, a useful distinction must be drawn between standards, styles, and what some call modes or fashions.[33] When we speak of living standards, we refer to a people's level of creature comforts. Either they do or they do not sleep on the floor, can or cannot heat more rooms than a kitchen, and have or do not have a second change of clothes. Lifestyle is something else. Anthropologists use that term to mean a culture's characteristic manner of doing something. Style results from a common understanding that pervades and invigorates everything a people does. As accepted convention, style uses a restricted vocabulary of words, forms, and actions to create a perceptible coherence in which self-acknowledged communities find consensus. Style is a cohesive force. It draws like-minded groups of people together and reaffirms their similarities.

By contrast, mode or fashion accentuates differences in society. It is the outlandish look adopted by individuals or groups who want to set themselves apart from their fellows. Fashion, if you will, is the style of subgroups. Often these have been wealthy or privileged elites, but not always. Religious sects and racial minorities sometimes choose and sometimes are forced to assume distinguishing modes of dress and behavior.

No people and no period have been devoid of style in this sense, certainly not the Anglo-American folk cultures whose standards of living had been improving steadily for several centuries. What historians find so surprising is the suddenness and speed with which fashion entered their lives in the first half of the eighteenth century. A grandson of an old Virginia bumpkin whose unadorned lifestyle had been cause for comment fifty years earlier wrote to a correspondent in London that "I w[oul]d willingly consult the present Fashion for you know that foolish Passion has made its bray, even into this remote region."[34] By 1760 George Washington could reproach his London supplier for palming off on the Virginia planter goods "that could [only] have been used by our Forefathers in the days of yore."[35] Sometimes the colonies seemed almost as à la mode as London itself. "The quick importation of fashions from the mother country is really astonishing," an English traveler wrote from Annapolis in 1771. "I am almost inclined to believe that a new fashion is adopted earlier by the polished and affluent American than by many opulent persons in the great metropolis." The good life was not just city life either. In rural areas he had also seen "elegance as well as comfort . . . in very many of the habitations."[36]

Such statements are exaggerated views from the top of society, but probate inventory studies and analyses of archaeological evidence bear out their diminished but essential truth further down the social scale. Wealthy families were the trendsetters, of course. But by the 1730s and 1740s people in the middle ranks of society were purchasing many newly imported "elegances" as well. By the Revolution even some of the poorer sort had made "necessities" of goods that had been their fathers' "decencies," their grandfathers' "luxuries," and before that were simply unheard of. All classes continued to acquire basic equipment—better beds and more bed linen most of all, but also tables and chairs, extra cooking utensils, lighting devices, and more. Yet, significantly, by midcentury many poor-to-middling householders forwent ordinary comforts in favor of equipment for specialized social activities—tea wares first and foremost, but also knives and forks, and some tasteful ceramic and glass tablewares, although usually in odd-lot assortments, not sets, among less-well-off consumers. For the privilege of taking tea in the parlor, more than a few families were content to continue pissing in the barn.

But less and less content after 1760, archaeologists tell us. Their investigations of eighteenth-century trash pits bring us one step closer to understanding people's motives for wanting certain kinds of artifacts, including, it appears, chamber pots in greater numbers as time wore on.[37] Where probate inventories usually only count "6 earthenware dishes" or lump together "a parcel of cracked china," archaeologists recover the actual broken pieces. From them we learn that many people increasingly took care to provide themselves, their families, and their social equals with individualized artifacts—that is, a plate, a fork and spoon, and a drinking vessel for everyone. Moreover, they insisted that all match. Sets of dishes, sets of chairs, suites of rooms, all fashioned alike, carried two messages: first that only a certain number of individuals could participate in the event for which the objects were needed and, second, that members of that exclusive company could be known by the similar appearance of the artifacts they used. The traditional, more-the-merrier, vernacular lifestyles were superseded—or, better, overlaid—by a fashionableness that divided society into finely calibrated user groups.

As archaeologists clearly demonstrate, fashion attached itself to some sorts of everyday activities more than others. Almost without exception these were those daily, weekly, and seasonal occasions when people consorted together in circumstances where accepted behavior was governed by an implicit knowledge of everyone's place in the social order—mainly mealtimes, group entertainments, public ceremonies, outings, and encounters among travelers. Written records, archaeological evidence, antique furnishings, and surviving eighteenth-century buildings all show the same thing, an extraordinary proliferation of goods and an efflorescence of forms in precisely those product lines that were instrumental to the performance of status-conscious social activities. One understands why many American householders were spending more on tablewares by midcentury than on the pots and pans used in the kitchen when one reads their orders to buyers and agents in England for dinner sets "of the most fashionable sort . . . sufficient for 2 genteel Courses of Victuals."[38]

Here then is one of the main conjunctions in consumer revolution scholarship. Here is the point where questions about consumer preferences merge with questions first posed by J. H. Plumb and his followers in Britain and subsequently by American scholars, questions about consumer behavior. This literature has been growing too. In essence, students of the English scene argue that men, women, and children experienced a dramatic expansion in the arts of social living in the eighteenth century. In larger numbers than ever before, ordinary middle- and upper-middle-class people engaged in entertainments and instructional activities that only the aristocracy had enjoyed before, if at all. Popular amusements included everything from pleasure tripping, theatergoing, ballroom dancing, and attending horse races, circuses, and freak shows to reading novels, buying prints, cultivating flower gardens, dabbling in science, collecting antiquities, and joining clubs. The list of diversions goes on and on.[39]

They were tastes that some Americans acquired as well—more of them after 1800 than before and townspeople sooner than country gentlemen, however much foreign travelers remembered otherwise. Social historians have taken a renewed, analytical interest in early American pastimes. Like their British cousins, a few colonists began indulging the passions of mind, heart, and body that sought fulfillment in social activities, self-improvements, organized sports, and recreational travel as early as the middle decades of the eighteenth century. At first such pleasant diversions found outlet in purely personal recreations or in activities that were easily organized by small groups of friends or confederates. Men and women with leisure time on their hands bought books for light reading, sheet music and artists' colors, dancing lessons, newspaper subscriptions, sporting gear for fishing, fowling, hunting, and racing, card and billiard tables, and books of rules for the games they played on them. Likewise, and in this case starting in the 1720s and 1730s, the smart set clubbed together in their pursuit of "Common Amusements," men in eating and drinking societies and sporting associations and both sexes at dancing schools, assemblies and balls, card parties, and concerts.[40]

Wherever leisured Americans could engage in playful activities with little specialized equipment and without extensive supporting services, their recreations resembled those enjoyed by their upper-middle-class English brethren at about the same time. What the colonies were slow to develop until the end of the century or later was a significant leisure industry in the service and manufacturing sectors of the economy. Commercial entertainments of the sort that British consumers spent vast sums on throughout much of the eighteenth century were relatively few and far between in the colonies. Playhouses and race tracks were among the first (fig. 1). Heavy capital investment in assembly rooms, mineral baths, and resort lodgings attracted few American entrepreneurs until the 1790s and not significantly for another twenty or thirty years thereafter (fig. 2).[41] Similarly, printers and booksellers only discovered a sustaining market for novels, children's books, fiction magazines, circulating libraries, and 150 newspapers at the end of the century. Popular sheet music printed in the United States and American-made musical instruments also became readily available for the first time after the Revolution.[42]

The reason that the commercialization of such activities in the colonies lagged behind Britain was basically a matter of numbers. Before the end of the century, playgoers, travelers for health and pleasure, library patrons, and sportsmen and sportswomen were often too few in absolute numbers and too small a proportion of the whole population to encourage potential entrepreneurs to invest in the production of recreational goods or supply leisure-time services. Just as successful storekeeping required minimum population densities in the regions from which customers were drawn, so likewise the development of commercialized pastimes appears to have waited upon the growth of population, urban centers being the first to reach the necessary minimum numbers.[43]

America's small population relative to Great Britain's exaggerated the effect of another obstacle to the growth of leisure industries in North America. Historians of popular culture have been at pains to remind students of modernization that folk customs and traditional lifestyles still flourished in the eighteenth century. When scholars look very closely at the book trade, for instance, or at popular sporting events, or at folk music and country dancing, they find that old favorites and old forms not only persisted throughout the century, but resilient folkways even invaded genteel and learned culture to create distinctive American forms of polite behavior.[44]

For example, four frequent social occasions at which a Virginia gentleman's social skills were put to the test included high society balls, but also lower-brow horse races, cockfights, and fish feasts. Even balls combined "minuets danced with great ease and propriety" with "country-dances," some in the English manner and others without manners at all. "Then came the reels," one Virginian recalled of an official ball held in 1774 at which only "the finest gentleman" and the mayor dared dance with three visiting English noblewomen until the musicians struck up a favorite country tune, "and here our Norfolk lads and lasses turned in with all their hearts and heels."[45] The seaboard American colonies were no more rustic than large parts of rural England. But, the population of North America being comparatively small and dispersed, the veneer of genteel culture was necessarily thinner. Vernacular culture bulked larger proportionately, a check on the commercial success of high-style entertainments until the end of the century.

Be that as it may, folk sports, folk music, and even the almanacs and chapbooks so popular with country readers developed in the course of the century in ways that lent themselves to commercial exploitation when eventually the marketplace grew large enough to be profitable. Gradually, traditional sporting events began to be held in permanent arenas and on custom-made playing fields. Jockeys left off drag racing on open roads in favor of oval tracks. Tavern keepers built bear pits, cockpits, boxing rings, and bowling alleys (fig. 3). Little by little, contests and games that once were open to the whole community were removed from public view, a necessary first step in converting onlookers into paying customers (fig. 4).[46]

So too with popular music. Folk singing continued to thrive alongside formal choral music, but increasingly both were learned "by Rule" in singing schools from tune books and music teachers and performed in concert. The popular press, historians tell us, printed and sold far more

FIGURE 1

Theater producer and impresario David Douglass built and managed a circuit of more than nine commercial playhouses from New York, Philadelphia, and Annapolis to Williamsburg, Charleston, and Kingston, Jamaica. Until the American Revolution closed him down, his American Company of Comedians followed the court calendar from town to town much as provincial theater companies did outside London.

Digital reconstruction of stage and auditorium, David Douglass Theater, Williamsburg, Virginia, c. 1772. Playhouses were planned with a keen eye for ticket sales. When Douglass opened his Williamsburg theater in 1760, the 350-person capacity auditorium sold cheap seats in a sloping pit separated from the orchestra by a row of iron spikes, more expensive boxes along the sides and back, and moderately priced seats in a second tier gallery above. Each had its own staircase.

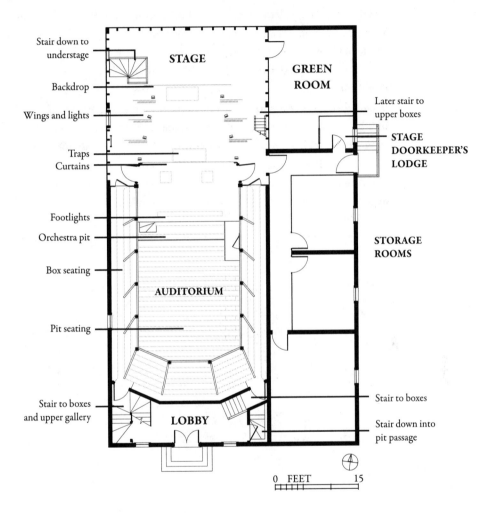

Stair down to understage

STAGE

GREEN ROOM

Backdrop

Later stair to upper boxes

Wings and lights

STAGE DOORKEEPER'S LODGE

Traps
Curtains

Footlights

Orchestra pit

STORAGE ROOMS

Box seating

AUDITORIUM

Pit seating

Stair to boxes and upper gallery

Stair to boxes

Stair down into pit passage

LOBBY

0   FEET   15

Plan of stage and auditorium, David Douglass Theater. By the early 1770s, when Douglass found that court season brought an abundance of well-heeled planters and merchants to the capital, he converted the gallery to upper boxes, jacked up the prices, and probably built a steep staircase directly from the stage as he had at his playhouse in Annapolis, another gentry watering hole during racing season.

FIGURE 2

Local entrepreneurs had already turned the healing waters of Warm Springs, Virginia, to commercial advantage by the 1760s. In addition to the original gentlemen's bathhouse, a separate and larger facility for women and a three-story hotel, complete with public dining room and ballroom, added to the popularity of the spa in the years before and after the Civil War. In 1837 a beguiled visitor to the springs described the original bathhouse as "a wooden building having an opening at the top, & four neat & comfortable rooms on as many sides for the accommodation of bathing [obviously for both men and women although separately]. . . . It is one of the most curious & beautiful objects I have seen, the water is pure and translucent to an almost dazzling degree, & rises in ceaseless flow, accompanied by showers of bright gleaming air bubbles."

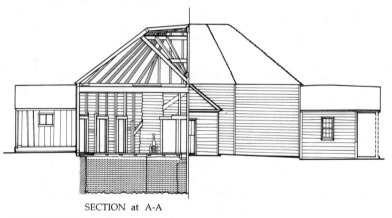

SECTION at A-A

EAST ELEVATION

Elevation and plan of gentlemen's bathhouse, late 1820s, constructed over the principal mineral pool at Warm Springs. As first built, this oldest of all surviving bathhouses, a clapboard-covered octagonal structure, was entered through two (soon four) identical porches, which also served as changing rooms. Later, as competition among spas promoted the development of special attractions, the west porch was enlarged to accommodate a spout bath after its invention in the 1830s, and the south porch was rebuilt after 1850 to provide a cold water plunge. Additional dressing rooms and a solarium or sun deck filled in three other sides of the octagon in the second half of the nineteenth century.

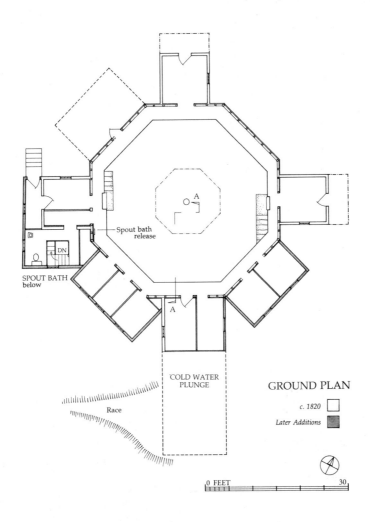

Spout bath
release

SPOUT BATH
below

DN

A

A

COLD WATER
PLUNGE

Race

GROUND PLAN

c. 1820

Later Additions

0 FEET   30

FIGURE 3

English immigrants of all ranks brought to the colonies a passion for blood sports. From early on, American tavern keepers built bear-gardens, cock-pits, and dog-fighting rings to pull in customers the way darts, skittles, and pinball machines do today. The appetite for animal baiting and the wagering that went with it was not sated at these public gathering places. Farmers and their neighbors, often including gentlemen "of character and intelligence," brought prize gamecocks and champion bandogs to make-do matchups staged in barns and stables throughout the colonies.

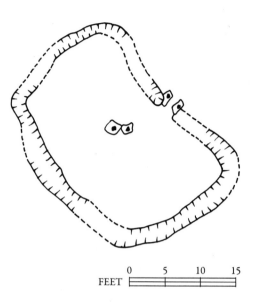

FEET | 0 5 10 15

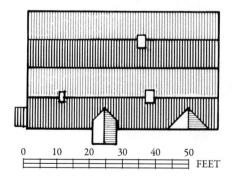

0 10 20 30 40 50 FEET

Archaeological remains of an animal-baiting ring behind the "Country's House," St. Mary's City, Maryland, a tavern by 1644 with a baiting ring not later than 1680. The shallow oblong ditch probably held a wattle-like fence to confine the fighting animals and protect bystanders. Bears or dogs may have been the sport here considering the large size of the ring, more than thirty feet across, and a sturdy center post or posts to which the set-upon animal was chained. A pair of narrowly spaced posts on one side of the ring suggests a chute gate through which attack dogs entered the arena.

Cockfighting pit or animal-baiting ring behind Marot's Ordinary, Williamsburg, Virginia, 1708–38. Smaller in size than the ring at St. Mary's City, this enclosure may have been built to stage cockfights (see fig. 4). Originally, or perhaps later, it too was fitted with a centered tether post whose function is unknown.

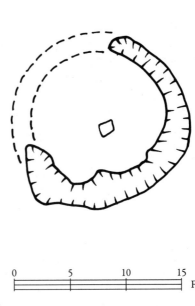

0   5   10   15
FEET

0 10 20 30 40 50
FEET

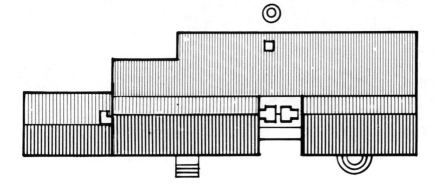

FIGURE 4

Genre painting of fighting gamecocks and brawling cockers allegedly at Berkeley Springs, Virginia, c. 1845–50. Unsigned, but probably by Christian Mayr (d. 1851), a German immigrant painter. The artist had a keen eye for the travesty of manners he observed at hillbilly spa towns in western Virginia, such as this cockfighting scene attended by ruffians who dressed better than they behaved. The painting shows a simple outdoor ring enclosed behind a high fence that kept out all nonpaying spectators except agile boys. The legitimate cocking clientele inside the yard lays bets on the birds and perhaps on the impromptu wrestling match as well.

sermons, primers, almanacs, and Domesday books than travelogues or fiction throughout the eighteenth century. Yet the remarkable careers of such bookmen as Parson Weems anticipated the shape of things to come—aggressive merchandizing, abridgments, and cheap "pretty" books crammed with "images." As in provincial England, although perhaps not so rapidly, ordinary country people discovered that middlemen were increasingly eager to help them enjoy their traditional pastimes and introduce them to new ones, always at a price.

The observation that men and women in England and the colonies created for themselves an earthly paradise with goods that modern archaeologists rediscover in fragments, curators collect in museums, and historians quantify from probate inventories brings my argument about an American consumer society to another useful point of summary. My recapitulation of recent scholarship on the seventeenth century described a people who enjoyed a slowly rising standard of living long before 1700. We recognize in these eighteenth-century studies a qualitative difference in material life. Thus my second set of observations takes into account that *sometime toward the end of the seventeenth century and accelerating into the next, many people began to acquire goods, use services, and engage in social, recreational, and educational activities that went far beyond meeting or improving basic physical needs. For the first time in Western history, considerable numbers of ordinary people deliberately assumed a personal appearance and demeanor and behaved themselves in ways that were more class-bound than culture-bound.*

J. H. Plumb borrowed Thomas Jefferson's phrase "the pursuit of happiness" to describe the delights that many took in their new pastimes. Its ring of rights inalienable has not, however, deterred other historians from grubbing in matters of fact to ferret out the economic fundaments underlying such pleasurable behavior. Numerous reasons have been offered to explain the extraordinary phenomenon of eighteenth-century consumer demand. The problem is that the English explanations are so different from those proposed by historians of colonial America that the answers are not easily reconciled. British historians have asked themselves why that country was so economically and socially ripe for a consumer revolution. They give several answers. Careful study of eighteenth-century political economists, for instance, has revealed an important shift away from outright opposition to the spread of luxury and even from the modified view that it was a necessary evil. By the third quarter of the century, by the time Adam Smith published *The Wealth of Nations,* theorists were of a mind to embrace a "doctrine of beneficial luxury" and concede that domestic consumption operated as a powerful stimulus to industriousness in all ranks of society.[47]

Here social historians make their contribution. They argue that England was prepared socially as well as intellectually for a consumer boom. They set great store by the fact that the structure of English society was composed of closely packed strata that bred competition, excited emulation, and encouraged upward mobility.[48] Contemporaries remarked on the "gradual and easy transition from rank to rank," a characteristic that made English society very different from others in which consumption of luxuries was confined to an exclusive upper-class market far beyond the reach of the masses.[49] The commercial opportunities inherent in a many-layered social order were not lost on entrepreneurs eager to spur on class competition and the spread of new fashions by making goods of different qualities and selling them over a broad price range.[50] English historians take account of other factors as well: the size and magnetism of London, the growth of population, high wages paid to young men and women who then married later when they could support themselves and their children, falling prices for consumer goods in relation to rising fuel and food prices (but improved food supplies), rapidly expanding markets, easy access to cheap money, a division of labor conducive to mass production, and so on and on in a recitation of "causes" that is reminiscent of textbook explanations for the coming of the Industrial Revolution.[51]

One historian, Jan de Vries, has worked out which factors were significant and which were not. In the end, he concludes that none by itself satisfactorily accounts for a seeming paradox that economists find very puzzling. Almost everywhere they look in England, the Netherlands, and North America they find people acquiring more and more consumer durables without reallocating their total wealth to pay for them. People's worldly goods multiplied exponentially while the value of their probated estates remained fairly constant. For some, this logical absurdity calls the whole notion of a consumer revolution into question. De Vries approaches the conundrum another way. He argues that consumption of marketed goods grew rapidly because large numbers of households reapportioned their most flexible productive resource, their time.[52] Underemployed labor, especially women's and children's, was put to harder, more constant, market-oriented work to earn the money income needed to purchase store-bought foodstuffs, manufactured goods, and commercial services. Women, children, servants, and (in the colonies) slaves produced much of the income-earning surplus needed to buy into this expanding commercial world.

So, as De Vries terms it, an "industrious revolution" preceded and prepared the way for the technology-driven Industrial Revolution by concentrating household labor on market production. Households thereby increased their yearly money earnings relative to individual daily wage rates. This growth in purchasing power occurred independently of technological advances or the growth of capital wealth. Busy hands account for rising demand. A political economist of the period put it as succinctly as any modern economic historian has since: in former times (he was writing in 1767) "men were . . . forced to labour because they were slaves to others; men are now forced to labour because they are slaves to their own wants."[53] Not just men, it turns out. Actually women and children first and foremost.

To this insight, De Vries offers another and complementary explanation for the fact that the stock of new goods purchased with this extra pin money failed to show up in probate inventories as a larger share of householders' total wealth. The reason, he theorizes, is that fashionable goods, often less durable, were not only cheaper, but more quickly depreciated and replaced. In effect, they came and went many times over before the consumer's death finally occasioned the making of an inventory. Thus, at last, can economists rest easy that a "resolution to the contradiction between the wage and probate inventory data" has been reached.[54]

For now De Vries's synthesis stands alongside the more familiar notion among British scholars that a happy combination of many circumstances conspired to create an ideal breeding ground for England's embryonic consumer society. The problem with all is their failure to explain how and why it happened, and Plumb's quip that "there was no simple causative factor—no trigger that released change, and so moved society into a higher gear, as a clutch does a motor" is no excuse for not trying to understand the operation of the larger engine that powered consumer demand.[55]

Historians seldom expect to find single causes for anything. Those who study consumer behavior in North America, especially in New England and the Chesapeake colonies of Maryland and Virginia, have isolated and investigated several "triggers." Their work shows that, within the broad time limits that bracket the advent of fashionable consumption everywhere, close attention to the timing of its appearance region by region can help historians distinguish primary preconditions from those that were only contributing factors. The key determinants in the South turn out to have been density of settlement, agricultural diversification, and the spread of chattel slavery.[56] At first Chesapeake tobacco planters were too thin on the ground to keep stores in business year-round. Instead English merchants shipped only such necessities as planters bought in bulk once a year in trade for their annual crop. As rural neighborhoods became more densely populated after 1700, storekeepers could afford to stock a larger inventory and a wider selection of goods. Thus protected against shortages, customers felt easier about spending discretionary income on nonessentials, especially as competition among a growing number of rival storekeepers kept the lid on prices.

The spread of mixed farming was a second factor that helped to stabilize local economies. Planting a variety of cash crops provided a hedge against the unpredictable ups and downs of the tobacco trade. The more reliable income planters earned from the sale of foods and forest products gave them confidence to invest in the tools and raw materials needed to start home industries such as shoemaking, weaving, and blacksmithing. The result was not greater self-sufficiency but a livelier local exchange in homemade manufactures and homegrown foodstuffs. Surpluses were sold locally. The profits augmented farm incomes. With ready money in their pockets, southerners were willing to spend an extra shilling or two on a chocolate pot or a Gothic novel. One thing led to another until by midcentury many Virginians were well launched as consumers of English luxury goods. In the words of the colony's governor, "These imports daily increase"—he was writing in 1763—"the common planters usually dressing themselves in the manufactures of Great Britain altogether."[57]

The conversion of plantation labor from indentured servants to enslaved Africans, coming rapidly after 1700, left many Chesapeake grandees no choice but to join the consumption rat race. Previously considerable numbers of affluent planter families had steadfastly eschewed expensive fashionable living during a time when they managed their plantations with relatively few slaves. But when bottom-line realities compelled them to acquire larger gangs of Africans, they began to feel the same pressures that their slave-owning neighbors had experienced a generation or two earlier. They found they needed slave drivers to manage the larger crews of forced workers. They felt obliged to house and feed them in separate quarters and erect other physical and psychological barriers between themselves and these minions. Most important of all, joining the ranks of confirmed slaveholders drove them into the select company of men who already comported themselves in a manner and fashion deliberately calculated to set them apart from and raise them above their provincial neighbors, wealthy or not. Acquiring a labor force of African slaves, it turns out, was the bellwether—and the trigger—to living large in the Chesapeake colonies. Plantation slavery not only earned the means to support a life of fashion; it thrust a growing number of large slave owners into association with men who wore the new-model gentility as a badge of rank and expected other slave owners to wear it as well.[58]

Local history research in Maryland, Virginia, and South Carolina has counterparts in studies of New England and the Middle Colonies. Northern farmers practiced various mixed agricultures from the very first. The component essential to the development of a capitalist economy in each locality was the capacity to accumulate liquid financial assets. Many northern farmers and stockbreeders bought and sold produce on the local market, and many were favorably situated to export grain and beef overseas and later also to feed the voracious appetites of the country's fastest-growing cities. The income they received from the sale of agricultural commodities not only supported consumer spending, it also provided venture capital to invest in new and more lucrative business enterprises.

Shipbuilding, shipping, coopering, chandlering, milling, and manufacturing in turn gave work to thousands of wage-earning sailors, clerks, artisans, and laborers. They all required additional goods and services, which further expanded the market for English and American manufactures.[59]

When regional comparisons are drawn, they demonstrate that different local circumstances differently shaped the social and economic environments where consumer cultures took root. Everywhere, not one, but a number of interconnected factors released changes that either slowed down or sped up the spread of consumer habits. Regional studies go far to explain a people's readiness to participate in an international consumer culture. In that sense they parallel the British research that has identified elements in the national economy that created a climate favorable to increased consumption of goods. Difficult as it still is to mesh explanations on both the micro- and macroeconomic levels, both describe developments that had to take place before growing demand for consumer goods could be met.

In the last analysis neither the American regional approach nor the larger treatment the subject has received from British scholars can tell us why so many ordinary people chose to spend discretionary income the way they did—not unless historians fall back on the view that the real revolution in consumers' ambitions occurred in some earlier age and that a frustrated demand for consumer goods remained bottled up until events in the eighteenth century finally released a long pent-up demand. Some have indeed advanced this case, arguing with Neil McKendrick that "the novel feature of the eighteenth century was not its desire to pursue fashion, but its ability to do so."[60] Later on in this volume I will try to show that proponents of this view misunderstand such evidence as there certainly is for fashionable living in earlier centuries.

The problem of explaining rising demand will simply not go away merely by pushing it off on historians of another period. On the contrary, the weight of evidence already presented strongly suggests that, whatever examples of conspicuous consumption may be traced back to the sixteenth century or earlier, responsibility for explaining how ordinary household goods and personal possessions became indispensable tools to the conduct of everyday social relations rests squarely on the shoulders of those who make the late seventeenth and eighteenth centuries their specialty. Even after unraveling the paradox between goods and wealth, Jan de Vries concedes that the irrepressible desire for ever more material things ultimately comes down to a "social decision," a choice defined by the chooser's cultural values.[61] Scholars today are closer to knowing how, when, and where Britons and Americans acquired the desire to consume, but the question *why* remains unanswered.

To understand the origins of consumer demand is still our quest. Before pursuing it in one last body of published scholarship, the important background research just reviewed first needs to be restated as a third set of assumptions, namely these: *A combination of social, economic, and intellectual circumstances came into play in eighteenth-century England, parts of northern Europe, and North America that set the stage for a consumer revolution. Thereafter its reception and progress from region to region depended primarily on the size, wealth, and stability of local economies.* This is the most guarded statement so far because it must not imply that scholars have adequately addressed themselves to Plumb's admonition that "what are so frequently . . . omitted from any discussion of one of the most momentous changes ever achieved in social living are the will, the desires, the ambitions, and the cravings of the men and women who wanted change and promoted it."[62]

Has nothing been written that throws light on the prime motives of those men and women who wanted change? Actually that is the oldest literature of all, and by far the largest. The debate for and against the spread of luxury goes back as far as the consumer revolution itself. It produced a prodigious number of tracts and countertracts. Four hundred and sixty catalogued books and pamphlets in the half century between publication of Bernard Mandeville's *Fable of the Bees* (1724) and Smith's *Wealth of Nations* (1776) are but a fraction of the total. It was said at the time that over five hundred pamphlets were printed in the 1760s alone.[63]

There is a pattern in this tidal wave of ephemera. Clear chronological stages can be discerned in the polemics. Some have no bearing on our inquiry into consumer demand because sometimes the disputants were less concerned with causes than consequences. Not so when the debate turned to social analyses. Critics feared that "the vast Torrent of Luxury which of late Years hath poured itself into this Nation" would spawn a dangerous insubordination in society.[64] There was little disagreement about the reason behind conspicuous consumption. The new consumers were social climbers. Emulative spending was the engine that drove the fashion trade. Listen once again to Henry Fielding: "While the Nobleman will emulate the Grandeur of a Prince; and the Gentleman will aspire to the proper State of the Nobleman; the Tradesman steps from behind his Counter into the vacant place of the Gentleman. Nor doth the Confusion end here: It reaches the very Dregs of the People, who [are] aspiring still to a Degree beyond that which belongs to them." The "frenzy of Fashion" was deplored from the pulpit, the stage, and the Houses of Parliament.

Similar jeremiads appeared in American newspapers. Many were reprinted from British journals, but there was no shortage of homegrown polemicists who found special reason to decry extravagance in the colonies. "All other Nations have their favorite luxury," wrote one, but in the American catch-basin "our Taste is universal," a potent distillation of all the sumptuary excesses of other countries pooled together.[65] In the colonies no less than in Britain unbridled ambition was unquestionably taken to be the social climber's motive and high living his unearned reward. The familiar refrain sounded exactly the same here as it did there: "The wife of the laboring man wishes to vie in dress with the wife of the merchant, and the latter does not wish to be inferior to the wealthy women of Europe."[66] A distraught correspondent to a Boston newspaper parroted words that had figured in Fielding's earlier lamentation, warning that "the baneful contagion" of luxury "spreads at last to the very dregs of the people."[67] The English-born physician, Dr. Alexander Hamilton, a resident of Annapolis, had no quarrel with "extravagant Living in general; I only say," he wrote in defense of privilege, "that if Luxury was to be confined to the Rich alone, it might prove a great national good, and a Public benefit to Mankind." Shared with the poor, however, it led to no end of mischief.

The doctor may have been remembering an incident that had occurred while he was making his famous *Itinerarium* to New England two years earlier in 1744. He and a gentleman traveling companion had stopped at a humble cottage outside New York, "clean and neat but poorly furnished." Yet even there they observed "an inclination to finery" in the presence of a looking glass, some pewter spoons and plates, and a teapot. Hamilton's scandalized friend pronounced them "superfluous and too splendid for such a cottage. . . . They ought to be sold to buy wool to make yarn," he blustered, adding that "a little water in a wooden pail might serve for a looking glass, and wooden plates and spoons would be as good for use and, when clean, would be almost as ornamental. As for the tea equipage it was quite unnecessary."[68]

The luxury debate produced more heat than light. Proponents and critics took their opposing stands largely with regard to the effects they presumed consumption would have on a social order they perceived in traditional terms. There were those who feared creeping egalitarianism most of all. Samuel Adams was alarmed lest affordable consumer goods erase "every Distinction between the Poor and the Rich."[69] Others saw greater danger in widespread poverty and unemployment unless the production of luxuries put the lower classes to work and gave them something to work for.

Only now, two centuries later, can scholars take a longer view. They see that English society was undergoing a realignment that not so much overturned the traditional order as it imbued the leisured squirearchy with certain cultural attributes that set them apart from the working classes below them. Known to contemporaries as "genteel taste," today's modern scholars call this code of conduct by various names: civility, sociability, politeness. It was something men and women had to take time to learn, time that working people could not spare. It required the mastery of prescribed social skills, which, when practiced, transformed the activities of everyday life into the arts of genteel living. Old-fashioned folkways followed rules too—implicit rules—but these were different from the artificial rules of etiquette. Folkways were second nature to people born into the fold. Gentility was a manner sought after and acquired only with diligent application. Its validity was certified by open demonstration. It was theater. Consequently it needed settings, costumes, props, and, not least of all, audiences. Those audiences were full of admiring, aspiring imitators. Often they saw only what was visual, missing the genuine refinements of thought and character underneath. For many, looks were enough. The trappings could be purchased in every price range. The consumer revolution inflated a gentleman's or lady's face value to heights previously unimagined.

Historians have made considerable headway in recent years in studying this realignment and cultural redefinition of Anglo-American society. Their findings, as I have just described them, can be summarized as a proposition that advances my argument an important step further: *Fashion became a badge of membership (or a bid for membership) in class-conscious social groups. As the outward signs of status, consumer goods and the social arts they were used to perform served, first, as shared symbols of group identity and, second, as devices that social climbers imitated in hopes of ascending the social ladder.*

This fourth statement, presented in the form of a working hypothesis, brings me to the end of the bookshelf that holds current publications dealing directly with the subject. The literature to date carries the search for an answer to the question—*why consumer demand?*—thus far and no further. True, we now better understand some of the factors that created a climate favorable to the spread of fashion in the eighteenth century and enabled ordinary people in ever greater numbers to satisfy their ambitions to acquire material goods. But, as I began by asking, why those ambitions in the first place? Why the late seventeenth and eighteenth centuries specifically? Why household goods and personal possessions instead of some other more intrinsically valuable measures of status? The halfhearted answer that a few historians have offered is that old saw about English and early American society transformed from age-old, collective, peasant communities into a dynamic, cosmopolitan, modern world order in which individuals, cut adrift from their traditional moorings, needed personal status symbols to compete in a social free-for-all for position, power, and prestige. The error is not in believing that such a transformation never occurred but in taking the fact of modernization as its own adequate explanation.[70]

What consumer revolution studies need now are explanations grounded in circumstances peculiar to the decades immediately before and after 1700. Furthermore, these explanations must apply to all those regions and countries where fashion flourished, regardless of their different stages of economic development. Finally, genuinely useful historical explanations will have to demonstrate that fashion-bearing consumer goods solved specific social problems better than any other conceivable form of expenditure.

To present my argument in full, I must advance my thesis three steps further, but without supporting research, at least not research undertaken by students working directly on this particular historical problem. The first four summary statements were deduced from a body of clearly relevant evidence. Three remaining propositions can be offered only as hypotheses in need of testing, as blueprints for ongoing research.

These hypotheses stem from the last substantiated statement, that consumer goods and services became the currency of social emulation. This much more may also be asserted: the need for individuals to communicate information about their status was nothing new. Traditionally, most people had lived their entire lives well within the compass of their local reputations. The estimation of a man's standing in his community was based on his family connections, his wealth in land and labor, his largesse, and the offices he held and through which he exercised authority. All were rooted in a particular place. Social emulation in traditional societies was literally a contest among neighbors. It did not remain so forever. Beginning in the sixteenth century and accelerating rapidly after 1660, significant numbers of people in Britain and northern Europe began moving far beyond the reach of reputation, to neighboring counties, to big cities, to foreign countries, and to overseas colonies. There newcomers and travelers inevitably found their worth measured against the worth of perfect strangers. There the old yardsticks were nowhere near at hand.

These statements of fact are appropriated from historical scholarship on subjects altogether unrelated to consumer behavior. They are linked together here to throw a bridge over the chasm of our present ignorance to a proposition that advances the central argument of this book. It goes like this: *In a world in motion, migrants and travelers needed a standardized system of social communications. They required a set of conventions they could carry with them that signified anywhere they went the status they enjoyed at home. So it came to pass that ordinary people adopted and then adapted to their own various special needs a system of courtly behavior*

*borrowed ultimately from a protocol developed in Italy and France and dis-
seminated through Amsterdam and London to provincial England and the
colonies. Standardized architectural spaces equipped with fashionable furnishings became universally recognized settings for status-communicating
social performances that were governed by internationally accepted rules of
etiquette.*

If future research substantiates the main points of this overarching
hypothesis, historians can explain the consumer revolution in terms that
meet four critical criteria: *time*—the mid- to late-seventeenth century
onward; *place*—Britain and northern Europe generally and their overseas colonies as each locality achieved social equilibrium and developed
a sustaining economy; *class*—the "middling sort" principally, but eventually even the working poor when they could afford small indulgences;
and finally *means*—a large selection of highly standardized, affordable,
and widely distributed consumer goods and a comprehensive set of easily
learned rules governing their use. Unproven theories can be a useful way
to organize historical research. To hold up they have to show that they
work when tested against real-world evidence. It remains to marshal that
evidence and make that case.

2

⫸⫸⫸⫷⫷⫷

FOLK CONSUMERS

To call a basic alteration in people's consumption and use of everyday objects a revolution implies a fundamental difference between the meaning users attached to material things before the events in question and the meaning ascribed to consumer goods afterward. Before I can advance the case set out at the close of the last chapter, it behooves me to pause and take a backward look at earlier times when almost everyone was born into a world governed by custom and tradition. Folk cultures, diverse as they always were, generally shared a system of beliefs in which physical things had a bearing on people's everyday lives in ways that the consumer revolution would change forever.

Surprisingly few attempts have been made to explain how personal possessions and ordinary household equipment figured in the lives of traditional peoples before England and its colonies began to respond to the consumer impulse. The question is not what goods they owned or how people used them. That *has* been studied. The problem is knowing what importance people assigned to artifacts, especially how their possessions defined status and how their use intervened in and affected the users' dealings with others. If goods eventually became high marks of esteem and essential tools necessary to perform activities of great social consequence, what had they been previously?

To take a stab at an answer, we can start by drawing a distinction between the different meanings of material things before and after the transforming event we are calling the consumer revolution. Because its timing and progress responded to so many complicated influences after the middle of the seventeenth century, investigators need to look as far back as the late Middle Ages to find English folk culture unalloyed. A backward glance at the attitudes of ordinary people toward their personal possessions in the two or three centuries preceding American colonization is justified because the profound differences to be observed are instructive in understanding why consumer behavior in the eighteenth century took the surprising forms it did. Considering that my fifth proposition turns on a correlation between geographical mobility and the spread of consumer habits, the following account of material life in fourteenth- and fifteenth-century Britain starts by making connections between a medieval villager's neighborhood and the social order in which he fit, between his social status and his reputation, and finally between his standing in the community and the value of his personal possessions.

Scholarship since the 1950s has punctured many sentimental stereotypes about medieval peasants and their descendants under the Tudors and Stuarts. The legendary English village—immutable, self-contained, and largely self-sufficient—now lies discarded on the spoil heap of history. In its place medievalists have reconstructed a picture of peasant communities ordered in a familiar hierarchy of yeomen, husbandmen and craftsmen, and poor laborers, but at the same time open to social conflicts, far-flung market forces, outside cultural influences, and a never-ending turnover of inhabitants. As early as the fourteenth century more than a third of all peasant families in villages in the East Midlands (where the matter has been studied) died out or moved away within a single generation. Native sons and daughters left home in ever-larger numbers after 1400, especially servants, craftsmen, and laborers in search of work. The pace of resettlement continued to grow at such a rapid rate in the sixteenth century that only one in four married men and one woman in three raised their children in the same village where they themselves had grown up. Staying put had become the exception for a majority of English villagers and moving around the rule.[1]

The homebound, hidebound swain of days gone by has been superseded in the literature by the footloose migrant worker. All the same, scholars who have carefully examined the geography of the social worlds in which medieval villagers lived and moved have discovered that the mobility of these men and women was usually confined to a fairly small area for property-holding yeomen and husbandmen, albeit less so for young craftsmen and farm laborers. Those roles were later reversed in the great overseas migrations of the seventeenth century, but before 1600 the most substantial villagers were also the most settled. Furthermore, their extra-village relationships took the forms of marriages, court battles, ownership of property in nearby parishes, and various kin connections that validated an individual's roots in the greater locality. They were the kinds of ties that expanded the range of a man's or woman's local reputation.[2] For most peasants, the village of their birth was still the center of the universe, however much they orbited around it. Relatively few escaped its gravitational pull altogether. Those who did— those who took themselves off to market towns, county seats, and sometimes even London—were responding, it should be noted, to forces of change that were to grow more powerful as the sixteenth century drew to a close. These few were forerunners of the genuine pioneers who became much more numerous after 1600. For the time being, though, and despite its ever-changing cast of characters, the English village and its neighborhood retained its ancient integrity as a vital community center.

Status, wealth, and power ran together in such face-to-face societies. And they ran principally to those same property holders with the oldest and deepest roots. That tended to exclude those on the top as well as those at the bottom of the social ladder. The wealthiest gentlemen landowners, being players in a larger county social scene, were the most migratory of all. Landless laborers and craftsmen had small stake anywhere and frequently wandered off in search of employment. The larger farmers and husbandmen formed the bedrock of village society. They settled down, they prospered, they sank their wealth into the land, they married back and forth, and they dominated local affairs. They also opened their ranks and shared their offices with newcomers of comparable social standing from neighboring villages, people whom they knew by reputation. Medieval and early modern communities were not closed, just close.[3]

Status among such village worthies was a matter of common knowledge. A man's reputation (or "estate," to use their word) resided in his neighbors' estimation of his worth measured in the only terms that mattered—in land, labor, livestock, precious plate, and capital improvements (such as barns and mills) among his property, reputable kinfolk and creditable neighbors among his relations, and the offices he held and the largesse he dispensed in the exercise of his authority. All but plate were indivisible from their locality, and gold and silver objects were safest locked away or else displayed in the stronghold of the owner's own house. A peasant's reputation was his letter of credit beyond the village boundaries. As we have seen, that network of acquaintances might extend some miles roundabout, but seldom farther.

Material things that lacked intrinsic value counted for next to nothing in establishing their possessor's social standing. Well-off yeoman farmers were, of course, likely to enjoy the convenience of larger dwellings to accommodate their larger households. They furnished them likewise, that is, according to need, which meant scarcely at all in the late Middle Ages. Everyday domestic life required relatively few pieces of furniture, cooking equipment, and tablewares among all classes of men and women from princes to peasants. The household goods of typical fourteenth- and fifteenth-century farmers included chests, tables, stools, ale stands, and an occasional cupboard, plus cooking pots and other kitchen gear, as well as plates and drinking vessels of wood, horn, earthenware, and leather. Chairs were far from numerous and bedsteads evidently rarer still in ordinary farmhouses.[4] Men of greater estate might own an aumbry (a food locker) or a bedstead with curtains. But by and large, as we already noted about living standards among American colonists in the seventeenth century, rich and poor lived fundamentally alike, the only difference being that the one generally enjoyed more of the same than the other.[5]

That is the first point worth remembering about household goods in traditional English village communities, that since no one's social standing was judged by the quality of his furniture, no one saw advantage in acquiring more or better pieces than use and convenience required. Before the seventeenth century, furniture was largely exempt from social pressures to conform to changing tastes.

Heavy wooden furniture and coarse earthenware vessels that had little value in themselves nevertheless were used in two distinctive ways as accessories to the display of real wealth and the affirmation of social precedence. Both are worth considering briefly because they stand in marked contrast to later uses of consumer goods as status symbols in their own right. Affluence took material form in articles of three or four kinds in medieval households: exotic and expensive foodstuffs, jewelry and plate, and textiles made into clothing or used as napery, upholstery, bedclothes, and wall hangings. Many quite modest householders could count a silver spoon or two among their liquid assets, spread the trestle boards with a tablecloth, or deck the hall with wall paintings or "pentyt clothes," a poor man's tapestries.[6] Furniture and ceramic tablewares were important principally as objects needed to store, display, and serve those few articles of conspicuous consumption. Valuables of all kinds, but especially plate, cash, and yard goods, were locked away for safekeeping in the most common containers to be found in houses everywhere, chests and boxes in the larger sizes and less frequently such smaller "cases of boxes" and cabinets "as Ladyes keepe their rings, necklaces, Braclett[s], and Jewells In."[7] Notice that the contents usually far exceeded the value of the container. There were other medieval forms which persisted well into the seventeenth century that functioned principally as display stands for plate or as sideboards for serving dishes and drinking vessels used at table. Cupboards (literally *cup boards)* were essentially open shelves on wooden frames, the prefix referring not to china teacups, but to goblets that sometimes appear in ones and twos even in quite humble householders' inventories, at least by the first half of the sixteenth century. Once again, such pieces of furniture were usually wooden structures of only small importance compared to the objects they displayed. As a matter of fact, much medieval furniture literally had to be dressed—that is, draped with status-bearing textiles—before it was ready to use. Carpets and cloths covered rough cupboards and tables, curtains and testors concealed bare bed frames, and upholstery and cushions softened hard wooden stools, chairs, and benches.

Furniture and tablewares that were to become showpieces by the eighteenth century were still showcases in medieval times. They were auxiliary equipment useful for displaying, presenting, and safekeeping other objects and substances of much greater account. Utensils made of precious metals could be cashed in on a rainy day, and expensive perishables could be shared with friends and neighbors as proof of the host's reputation for hospitality. Showing them off was the first use of medieval furniture.

There was another. Certain kinds of household equipment could sometimes be used to assert and reinforce an individual's degree of estate. In particular, seating furniture, bed hangings, standing salts, and various covered table vessels expressed social realities very precisely. Always the controlling factor was precedence rather than rank. Precedence was based on immutable qualities attached to occupations, offices, or other preferments. Status defined by rank was inalienable from the person himself or herself. Its perquisites went wherever the rank-holder went unless modified by something else. Rules of precedence were the modifiers in medieval society. The status that precedence conferred on an individual was relative to the estates of everyone else who was present on occasions where social formalities were observed. Thus, in practice, a yeoman farmer might sit in an armchair in his own hall and drink from a covered cup at his own table, but he would expect to occupy a stool or form located below the salt and drink from a tankard in the house of his seignorial lord. Precedence overruled all other measures of rank in the use of objects that had ceremonial significance. Not even ownership, let alone conversance with ritual furniture and utensils, entitled a person to use them in every situation.[8] Let us note in anticipation of later events that the rule of precedence was to be thoroughly swept away, except on state occasions, by the scramblers after luxury in the centuries still to come. Little by little, gentility would supersede precedence as the chief regulator of men's and women's social interactions.

Every peasant household was also equipped with utilitarian objects seemingly too mundane to be adjuncts to ceremony. The historical sources that tell us what meaning people attached to furniture of estate throw no light at all on their attitudes toward all the other things recorded in probate inventories. If there were some way to discover how English and other folk cultures accounted for commonplace artifacts in the experience of everyday living, we might better understand how completely the consumer revolution altered the traditional relationship between men and women and their tools in favor of the rank-conscious uses to which fashionable goods came to be applied in later times. Some documents have a little to say, but the most explicit and revealing information on this aspect of popular culture comes curiously from artifacts that quite literally speak for themselves.

In the long ages before empirical thinking invaded the realm of folklore, the belief was nearly universal that the cosmos was an organic unity in which every part—physical as well as spiritual—bore a harmonic correspondence to every other part. The difference between matter and spirit was blurred. The elements themselves, ordinary people believed, were literally alive. Trees, rocks, rivers, and animals were endowed with supernatural properties. Some held truly magical powers, which could be enlisted on a man's or woman's behalf or turned against them. Others, it seems safest to say, were simply felt to embody humanlike qualities over and above their physical attributes. Sometimes they were given personalities and the gift of speech, as well as limbs, wings, and anthropomorphic faces in visual representations.[9] The earliest English and European newcomers to North America shared such beliefs with bondsmen from West Africa. For instance, it was said of Igbo people, who were enslaved in considerable numbers on Chesapeake plantations, that, as they worked, they "continually talk to their tools and that in an earnest manner, as they were addressing a human being."[10]

The doctrine of correspondences among all physical things pertained as well to man-made houses and everyday objects. Dwellings were likened to the human body. The analogy was not just a literary metaphor invented by seventeenth-century poets and sermon writers who were the first to set down in print these ancient superstitions. To the folk imagination the similarities between windows and eyes, doors and mouths, and roofs and heads were plausible beyond all question. Just as the body's orifices were the weak points in its defenses against witchcraft and disease, the corresponding openings in a house were prudently fortified against evil spirits by burying "witches bottles" under doorsteps and hearths, concealing horse and cow skulls behind walls and over entrances, and mounting cherubs' heads on gate posts. These and other objects imbued with magical powers have been found in association with dwellings belonging to European settlers in the American colonies as well as in cabins and workplaces used by enslaved African Americans (fig. 5).[11]

Spirits and other personifications lived indoors as well as out. From antiquity the hearth had always been a place where the presence of the

FIGURE 5

Jujus and talismans. European settlers who were heedful of the supernatural world used horse and cow skulls, bottles, old shoes, and other objects imbued with magical powers to stand guard over their dwellings. Enslaved African Americans, property themselves, usually did not have that choice. Instead they were sometimes disposed to protect their persons with amulets—shells, bones, beads, and small household trinkets worn as charms. Occasionally archaeologists find totems cached in hidden locations inside slave spaces that suggest ritual concealment rather than mere storage.

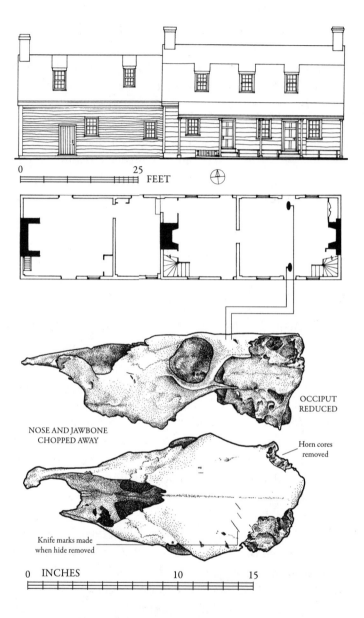

OCCIPUT REDUCED

NOSE AND JAWBONE CHOPPED AWAY

Horn cores removed

Knife marks made when hide removed

Elevation, plan, and cow skulls hidden above the ceiling over front and back doors at Godlington Manor, Kent County, Maryland. The house, built c. 1740, was enlarged in the course of the eighteenth century, the last time c. 1800 when these talismans were concealed over the entrances. A zooarchaeological study of the scars left by knives and cleavers showed that the cow heads had not been butchered in the usual way for food. They were deliberately chopped down to fit the narrow space above the plaster ceiling and under the floorboards upstairs.

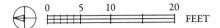

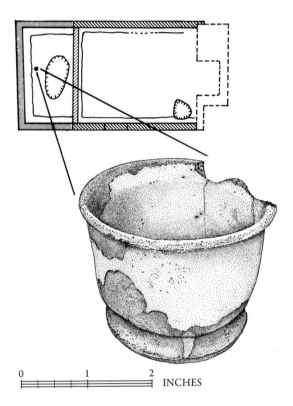

Archaeological plan of the kitchen behind the Thomas Everard House, Williamsburg, Virginia, and a mid-eighteenth-century salve pot buried in the earthen floor after 1774. Archaeologists discovered this small commonplace delftware container in a shallow hole scarcely larger that the vessel itself. The cavity appeared to have been custom-sized to fit the object it held. The pot itself was empty when found. Its location in an unheated ground-floor chamber built off the cook-room in 1773–74 suggests a private space occupied by Everard's enslaved cook or other kitchen help.

domestic genie was strongly felt. Folklorists might suspect that the table was another. Eating and drinking are often activities where important social exchanges take place. Vessels for food and drink assist in that interchange. Therefore the possibility must be entertained that, where commonplace objects meddled in the affairs of men and women anyway, tablewares were welcomed into the company of eaters and drinkers perhaps little differently from the other messmates who sat around a peasant table.[12]

Written records remain noncommittal on this point. Fortunately, their silence is uproariously broken by testimony from a multitude of garrulous artifacts. Most major collections of English ceramics contain at least a few slipware and salt-glazed bottles, jugs, and pitchers bearing inscriptions that give the vessels actual speaking parts: "I by my Master heare am Sent / to make You merrey is my Intent"—to cite one example among many.[13] Such pot laureates were meant to be droll, no doubt about it. But humor is culture-bound too, and full of insights. If historians are prepared to collect evidence from these gallipot informants, they will observe several qualities in them that say worlds about English and American folk material culture before the consumer revolution (fig. 6).

First of all, most were communal drinking vessels, usually harvest pitchers, puzzle jugs, or stoneware bottles. They were brought out at those times of day and seasons of the year when peasants regularly consorted together in activities that reinforced their commonality. The vessels addressed their users as they would good neighbors, sometimes as they paused from work ("Now I am Com for to Suply / the Harvismen when they are Dray") and other times when the village lads were wiling away empty hours tippling and gaming ("Gentlemen now try your Skill / Ill hould you sixpence if you Will / That you dont drink unless you Spill").[14] Jug and Bottle were just two more good old boys who helped with the harvest and afterwards joined the merrymaking that included all villagers regardless of rank.

They were not, however, unconscious of rank. The act of eating and drinking together was always an occasion to acknowledge the village social order. Harvest jugs could show great social acumen when paying the respects of their "Masters" to the recipients of their proffered hospitality. One North Devon pitcher, which was imported into Sussex County, Delaware, after 1698, recites a pretty little speech: "Kind Sr: i Com to . . . Sarue youre table with Strong Beare / for this intent i was sent heare" (fig. 7). The sender, however, anticipated that "Kind Sr" might prefer to share his gift with his own lower-ranking field hands. So the vessel was further instructed to say, "or if you pleas i will Supply / youre workmen when in haruist dry / when thy doe Labour hard and Sweate / good drinke is better far then Meate."[15] Pots—like other peasants—knew their place and everybody else's in the intimate, face-to-face jug, village communities they all inhabited together.

Their testimony is sufficient to support at least a strong presumption that these and probably a larger menagerie of unlettered domestic utensils were part of an animated world that we moderns know only as children. It was a small world, as we have seen, larger than a village, but usually not wider than the circle of acquaintances that a person could meet or know by reputation in a lifetime of moving around its environs. Its landscape—real, imagined, and blurry in between—was as crowded as a canvas by Hieronymus Bosch. Like his paintings, its denizens included a fantastical fellowship of human beings, spirits, animals, artifacts, and a veritable zoo of halfling hybrid combinations. Animal, mineral, or vegetable, all were inseparably linked in a harmonic, though often not harmonious, unity. In ages long ago, before ordinary men and women learned to give notional values to utilitarian objects according to their capacity to reflect flatteringly on their owners and do their bidding, the material world was an infinitely lively place where cats played fiddles and little dogs laughed and a dish could elope with a spoon.

This patchwork quilt of commonplaces that covered the British Isles in the Middle Ages began to come unraveled, and the local colors run together, as economic pressures further accelerated the movement of peoples and expanded their cultural horizons in the sixteenth century. Folklife and folklore, including traditional ideas about material things, persisted centuries longer, of course, surviving well into our own times in pockets of rural England and in the hills and hollows of backwoods America. All the same, it is also fair to say that the singular habits of personal acquisitiveness that later came to characterize consumer behavior can already be detected by the second half of the sixteenth century.

FIGURE 6

Face vessels and other anthropomorphic objects had fraternized with people at all levels of European society since the Middle Ages. Not surprisingly, many later stowed away to the colonies in immigrants' personal baggage. Others came in trade. In North America they met and mingled with ceremonial and everyday objects used by other folk cultures, African and Native American, where beliefs in animism also had deep roots. Such vessels gradually disappeared from polite company after 1700. Commercial potteries in Britain went on producing Toby jugs and puzzle pots for taverns and other vernacular haunts, although none has turned up on American sites. Folk potters in this country continued to find ready markets for face vessels wherever folk customs persisted.

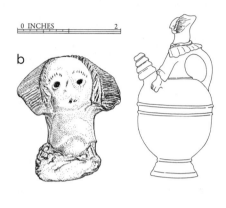

b

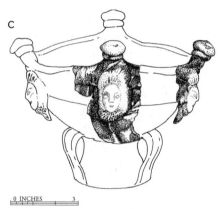

c

a

Aachen (Germany) stoneware bottle (*a*), made c. 1475–1525 in the form of a bagpiper. German and Belgian jugs and bottles were widely exported and fragments are found frequently on early Tudor archaeological sites from palaces to peasant houses. Immigrants to America left behind a host of personable face vessels like these.

Saintonge (France) figurine bottle (*b*) used in the second quarter of the seventeenth century in the household of Walter Aston, "Gentleman," militia colonel, and first owner of Causey's Care in Charles City County, Virginia. Made after c. 1610 and discarded before c. 1640. Polychrome chafing dish (*c*) from southwest France, probably exported through La Rochelle, the chief supplier to the Arcadian fur trade post at Fort Pentagoet, Castine, Maine. Not a brazier for cooking, the basin contained steaming water to warm food in dishes supported on the knobs above the relief molded masks. Stylistically c. 1550–1650, but from the table of the garrison commander Charles d' Aulnay, 1635–54.

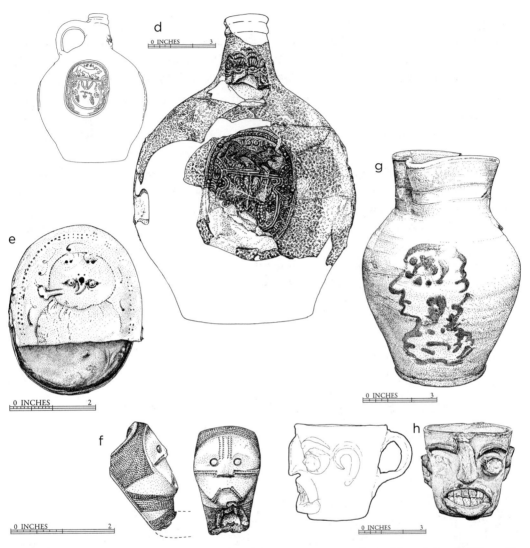

Bartmann stoneware bottle with a double mask (*d*), dated 1661. This German vessel remained in use in a fashionable Jamestown rowhouse (structure 17) until c. 1720. Copper tobacco can (*e*), punch-decorated with the figure of an owl smoking a 1620–60–style pipe. Its unknown owner lived at Littletown Plantation, James City County, Virginia, the home of Col. Thomas Pettus. The farmstead was occupied c. 1640–1700. Indian effigy tobacco pipe (*f*), probably made by a Piscataway potter using a gear wheel from a watch to roulette the human face. Discovered at St. Mary's City, Maryland, probably from a deposit of c. 1650.

Stoneware pitcher (*g*), made locally at Alexandria, Virginia, possibly by John Swann, 1813–21, and thrown into a privy behind an artisan's shop near the Market Square. Stoneware face cup (*h*) with kaolin teeth and eyes made by slaves working at the Thomas Davies Pottery, Bath, South Carolina, c. 1860. Davies explained that "weird-looking" vessels made by his black potters were "modeled in the front in the form of a grotesque human face evidently intended to portray the African features."

FIGURE 7

Sgraffito-ware harvest jug, 1698, North Devon, England, with a history of ownership in Sussex County, Delaware. Inscribed *Kinde Sr: i Com to Gratifiey youre Kindness Love and / and* [sic] *Courtisey: and Sarue youre table with Strong Beare for this / intent i was sent heare: or if you pleas i will Supply youre workmen when in / haruist dry when thy doe Labour hard and Sweate good drinke is better far then Meat:*. The pitcher's decoration catches the last rays of one era and the first of another in its schizophrenic combination of folk elements—the birds, tulips, and unicorns—with a stylish baroque portrait medallion enclosed in a wreath of fruit. Even the ancient spout effigy now wears a fashionable hat and periwig.

Such anthropomorphic vessels and verses continued to perform their original functions for at least another generation in rural Delaware, where it was still common practice in the 1720s for smallholders and gentlemen to work side by side helping each other bring in the harvest, repair barns, and whitewash houses. No wages were paid in these circumstances, it was said. Caesar Rodney, one of the region's prominent shirtsleeve gentlemen, recorded that a shared pipe and a draught of rum were often his neighbors' only reward for helping out—that and the "old Seremony of fiddling and Dancing" in the evening.

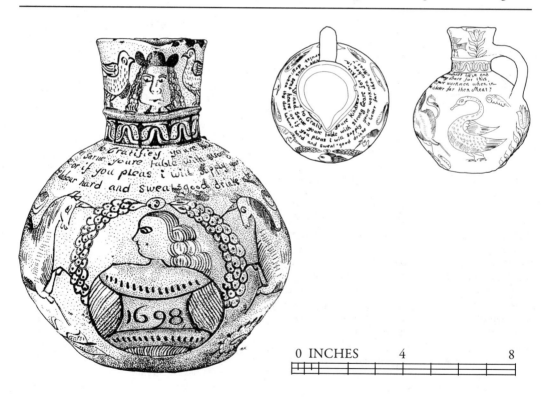

0 INCHES   4   8

The complex causes are much studied by historians of early modern Europe. Some emphasize the pressure of a rapidly growing English population on food resources after about 1520. Higher prices and lower wages pushed the unemployed and underemployed off the land toward cities and colonies where opportunities looked brighter.[16] Other historians prefer to see the impetus to these events coming from the opposite direction, pulling people away from their ancestral homes more than pushing them. These writers understand the expansion of Europe in the sixteenth century to have been an expansion in the capitalistic mode of production. Capitalism required a global redistribution of labor to cities at the commercial centers of the system and to overseas colonies at the peripheries, there to be populated by suppliers of raw materials and buyers of finished goods.[17]

Proponents of both explanations identify two consequences of these events that bear on our search for the origins of consumer demand. Each left its mark on village life. Rising prices filled the pockets of the growers of agricultural commodities while at the same time emptying the pockets of those with only their labor to sell in a crowded labor market. A social gap opened between landholders and wage earners, which the spread of international Protestantism and formal education widened into divergent and distinctly different cultural outlooks between parish notables and their poorer neighbors. To Marxist historians, the polarization of two cultures resembles nothing so much as the division of society into separate classes of employers and proles. Either way, the much older rule of precedence began giving way in the sixteenth century to differences based on perceptions of class and associated lifestyles.

The second consequence could be seen everywhere on tracks and highways leading from villages to provincial towns and from towns to the great metropolis. The ceaseless movement of people that historians now know began centuries earlier accelerated still more in the sixteenth century. Besides landless farm workers looking for employment in nearby parishes and the ever-circulating population of young men and women in local service, the roads filled up with others traveling longer distances. Younger sons of established country families journeyed to larger towns to seek apprenticeships and follow trades that seldom brought them home again. Migration that removed people from their immediate localities was further swelled in the sixteenth and early seventeenth centuries by a stream that became a torrent of desperately poor wage laborers unable to find work in the countryside and forced to wander far and wide to eke out a bare living.[18] Better poor relief and increased food production reduced their number after the English Civil War, but aggregate mobility rates remained high. Furthermore, and of greater importance for the study of material life, movers in the latter half of the seventeenth century tended to be more affluent and respectable than previously—lesser-gentry families drawn to the bright lights of provincial towns, apprentices to the professional and higher-status trades, skilled artisan refugees from the Continent to the safety of tolerant England, and women to domestic service in the town houses of merchants, gentlemen, and professionals.[19]

Throughout the entire period the magnetism of London exerted a tremendous influence on local and regional migration patterns. The metropolis grew enormously—sometimes it seemed exponentially—from 60,000 inhabitants in the early sixteenth century to 200,000 by 1600, 350,000 by 1650, and more than half a million by the end of the seventeenth century.[20] Reliable estimates make 11 percent of the total population of England and Wales resident in greater London by 1700. The capital was a catch-basin for tens of thousands of migrants, who may not have left home intending to move far, but, not finding opportunities nearby, drifted from place to place and eventually gravitated into the sprawling London labor market. Bernard Bailyn has described early modern England and northern Europe as "a world in motion." It can be added that it was a centrifugal motion expanding the tight little circles in which medieval migrants had moved mostly from neighborhood to neighborhood. That was one difference. The movers themselves were another. They ceased to be principally the poorest people in society after the Restoration. Furthermore and apropos to the question that drives my inquiry here, *why demand,* this better class of migrants was not long discovering that they needed an altogether new approach to integrate themselves into the unfamiliar communities they traveled to and sought to join.

At first the colonization of North America was simply a spillover from these local and regional movements of people across England, Scotland, and Wales and eventually large parts of the Netherlands, Flanders, Scandinavia, the German states, and Switzerland as well.[21] Bailyn, whose multivolume treatment of the subject provides a framework for understanding these national migrations as parts of a global resettlement of British and European peoples, identifies two categories of emigrants. Each came from different backgrounds and sought different fortunes overseas in ways that were to bear directly on their material living standards in America. One group consisted mainly of young, unmarried men, frequently in the seventeenth century the sons of yeomen and husbandmen or rural craftsmen. A hundred years later their ranks were swelled by disappointed artisans and runaway apprentices from urban employers. Usually impecunious, they earned their passage across the Atlantic by indenturing themselves to American masters who badly needed their labor and specialized skills. They tended therefore to settle first in the older agricultural regions and somewhat later in the growing seaport cities. As bondsmen, they earned little income during the period of their service, which had the effect of delaying for four years or more their entry into the market as consumers of anything beyond the maintenance and freedom dues they were owed by their masters. Nonetheless, coming originally from London or from one of the larger provincial English cities, as many of them had by the middle of the eighteenth century, freedmen often were well acquainted with the "decensies" and "luxuries" that poverty and servitude had long denied them.

The other group of emigrants was older and more prosperous. They paid their own passage to North America in family groups that included women and children. Most were farmers. The English among them came at first from the Home Counties and the south generally. Their destination was overwhelmingly New England before 1650, although some ended up in the proprietary colony of Maryland. A hundred years later the center of family emigration from Britain shifted northward to Yorkshire and Scotland, again in response, it seems, to changing patterns of internal migration caused in part by commercialized farming and the breakup of the Scottish clans. In America the lure of cheap, empty land drew these British farmers to the vast backcountry tracts of Nova Scotia, New York, Pennsylvania, and North Carolina. There they were thrown together with individuals and families from lower Germany, Switzerland, Ulster, and the Netherlands, many of whom, like themselves, had been uprooted by dislocations at home that predisposed them to the blandishments of recruiting agents working for American speculators in western lands.

Few families were wealthy, but, being free, they contributed immediately to the American economy, not only the foodstuffs and handcrafts they sold at market, but, after their initial investment in necessary capital improvements, also the durable goods they purchased for their own consumption. Country people may not have been fashion setters by city standards, even those of artisans, but many of the middling sort had already developed certain genteel appetites before emigrating. They transmitted those cravings from their homelands to the hinterlands of America. Travelers' journals are replete with accounts of backwoodsmen who served a proper English tea in the howling wilderness. As one intrepid Englishwoman reported, it was "droll enough to eat out of China and be served in plate" in the hovel of a mere sawmill operator in the wilds of North Carolina, for the "house [was] no house" and hardly bigger or better than one of the man's slave cabins. Yet, she conceded, "the master and the furniture made you ample amends."[22] Drawing-room manners, however watered down, were no mystery to many immigrant families who flooded into the backcountry that began filling up after 1763. Meanwhile in the cities, skilled indentured servants marked time until they too would be free to set up as journeymen, tradesmen, or clerks and share in the world of goods they saw all around them.

I have let this moving picture of uprooted peoples roll forward two hundred years from the sixteenth century to the eighteenth to show how the settlement of colonies was but one episode in a massive global redistribution and relocation of British and European populations, not to mention the several million enslaved Africans who were redistributed and relocated against their will. So far as Western European history goes, here without doubt was an event that reshaped the lives of a multitude of the same "middling sort" of people who by the eighteenth century were becoming participants in an emerging pan-atlantic consumer society. Here at last are the highly mobile, ordinary people who must be present to sustain our hypothesis about a standardized and widely distributed mass material culture. Moreover, their journeys start and end in precisely those locations where the drama took place—northern Europe, the British Isles, North America, and the Caribbean islands—the same places where consumer spending and fashionable living reached epidemic proportions by the closing decades of the eighteenth century.

The strands of the argument played out in the fifth proposition are drawing together. If mobility data were more complete and if the most sensitive evidence of early consumer behavior could be reduced to a head-count, we would almost certainly see a pair of trend lines rising suggestively in parallel tracks. One would show a burst of population growth during the period of initial settlement followed by a diminished but consistently strong stream of English immigration into mainland North America through the 1680s. It would coincide with the earliest measures of fashionable consumption among American elites. Migration rates fell off sharply in the 1690s but recovered again after 1700. Both indicators would then veer sharply upward, the number of free white immigrants from the 1710s onward and consumption levels from the 1720s. Both skyrocketed to 1740.[23]

The correlations invite speculation about possible explanatory connections, but they are suggestive and no more. These trends might also correlate merely by coincidence or might perhaps be better explained by some third factor—by the growth of wealth, for instance, or by growing extremes in wealth, or, as some scholars have argued on the American side, by a re-Anglicizing of colonial culture. If there really is a case to be made that geographical mobility, as it became an ever more commonplace experience, diluted and eventually dissolved the traditional links between neighborhood, personal reputation, status, and power and in their place substituted an altogether novel system of values that measured reputation and social standing by the possession and prescribed use of relatively inexpensive and socially significant consumer goods—if that is the case that has to hold water—then it must be demonstrated that the meaning of material things and the uses to which they were put changed, not just for the migrants and movers, but for the stay-behinds and stay-at-homes as well. The thesis presented here cannot be confined to a mobile population alone, if for no other reason than because participation in the new consumer culture clearly was not limited to migratory populations exclusively, however large they may have been. The argument applies more broadly than that. The fifth proposition is addressed to Anglo-American, even Euro-colonial, society as a whole. It holds that the sheer volume of increased travel and migration reshaped basic cultural norms throughout northern Europe and European nations' overseas colonies. The fact of geographical mobility, if not always the personal experience of it, enforced on virtually everyone to some degree or other new standards and practices of social intercourse.

The immediate beneficiaries were the travelers themselves, the merchants, itinerant tradesmen, immigrants, colonists, army officers, crown officials, churchmen, tourists, scientists, sportsmen, convalescents, and a host of other footloose men and women, especially those of some little reputation, whose journeys nevertheless carried them outside the effective range of their reputations. In their need to make themselves known in strange places they adopted a different system of social communication. For it to work, the information they transmitted had to be taken in, digested, understood, and heeded by those who received them. Increasingly it was. The presence of travelers and migrants altered the chemistry of everyday life in the settled communities into which they and their affairs intruded. Their traffic, whether for business or pleasure, brought advantage to the settled individuals with whom they necessarily had dealings. The locals soon discovered that they could advance their own fame and fortune by welcoming outsiders into their circle of acquaintances on these new terms. Thus a value system prized initially for its portability spread far and wide among peoples who were less traveled and otherwise appear little different from the inhabitants of the medieval villages that we looked at earlier, except that now some of their affairs and some of their associates were farther flung.

The old-fashioned measures of personal reputation were not immediately overthrown. But they were no longer enough by themselves. The chiefest men and women in any particular locality where those who possessed the wherewithal and wielded the influence that usually brought them to the attention of strangers in the first place. Their accommodation to fashionable living therefore often merely reaffirmed the old pecking order based on landholding and lineage. Indeed the good manners that newcomers offered as their principal letters of credit were honored in no small part precisely because local worthies had already been observed to behave after the same fashion. Gentility was like paper money. It was presumed to stand for tangible social assets that unfamiliar bearers kept stashed away at home, and it was generally accepted at face value because it was currency that homegrown ladies and gentlemen traded in as well. In short, gentility and the consumer goods required to practice the arts of fashionable living were a social compact into which more and more covenanters were drawn as they perceived that the opportunities for personal betterment in a more open society outweighed any advantage to be gained from stubborn adherence to tradition. Visual literacy was as much a prerequisite to getting a piece of action in the expanding world three hundred years ago as computer literacy is our entré to a shrinking world today.

Neither events nor inventions precipitate cultural changes so fundamental and so far-reaching. They happen cumulatively, occurring slowly and haphazardly at first and only gaining momentum as time goes by. Assigning a starting date to the consumer revolution is, therefore, much less instructive than narrowing to two or three generations the era when consumer culture became a pervasive social force. My account proposes that that moment occurred throughout large parts of provincial England and North America in the hundred years or so between, say, the Restoration and 1760. To test the validity of the fifth proposition—and to sharpen the focus of our search for the origins of demand—we must therefore look most carefully for evidence of this transformation in consumer behavior in the several decades around 1700.

First, though, we need to take account of a body of scholarship that would push the dating of these developments back to Tudor times, a century or more before the period where we will concentrate our search. Some historians have argued that the ambition to cut a fashionable figure was widely felt among even common folk not later than the sixteenth century.[24] They are not talking about an improving standard of living, which we have already acknowledged to be an important consequence of Elizabethan prosperity. These historians have in mind out-and-out conspicuous consumption, and they point to a flurry of Tudor sumptuary laws as proof that Phillip Stubbes wrote the truth in 1595 when he said that "no other nations take such pride in apparel as England."[25] His evidence is undeniable. But when historians ask *what* was consumed and *why,* the village jack-a-dandies who so excited the displeasure of their Elizabethan superiors turn out to resemble only remotely their descendants in the eighteenth century for whom gentility with its wardrobe of fashionable clothing and toolbox of newfangled housewares would eventually become a total way of life. The hallmarks of the consumer revolution, we must keep in mind, were not just a profusion of attractive and affordable personal possessions but also a code of easily learned rules governing their use on prescribed occasions.

The importance that people in Tudor and Stuart times attached to clothing appears on close inspection to have been decidedly more traditional than innovative. Sumptuary laws were aimed overwhelmingly at excesses in dress, at what Stubbes called "pride of apparel." Such "new fangles" offended propriety in two ways: by extravagant use of expensive materials by those who could ill afford them and by misuse of fashionable clothing reserved for those who could. A lowly collier's wife in Jamestown, Virginia, broke both rules in 1618 by wearing a "rough bever hatt with a faire perle hatband, and a silken suite thereto correspondent."[26] Her higher-ranking neighbor, William Harwood, was measured by a different yardstick. As "governor" of nearby Martin's Hundred, he was entitled by executive order of the Virginia Company to wear the woven gold garter points that archaeologists found on the site of his house.[27] Statute law in Massachusetts expressly forbade persons worth less than £200 to buy or wear "gold or silver girdles, hatbands, belts, ruffs, [or] beaver hats" as well as "any slashed clothes other than one slash in each sleeve and another in the back."[28]

In Old and New World alike, there was a rising tide of infractions against decorum. Its magnitude *was* new. But the forms extravagance took were not. Woven textiles, precious metals, jewelry, and exotic furs and feathers had always marked the high status of their owners and wearers. Made into clothing, often styled with cutwork and slashes to show off wasteful consumption, textiles were the most ancient personal status symbols of all. Why did coxcombs spend every farthing on such frippery? Was it a bold stroke to launch themselves into polite society? Not in 1600, not according to William Vaughan, who had interviewed numerous servants who, he said, had bestowed "all the money they had in the world on sumptuous garments." When he had asked these men "how they would live hereafter," they invariably replied that "a good marriage will one day make amends for all."[29] Here was self-advancement accomplished the old-fashioned way, by making advantageous family alliances. Both dress and success were still viewed in very traditional terms. As a matter of fact, sumptuary laws were medieval legal instruments for the defense of privilege by precedence, despite their apparent obsession with rank alone. Precedence, as we saw in connection with ceremonial furniture and tablewares, entitled individuals to use certain objects, or disallowed their use, depending on specific social circumstances. That was the trouble with clothing and the reason it had to be strictly controlled. Clothing was too portable and too inseparable from the wearer. A man could not remove or change his clothes, except to doff his hat, at the sudden appearance of social superiors. So there had to be laws to prevent common folk from ever wearing articles of clothing that might conceivably—somewhere, sometime—give offense to someone who had greater precedence. Sumptuary laws provided those blanket proscriptions. They were not intended primarily to check the spread of fashionable living.

To answer the historians who detect consumer impulses as early as the sixteenth century, it can be said in summary that *standards of living* were indeed improving rapidly on the eve of American colonization. *Lifestyles* changed more slowly where they challenged traditional attitudes about the value and use of material things. But challenged they were. There is no question that the identification of individuals with their personal possessions grew closer in the sixteenth and seventeenth centuries. Nothing in earlier times resembles the remarkable variety of affordable haberdashery that flooded popular markets fully two hundred years before the appearance of machine-made textiles. Studies of the stocking knitting industry in the sixteenth century estimate that a work force of maybe 200,000 part-time cottage knitters produced upwards of 20 million pairs of stockings annually. The selection of colors, qualities, and styles was so "wanton" that "no sober chaste Christian" could put on some of the really tawdry pairs of hosiery offered for sale without risking eternal damnation—again the opinion of the censorious Stubbes. Pretty gloves, ribbons, hats, and caps became plentiful as well, all at prices to suit every purse.[30]

Sensitivity to customers' personal preferences and attention to price points anticipated market strategies that Josiah Wedgwood and others made famous in the eighteenth century.[31] Variety and affordability both show concern for something else that had to happen before the meaning of material things could change. Englishmen had to develop the modern notion of the individual's right to property ownership. This is no place to blunder unwarily into the thicket of historical controversy surrounding the origins of English individualism.[32] My particular interest in showing that expanding consumer choices went along with an enhanced regard for personal property need only take passing notice of pertinent work by political economists. They find that a key prerequisite to England's maturing market economy was recognition of the fact that individuals were the sole owners of their resources to be employed however they saw fit.[33]

Usually when historians write on this subject they cite heavyweight authorities like Hobbes and Locke. I would simply observe that far beneath the notice of those erudite philosophers a kind of rough-and-ready possessive individualism spread rapidly throughout English and American society, leaving its signatures written all over the everyday objects that individuals possessed. Personalized marks of ownership appear everywhere starting quite abruptly in the 1580s and 1590s. House-proud men and women carved, stitched, stamped, chased, and painted their initials, names, significant dates, and other identifying devices on personal possessions in the seventeenth century as never before or since.[34] Name plaques and date stones, mounted on houses and barns, broadcast to every passerby facts of village life that previously had been common knowledge (fig. 8). Indoors, householders carved their initials on cupboards,

FIGURE 8

Overmantel painting, *Samuel Harrison's Land Near Herring Bay*, Holly Hill, Anne Arundel County, Maryland, painted before 1733, signed *AS*. Not content to leave any room for doubt among guests invited into his parlor, the Maryland planter proudly displayed a double portrait of both his inherited estate and his newly enlarged brick house in a framed painting hung on the chimneypiece. A banner headline proclaims his ownership while sidebars record the metes and bounds. Harrison's stylish renovations made portrait-worthy what had been a 1699 clapboard-covered timber dwelling little better than the tenant cottages seen in the background in this panoramic view of his holdings.

cabinets, and expensive armchairs as if the forms by themselves no longer confirmed unequivocally their users' importance.[35] Chests identified by names or initials the owners of their increasingly valuable contents, and more and more were fitted with locks to secure a little bit of personal storage space in what were otherwise still communal rooms.[36]

Actually, some rooms were becoming less communal. For the first time inventory takers were shown into chambers known not by their location over, behind, or within other rooms, but by the personal name of their principal occupant, which they dutifully recorded as the "roome called Mr. Wm ffarvar['s] roome," to take one Virginia example from many hundreds.[37] Coats of arms, family devices, and still more initials were engraved on silver plate and pewter, embroidered on bed hangings, etched in glass, pressed into bottle seals, and scrolled into stump-work pictures. The bond between owner and object grew closer, but at the same time the social distance between them widened into a gulf. Face jugs and vessels carrying first-person inscriptions remained imprisoned in unregenerate folk culture (see fig. 6). One senses that more worldly users were fast learning the modern practice of treating inanimate objects strictly as possessions, mere goods and chattels, one more resource to be employed, as the economists said, however their owners saw fit. Artifacts ceased to be actors in their own right. Instead they were acted upon by makers and users. Inscriptions on ordinary utilitarian objects bespeak not comradeship but ownership. They sound more and more like dog tags— "Roger Smith his Bottle," "Mrs. Mary Sandbach her Cup"—or, alternatively, like shopkeepers' receipts—"Made for Mrs. Hugs by Jos. Hollamore, Barnstable."[38]

A transformation was taking place, as mundane as it was also profound and far-reaching. A few household goods and articles of personal apparel had always been highly valued because they were made of precious materials, were hard to get, or represented their owner's ability to pay lavishly for other people's labor. Now little by little that small assortment of prized possessions was supplemented and expanded by whole categories of things whose worth was more notional—ascribed—than real. The fact of ownership became ever more its own reward. In life and death alike a man's or woman's estate came to be regarded as the sum total of old wealth and new, of land, its products and improvements, cash, plate, and uncollected debts. But increasingly a decedent's worth did not stop there. As probate inventories attest by the hundreds of thousands starting in precisely this period, household gear and personal possessions were often itemized down to the last linen handkerchief and appraised to the final ha'penny. Quality and quantity became twin ladders to greater reputation and upward social mobility. "Gentry or gentilitie is taken two waies," wrote Francis Markham in 1625, "that is to say, either by acquisition or descent."[39] The old way was tried and true, the new way strictly parvenu. Yet to many men and women who set out on the road to Bristol or London or set sail for Massachusetts or Maryland, the brave new world of material goods offered an irresistible shortcut to the good name they lacked at home or left behind.

3

꠹꠹꠹꠹

NEW CONSUMERS

Looked at backwards in historical perspective, the contrast between material life in medieval times and the early modern period appears so striking that the term *revolution* seems well deserved. Certainly the eighteenth-century champions and critics of luxury saw their era as the dawn of a new age, for better or worse. In reality the course of change was evolutionary. It only seemed otherwise because its pace sped up so dramatically. It burst on people's consciousness all of a sudden in the early eighteenth century even though it was already well advanced. Consequently, explicit discussion of fashionable living appears relatively late in conventional literary sources, and usually they describe the phenomenon in its more mature stages of development. It follows that historians who seek the earliest ancestors of *Homo gentilis* must undertake a kind of paleontological research among the fossil tools they left behind to discover a story that is seldom touched on in the standard texts. This chapter and the next take a close look at a curious assortment of newfangled personal and household objects whose acquisition answered a need that was different from the age-old itch simply to outshine one's neighbors by imitating one's betters. Drawing a distinction between emulation and fashionableness takes us one step closer to understanding the essential nature of demand for the kind of goods that eventually only an industrial revolution could satisfy.

The fossil analogy is not so far-fetched as it may sound. Our quarry from the beginning of these pages has been man the modern tool user.

What earlier states he evolved from and what new uses and meanings for material things he discovered along the way were usually not matters that he—or she—put into writing. They can, however, be strongly inferred from careful study of obsolete tools, which, when newly made, were full of uses, but, gradually aging into junk, were eventually discarded into trash pits, attics, and museums and replaced by later models. The replacements performed their tasks better in a utilitarian sense, or else they better equipped their users to compete successfully in a faster social tug-of-war. To understand demand is still the goal. To succeed, written-record historians must pay attention to the very artifacts that in their day satisfied that demand. Their materials, forms, ornamentation, and especially their uses are a prehistorian's earliest clues to the evolutionary history of consumer behavior.

The story early American artifacts tell about the origins of demand picks up where the foregoing account of material life in provincial England left off in the sixteenth century. The landscape that English and European immigrants and African slaves carved out of the North American wilderness appears remarkably traditional at first glance. Farmers in New England sited their barns alongside public roads, usually well forward of the house, in an age-old demonstration of wealth and prominence that no one in agricultural communities mistook (fig. 9).[1]

Likewise, early tobacco plantations in the Chesapeake colonies were conspicuous for buildings that emphasized their productive capacity, not the owner's claims to gentility.[2] A planter's own dwelling often nestled in a litter of nearly identical clapboard-covered structures, one hardly distinguishable from the others. Besides their own houses, planters frequently built numerous outbuildings and quarters, the most typical of which one early traveler in Virginia itemized as "a separate kitchen, a separate house for the Christian slaves [that is, indentured servants], one for the negro slaves, and several to dry the tobacco, so that when you come to the home of a person of some means," he explained, "you think you are entering a fairly large village"—and in 1686 he still meant an old-fashioned village.[3] Buildings everywhere in the colonies were so thoroughly vernacular—place-bound—that today architectural historians can often trace the traditions they embodied back to specific regions in England. Most exhibited no fashionable pretensions whatsoever. Contemporaries used words like *homely* and *slight* to describe cottages that people back home best understood when correspondents writing from the colonies likened them to barns.[4] There were a few larger and better-built houses, some substantial and commodious enough to remain serviceable for three hundred years. But, as we have seen, even they provided only such amenities as were already transforming late medieval houses in England—namely, chimneys, upper floors usually given over to bedchambers, and various arrangements of ground-floor rooms that had hardly begun to separate work spaces from those increasingly reserved for dining, sitting, socializing, and retiring.

Material life in the earliest American colonies remained rooted in the traditions of the English countryside and to a lesser-known extent in the folkways of African villages. Only when architectural and furniture historians add up the cumulative effect of many small improvements and innovations is it possible to detect an unmistakable drift toward true fashion consciousness, that radically new way of thinking that deployed personal possessions in support of social hierarchies built not upon precedence but on manners. The popularity of monograms is a tip-off to students of material culture to look for other attributes of everyday objects that refined them into symbols of class consciousness. There is an intelligible pattern in their development. And while this yardstick admits many exceptions, it exhibits notable congruities between furniture history and the history of gentility starting approximately in the middle decades of the seventeenth century. Several features of furniture in this period bear looking into one at a time—a tendency toward greater use of costly and exotic materials, the standardization of ornament, a proliferation of new forms, and eventually the combination of furnishings into sets and suites intended for use by ladies and gentlemen who regularly engaged in well-rehearsed social performances. Each bears closer investigation.

I am not the first to attach significance to these novelties, nor will I be the last to concede that buyers found newfangled goods desirable for a host of strictly personal reasons, including their beauty, convenience, comfort, utility, and sometimes good value.[5] As the saying goes, there is no accounting for taste. What most certainly must be accounted for was

FIGURE 9

Daniel Cushing Sr., a well-to-do Massachusetts farmer, bought this South Side property in 1675, built his "Dwelling house" four summers later, and a "Barne and all other Buildings standing there upon" by the time of his death in 1693. Originally, the hall-and-parlor house rose one and a half stories high, two large front-facing gables giving extra headroom to the attic bedchambers. A cooking hearth and built-in oven equipped the hall. Cellar stairs in the lobby led down to a cool storeroom for foodstuffs and dairy products underneath the parlor. One or more renovations, starting c. 1740–62, removed the gables, raised the roof to two full stories, and added a lean-to kitchen across the back. Cushing's farmyard lay along the road leading into town. There he built a five-bay, plank-sided grain and cattle barn with an aisle or lean-to along the south side perhaps for a stable, a porch too narrow for carts, and a gable on the rear roof to provide light for threshing and air for winnowing.

SOUTH ELEVATION *1679*

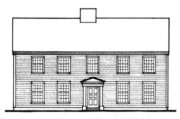

SOUTH ELEVATION *BEFORE 1762*

0 FEET   30

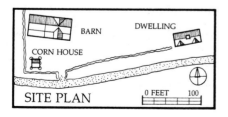

SITE PLAN

0 FEET   100

Cushing farmstead, Hingham, Massachusetts. House built July 1679 (diary), enlarged with lean-to addition and modernized c. 1740–62 (inscription) and perhaps again shortly before c. 1800, enlarged for the last time and restored 1936. The unusually large and handsome parlor must have held the best bed and assorted seat furniture. Upstairs, those who slept in the bedchamber over the parlor enjoyed warmth from a fireplace while lodgers in the hall chamber shivered. Despite differences in the status and uses of the four rooms, the exposed ceiling frames in all were expensively embellished with quarter-round chamfers, and the fireplace walls were sheathed with planed boards heavily shadow-molded along the joints. Black and marbleized beams in the hall and yellow walls spotted with brown polka dots were probably painted c. 1700–1725. Above average in their day, such refinements failed to meet the tastes and social requirements of later Cushings. A fashionably renewed staircase installed in the lobby and raised panels mounted on the fireplace walls in the parlor and former hall (a sleeping and dressing room by 1783) marked these as genteel spaces suitable for company. Farmhands and domestics could be restricted to the back rooms, coming and going to the cellar and the lean-to chambers via a service stair.

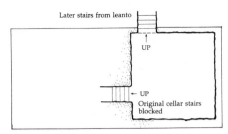

Later stairs from leanto

↑ UP

← UP
Original cellar stairs
blocked

CELLAR PLAN

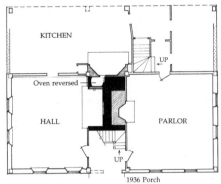

KITCHEN

UP ←

Oven reversed

HALL

PARLOR

UP ↑

1936 Porch

GROUND PLAN

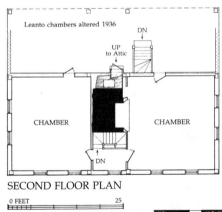

Leanto chambers altered 1936

DN ↓

UP ↑
to Attic

CHAMBER

CHAMBER

DN ↑

SECOND FLOOR PLAN

< (° 1762

INSCRIPTION
SCRATCHED ON BACK STAIRS

SHADOW MOLDED BOARDING *1679*

0 INCHES   2

A ———⌒⌒⌒——— A

0 FEET   25

FRAME   BRICK

☐ *1679*

▦ *Before 1762* ▨

SPONGE PAINTWORK IN
HALL, NE CORNER
c. 1700-25

0 FEET   2

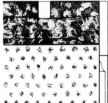 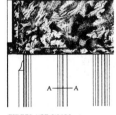

A — A

NORTH WALL   *FIREPLACE WALL*

FIGURE 9 (*continued*)

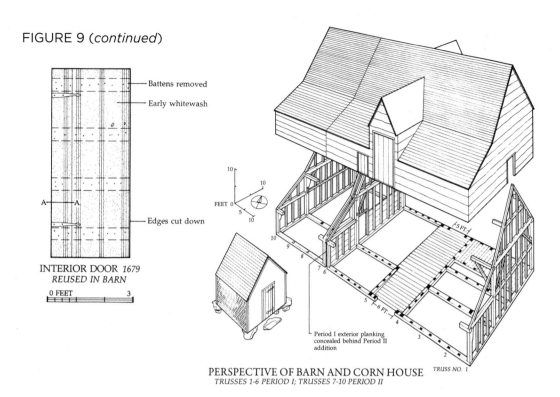

Battens removed

Early whitewash

A —— A

Edges cut down

INTERIOR DOOR *1679*
REUSED IN BARN

0 FEET   3

FEET 0

Period I exterior planking
concealed behind Period II
addition

PERSPECTIVE OF BARN AND CORN HOUSE
TRUSSES 1-6 PERIOD I; TRUSSES 7-10 PERIOD II

TRUSS NO. 1

Perspective of Cushing's grain and cattle barn and corn house. An oak-planked threshing floor divided the barn between storage space for harvested crops and open stalls for dairy cows. That combination was a new development in mixed farming regions in seventeenth-century England as well. Stalls used for milking and feeding were floored for cleanliness; those for bedding cattle had dirt floors for easy mucking. Soon after the barn was built, Cushing lengthened it by another three bays to store larger harvests. A surviving corn house, standing on staddle stones and fitted with two adjustable corn bins, is undated, but may have numbered among "all other Buildings" on the farmstead in 1693. It was standing by 1783 (inventory).

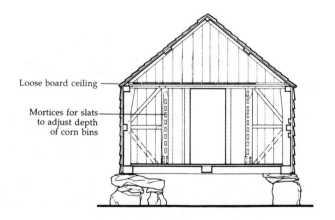

Loose board ceiling

Mortices for slats
to adjust depth
of corn bins

SECTION THROUGH CORN HOUSE
LOOKING EAST

0 FEET   7

the growing disposition of clients and craftsmen to prefer those design innovations that refashioned household artifacts to enhance their recognition and shared use by a universe of gentlefolk. By the same token, consumer choices reflected a spreading dissatisfaction with things that were meaningful only locally. Modernity gradually superseded memory where social sorting took place. Canon challenged custom. Brand names banished folk art to the cultural boondocks.

The first signs of fashion were nowhere visible on the rural American landscape or along the colonies' earliest city streets.[6] Outwardly, neither farmhouse nor town house revealed the first stirrings of the consumer impulse. Instead it incubated in the innermost sanctum of a yeoman's or merchant's physical world, namely, in his domestic parlor. Parlors still retained their ancient functions as ground-floor strongrooms and sleeping chambers, but, given hearths of their own, they were becoming withdrawing rooms and sitting rooms as well (see fig. 9). Here, behind closed doors, master and mistress felt most at home. Here, removed from the lesser inmates of the house, they entertained their social equals. Here, not surprisingly, they amassed those material things they prized above all else.[7] It is here, then, in the early American parlor that historians should seek the first telltale signs of fashion transformed into a total way of life.

Let us open the door into a parlor chosen at random from households in rural Massachusetts whose contents were inventoried by order of the Suffolk County court in the last quarter of the seventeenth century. Random, of course, does not mean average, and John Weld, a yeoman farmer of Roxbury, left a slightly larger estate than many of his neighbors when he died in 1691. But his was not the largest, not by far. Most of the furnishings that the inventory takers recorded in Weld's parlor were in no way extraordinary for the time or place or for men of his standing in the community. The most valuable piece in the room was "a fether bed." As we saw earlier, good beds had once been an uncommon luxury among ordinary farmers in England, but, ever since the sixteenth century, they were becoming favorite acquisitions for both English and American householders who could afford to improve their standard of living. The featherbed in Weld's parlor was well supplied with "a pair of sheets, Rugg, Coverlid, Blanket, Curtaines and Valines, Bolster, Pillows, and [a] Bedsted" (a frame) to raise the whole affair off the ground. The many textiles, not the plain, wooden bedstead, brought the total valuation to £6. That was a tidy sum, but nothing that other farmers could not match. "One standing Cupbord" was worth another pound (a fairly standard valuation for such pieces) and "a pair of tongs and a pair of small Andirons" on the hearth five shillings more. Everything else in the room came to £1 10s., inclusive for "A table, 5 Joynt stools, a wicker Chair, two other Chairs, 2 wrought stools, a wrought Chair, and a Glass-Case."[8]

A furniture historian, thus admitted vicariously into John Weld's parlor, recognizes first of all its ancient use as the principal sleeping chamber in the house.[9] But no longer was it merely an "inner room" partitioned off the hall, a cold retreat come end of day. A fireplace equipped with tongs and "small Andirons" (not the larger kind cooks needed) made the parlor a comfortable gathering place for family and friends to share their leisure time. Leaving servants and hired hands to eat at the "old Table" and sit on an "old setle Bench" in the adjoining hall alongside a cheese press and skeins of linen yarn, the parlor-users seem to have taken their meals seated around a newer table. It was set with drinking glasses and other tablewares (unrecorded but presumably the things stored in the "Glass-Case" and the "standing Cupbord"). There were stools and chairs enough for a company of eleven. All the same, the seating furniture was a motley assortment that reveals Weld's disinclination to provide the occupants of his parlor with matching chairs that accorded every sitter equal status. The one upholstered "wrought" chair, if it was his own, may indicate that the senior Weld observed the old rules of table to his dying day.

Much can be read into this one room in one house in one village in rural Massachusetts that applies to furnishings and fashions in comfortably well-off households all over the American colonies toward the close of the seventeenth century. Prestige was still conspicuously attached to expensive textiles like Weld's bed hangings and to cupboard plate. Textiles still imparted most of the value to the joined furniture they covered or cushioned. Other important distinctions were observed as well between the men and women entitled to sit on chairs and those consigned to stools and benches. These all were backward-looking customs. The Roxbury parlor also incorporated some of the innovations that had begun to alter everyday house life in the preceding hundred years and were becoming fairly commonplace by the end of the century. The householder's socially superior high table had removed into the privacy of the parlor, physically segregating persons of quality from the "mess" left behind in the hall. The display furniture had lumbered after, and some of the newer pieces were curiously "wrought" or otherwise embellished in ways that so excited the admiration of beholders that a proud owner, such as John Weld may have been, might instruct his joiner to carve "IW" on a drawer front or on the cresting rail of a chair.

What else can we learn about ordinary household gear in this period? What can a thorough knowledge of artifacts tell us about the way class consciousness eroded the old rules of precedence and laid the groundwork for that exclusionary aesthetic we call fashion? To examine the materials from which everyday objects were made is one useful place to start. Although the neighbors who compiled Weld's inventory saw no need to say so, we may safely assume that his furniture was oak, the favorite building material of joiners going back hundreds of years. Oak did not necessarily mean clumsy or plain. The "wrought" stools and chair, upholstered with needlework or Turkey-work seats, may have been carved with a flat, leafy, strapwork decoration that was also popular throughout the seventeenth century. The case pieces in Weld's parlor, the cupboard and the glass case, although not exceptionally valuable, are hard to imagine without at least a smattering of another common variety of mannerist-influenced ornament concocted of turned spindles, bosses, and applied architectural moldings. Such elements, glued and nailed to the oak carcasses of a farmer's cupboards and chests, were usually dabbed with black paint in imitation of ebony. Sometimes real ebony was used, one of several exotic woods from South America, Africa, and the Far East imported by timber merchants into Amsterdam and London and transshipped to joiners' shops in the colonies.[10]

For the first time ever, familiar pieces of farmhouse furniture were turned into eye-catchers before so much as a "cuberd cloth" was draped over top or the family plate put on display. Livery cupboards, court cupboards, chests, and boxes were deliberately made to look expensive by the extra workmanship they received, by the use of rare and unusual materials, and sometimes by application of brightly colored paint. As a matter of fact, relatively speaking, they *were* expensive. True, John Weld's bed hangings were worth six times more than the standard cupboard in his parlor, but he was a traditionalist. Even so, at £1 the cupboard represented two-fifths of the total value of all the parlor furniture used for dining, sitting, and storage. Elsewhere, even among some of his Roxbury neighbors, it was not uncommon for cupboards to be appraised at two, three, and four times as much. In settled communities everywhere, the price and value of good furniture were going up.

More significantly, imported woods and jazzy paintwork represented a different kind of value from investments in silver plate, gold threads, or latten spoons. Fancy furniture had little intrinsic value. It was not readily negotiable. It stood for money spent and gone forever. It implied reserves of wealth only marginally depleted by "wasteful" expenditures on property that did not appreciate in value or possessions that could not be melted down and coined. In that respect fine furniture resembled sumptuous garments. Costly ornament lavished on otherwise mundane stands and storage boxes advertised the owner's superior ability to squander his wealth, to use it frivolously, literally to consume his assets. Social symbolism that once resided in the things that case pieces and seating furniture displayed or stored came to be attached to the furniture itself, indeed at first to the selfsame pieces that had long assisted in public demonstrations of social precedence, namely, open cupboards, storage containers, and chairs of state.

The observation that such formerly utilitarian fittings acquired trappings that were aimed deliberately at impressing denizens of the parlor directs attention to this audience of privileged spectators. Who were they? Obviously those with eyes to see and minds to comprehend. But see and understand what? The literal answer, of course, is the physical appearance of the artifacts they looked at, the visual components and overall composition that formed the design. Furniture historians have made an interesting discovery about the design of household articles in the seventeenth century. Craftsmen then, like medieval craftsmen earlier, used geometry to lay out their work. The difference was that its later use was based on a system of proportions derived from classical architecture. It was a brand of northern European classicism, blended with lingering medievalisms, that art historians call mannerism.[11] First Antwerp and Germany and then Amsterdam after 1590 had been the principal artistic centers from which prototypes, patterns, publications, and eventually artisans themselves had spread the mannerist aesthetic throughout northern Europe and across the English Channel to become the dominant taste of the seventeenth century. Popular initially in court circles, this extravagantly decorative style was picked up and purveyed to bourgeois merchants and affluent yeomen by countless joiners, weavers, metalworkers, printers, and potters, many of whom were religious refugees from France and the Low Countries. Others, mostly English, joined the Protestant migrations to North America.

Artisans were not aestheticians. They did not have to be. Mannerist motifs were easily reduced to formulas that craftsmen could learn by rote and then replicate over and over again by using an ordinary rule and compass. Careful examination of pieces of American-made furniture reveals the lightly scribed lines and compass arcs that joiners scored across the surface of their work as they laid out mannerist-inspired strapwork, S-scrolls, and decoration in the applied molding style (fig. 10).[12] Tools and templates took some of the guesswork out of craftsmanship.[13] Not only could artisans make more objects in less time to meet the growing demand for quality household furnishings, jigs also guaranteed clients a higher degree of design consistency. Without consistency there can be no standardization. Mannerist geometry gave artisans a compositional strategy that they could follow using ordinary hand tools to create look-alike products for sale to what was already becoming a mass market without borders. Mannerism was the first international style to impress its image on city and village cultures alike. It was expressed in a thousand different forms and motifs because individual shop masters still controlled the design process.[14] But the look became recognizable the world over because the work all proceeded from the same design principles.

Those principles amounted to more than just syntax for a new language of ornament. They fundamentally reorganized the composition of mannerist images and objects to serve a purpose that art and architecture had not been called on to perform hitherto, certainly not pieces of household furniture. Mannerist forms deliberately created an illusion

FIGURE 10

William Searle emigrated to New England from Devonshire, England, and settled in Ipswich by 1663. His younger partner, Thomas Dennis, also learned his trade in Devon. They brought with them a popular mannerist design idiom composed of geometrical strapwork and foliage.

Carved chest, oak, attributed to Thomas Dennis, Ipswich, Massachusetts, before 1680. Mechanical and therefore replicable as the layout practice was, grids and compassed circles still gave joiners and carvers leeway to be creative. While geometry provided preindustrial workmen with convenient templates, it left them room to cater to the individual tastes of local and regional customers.

Joiners' scribed layout lines. Box, oak, attributed to the Searle/Dennis workshops, Ipswich, Massachusetts, 1663–80. The maker of this box used a pair of compasses to walk off the front into six equal units without measurements or arithmetic. He further divided the space in half the long way with a marking gauge. The dividers and awl came in handy again to lay out circles and strike quadrants. The rest he carved freehand using chisels, gouges, and a V-tool.

of perspective and interior space while scrollwork, balusters, and columns mimicked stage design to give onlookers a viewpoint of their own and the sensation of being an audience, be it only the audience of friends and neighbors that John Weld entertained in his parlor. As never before, paintings, prints, book illustrations, chimneypieces, architectural facades, and, yes, cupboards, chests, and armchairs affected a theatricality that increasingly came into play among people who valued performance over reputation.[15] Little by little, manners and mannerism commingled to become a European-wide culture of conspicuous demonstration, social playacting that required and produced domestic stage props appropriately designed. Mannerism was both medium and message in a new system of communications that historians can understand a little better by inquiring further into the uses to which people put their ever more numerous and newly valuable possessions.

There will be some who object that a functional analysis of household goods belabors the obvious. This volume set out to explain consumer behavior. Why make the problem more complicated than it has to be? Why not simply recognize that, as divisions in English and American society became more pronounced for reasons having little or nothing to do with consumption, the upper classes deployed consumer goods along a broad front to mark the social boundaries between themselves and those below them? Why not accept the obvious explanation that this passion for domestic paraphernalia was just the newest wrinkle in the age-old contest between the haves and the have-nots?

I tried earlier to rebut the commonsense assertion that the rich always have more toys by looking back at the fourteenth and fifteenth centuries and discovering that that statement is not a very useful way to understand material life in the Middle Ages. Four hundred years later a fuller historical record supports another observation. By the eighteenth century, however much wealthy consumers outspent their social inferiors, it is more important to recognize that the things they bought were significantly *different in kind* from the things other people had. Ownership enabled them to participate in activities that were impossible for the unpossessed. These were choices freely made by men and women who could afford to buy and learn to use the necessary accoutrements to fashionable living. It therefore follows that those artifacts are a faithful record of activities deliberately engaged in, and their uses are a guide to motivations more complex than the desire merely to outspend the competition.

Attentive students of material culture can read between these lines the logic that underlies the research strategy employed throughout these pages. Like any other historian's set of working assumptions, mine too require some leaps of faith. All are consistent with my understanding of human nature. The line of my reasoning starts with the function that artifacts perform, the things they assisted their users to do. Those intended functions indicate the primary uses to which the artifacts were put; uses imply choices; choices point to motives; and thus it logically follows that the reasons people chose to acquire certain goods and use them as they did are as close as historians can usually come to understanding the meaning their owners attached to material things. The trick, of course, is to identify correctly the use, the user, and the period of use. The attention I give to people's deliberate choices is not meant to dismiss the valid observation, usually made by anthropologists, that every culture perceives a narrower range of possible designs and uses for artifacts than their tools could make or the human mind imagine. Nor does it deny that there are distinctive cultural patterns to be observed in people's selections from the limited repertory of alternatives they perceived. Those patterns are clues to the many meanings that *we attach* to their material things. But that simply is not my assignment here. To answer the question, *why demand?*, I need to explain *their* motives. The men and women whose lifestyles I describe acquired and learned to use household goods that they either already knew would help them achieve whatever result they sought or they hoped would. Things that worked, they kept and used again; unsuccessful products and ineffective behavior were forgotten. Popular artifacts (in the sense of socially successful artifacts) can therefore be regarded as individual choices that happily conformed to lifestyles that found favor with some larger number of people in society. For students of material culture, popular artifacts thus become evidence from which it is reasonable to infer generally the motivations of the lifestyle group as a whole.[16]

Which brings me back to the matter of emulation. Had the old rules of precedence remained fully in force, we would expect few additions to the inventory of ceremonial furniture and tablewares that had served adequately for several centuries. Indeed, as we have already seen, traditional pieces of status-displaying furniture enjoyed continued high favor long enough to receive a thorough face-lifting in the mannerist style in the seventeenth century. So did the glass and ceramic vessels customarily used to establish protocol at table. Archaeologists working at Jamestown, St. Mary's City, and other early seventeenth-century sites in the Chesapeake region have found fragments of exquisitely delicate standing cups made in Venice or by Venetian-trained glassblowers working in London and the Netherlands (*a* and *b* in fig. 11). The elongated stems were twisted into mythological animal shapes or molded into swollen balusters and grotesque lion masks.[17] The Jamestown excavations also yielded pieces of two rare Rhenish (or Raeren) stoneware jugs, one with biblical scenes, the other decorated with the seven electors of the Holy Roman Empire, the figures on both set in an arcaded mannerist frieze (*c* and *d* in fig. 11).[18] Made about 1610, these magnificent drinking vessels were probably covered with lids befitting their superior size and status and may have been "tipped" with silver or pewter mounts, a technique much employed by mannerist craftsmen to enhance the preciousness of objects made of baser materials.[19] Heirlooms by the time they were broken, they must have been cherished like the "old fashioned guilt Canne [tankard] with a lidd" that was still one of the proudest possessions of a neighboring York County planter in 1659.[20]

Shards found on archaeological sites from Pemaquid to Poquoson tell the same story.[21] Cloisonné enameled knife handles, polychrome delftware platters and drug pots, imported Chinese porcelain curios, colorful Spanish and Portuguese majolica, slip-decorated serving dishes, sgraffito wares from the west of England, Rhenish and Flemish stoneware jugs and pitchers emblazoned with fantastical human masks and spotted with the usual mannerist bumps and bosses—all these treasures were brought to America by first- and second-generation colonists (see fig. 11). They tell archaeologists what historians only guess at from later probate inventory references to such tantalizing curiosities as one painted Dish, a "Chaney [China] saltcellar," "Holand juggs," "portingale [Portugal] ware," and a "white cupp with a silver tip" that belonged to one of John Weld's Roxbury relatives. These were not everyday utensils. They were showpieces. One Virginia inventory described the location of "two glasses and whyte Earthen Ware"; they were displayed on the planter-owner's "Cupboards-head," the cupboard itself being a "Court Cupboard with Drawers" worth a whopping £5.[22] Shards and inventories bring us to the same conclusion. Up-to-the-minute status symbols were present in American homes from the very beginning and were treasured for years thereafter. Furthermore, they were the same covered drinking cups, standing salts, knives and spoons, platters, chargers, drug jars, and assorted freakish knickknacks that had customarily set peasant tables and garnished their cupboards going back a long, long time. In short, there were already status symbols aplenty in the colonies—enough, it would seem, to satisfy even the ambitious social climbers whose success by the second half of the seventeenth century propelled them far above their less fortunate neighbors.

How very curious, then, that they wanted more. How inexplicable is the sudden appearance of so many new and different household goods in the middle decades of the seventeenth century if their insatiable buyers only sought to acquire things that signified their superior ability to spend with abandon. Those things already existed. They were still the height of fashion. The demand for more things, different things—*many more and different things*—must therefore be owing to something besides social competition. Inescapably the search for an explanation of consumer behavior comes down to understanding how a whole host of new inventions equipped their owners and users to meet social needs and solve social problems that had arisen more or less recently. Demand has seldom been satisfied merely by ownership or possession. Ultimately historians must ask specifically what new housewares were "needed" and acquired, and specifically how they altered age-old habits and household routines.

To list all the furniture forms and ceramic- and glass-vessel types that were created brand new or entered mainstream popular culture between approximately 1650 and 1750 is to demonstrate with astonishing clarity precisely when the modern domestic environment was born. These are pieces of furniture and tablewares that have been taken so much for granted by those who could afford them since the eighteenth century that a house without them mocks the very meaning of the word furnished.

FIGURE 11

High-quality mannerist tablewares and domestic utensils excavated on American sites. Faces, figures, and animal heads—realistic, mythical, and grotesque—appear on these and other objects in the mannerist idiom. While the convention and even specific motifs can be traced directly to the high-style sources that inspired serious mannerist artists and decorators, the runaway popularity of the style with lower-brow consumers must have owed much to its affinity to the age-old anthropomorphic character of animistic folk art. Exuberant floral festoon and strapwork decoration on handles of different shapes shows how ingeniously mannerist designers adapted standard motifs to meet customer demand for overloaded ornament.

a

0 INCHES 3

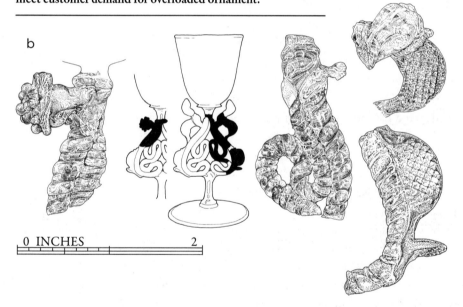

b

0 INCHES 2

One of several identical wine glasses (*a*) recovered from the c. 1676 wreckage of structure 112 at Jamestown, Virginia. The swollen baluster stem, molded with lion masks, floral swags, and heavy gadroons, was a widely used element in Venetian and Venetian look-alike cups, goblets, bowls, and tazzas. Netherlands or possibly England, late sixteenth or early seventeenth century. Stem fragments (*b*) from two or more delicate Venetian-style *flügelglas* wineglasses. They probably set Gov. Charles Calvert's table at St. John's, St. Mary's City, Maryland, at the end of the seventeenth century. Excavations at St. Mary's City have yielded large quantities of refined *façon de Venise* table glass, most of it probably Dutch, from the households of prominent officials and gentlemen lawyers, but not from the city's taverns. Last quarter of seventeenth century.

Two pieces of a large, Westerwald-type, blue and gray stoneware jug (*c*) excavated at Jamestown from a c. 1650–60 context. A frieze of arcaded panels depicts scenes from the biblical story of Judith and Holofernes. Besides the tapered columns paneled with scales and winged cherub heads in the spandrels, mannerist elements include rosettes and medallions on the shoulders and neck band of this 13-inch drinking vessel, c. 1610–20. Body fragments of a Westerwald stoneware panel jug (*d*) discarded at Jamestown c. 1650–60. Busts and strapwork shields of the Seven Electors of the Holy Roman Empire appear in an arcaded frieze supported on mannerist tapered columns with lobed baluster capitals. The smaller shard depicts the "Römisher Kaiser." Identical jugs in other collections are dated 1602 and 1603.

c

0 INCHES 3

d

0 INCHES 2

FIGURE 11 (*continued*)

Table knife handles (*e*) of brass and black-and-white cloisonné enamel found at Jamestown in a context that indicates that the knife remained in use to the middle of the eighteenth century. Probably Dutch, c. 1650. Brass fruit knife handle (*f*) with cloisonné decoration in green, black, white, and blue enamel. Excavated at Kingsmill Tenement, James City County, Virginia, a farmstead belonging to tenants or servants of Richard Kingsmill, a resident of Jamestown. Principal period of occupation 1625–50. English or Dutch, c. 1575–1650. Brass cover to a pair of snuffer scissors (*g*), originally tinned to resemble silver, from Causey's Care, Charles City County, Virginia. The snuffer may have been owned by gentleman Walter Aston as early as the 1620s, eventually passing into the possession of his lower-status son, who used it until his death in 1665. A well modeled and finely cast head of Mercury makes the centerpiece of a sophisticated composition incorporating a lion mask, two elongated human figures, and a profile Roman head in medallion. Germany, Netherlands, or Belgium, late sixteenth century.

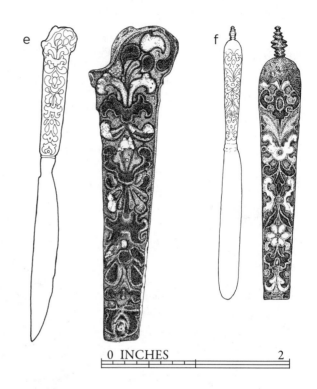

0 INCHES 2

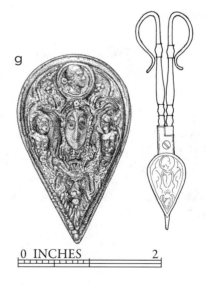

0 INCHES 2

Among the earliest inventions it is worthy of note that many were accessories to people's dressing activities and toilet preparations. That is hardly surprising considering that the human body, when it came to clothing, had long been treated like a medieval cupboard, a bare frame to be draped and adorned before it reflected the glory of him or her to whom the face belonged. Faces became the ultimate insignia of the possessive individual consumer. They bore endless looking at and looking after. Among the new furniture forms that appear in inventories between 1660 and 1690 are *chamber tables* and *dressing boxes,* both accessories to the serious work of self-beautification.[23] The one was less a table than a chest raised on a frame, the container too small to store textiles and the legs too tall to use conveniently except while standing. Furniture historians believe that chamber tables held the innumerable "basons and ewers" that are listed in inventories and were used for washing hands and face. They may also have been a place to put away the handsome new *barber bowls* that were available by the 1680s.[24]

Dressing boxes, sometimes worth as much as £5, were divided up inside into tiny compartments for the cosmetics, powders, and unguents needed to improve on nature. Sometimes they were fitted with a "Myrour" under the lid to assist the user in performing the kind of close-up facial renovations that old-fashioned country people had little time or use for.[25] Dressing boxes first appear in New England inventories in the 1670s among the belongings of Bostonians, men as often as women significantly. Well-off Philadelphians had them by the last quarter of the century. Frequently the trendsetters were sea captains, mariners, and merchants, the very men whose affairs were advanced not so much by a familiar honest face as a fashionably pretty one.[26] Conversely, just outside Boston in Roxbury, the one and only dressing box in John Weld's village belonged to the neighborhood's one and only gentleman, a man of considerable estate and, judging from his "Goods in the House," no stranger to high living.[27]

These containers for cosmetics, combs, and brushes were usually placed on top of another piece of furniture low enough to permit the user to sit before the glass. The term *dressing table* was not used in Boston inventories until the year 1700 and then in reference to a table so modestly valued that it seems likely that stands for dressing boxes were undecorated at first. Instead they were draped with a piece of cloth called by the borrowed French term *toilet,* which the English defined as "a Kind of Table-Cloth, or Carpet, made of fine Linnen, Sattin, Velvet, or Tissue, spread upon a Table in a Bed Chamber, where Persons of Quality dress themselves; a Dressing-cloth."[28] Sure enough, "twilights" show up in a probated New England estate of 1711 and a "table & twilight" by 1718, once again in each case the property of a cosmopolitan Bostonian with connections abroad. Dressing furniture reached maturity with the appearance of twilight tables in the 1720s, progenitors of the long line of *toilet tables* that continues to the present day.

A companion piece to the dressing table and another commonplace furniture form with an unusual history in this period was the *chest of drawers,*[29] which was destined to become the principal storage container for clothing and other textiles in fashionable Anglo-American households in the second half of the seventeenth century. In so doing, it sent the long-lived family of chests, trunks, and coffers into permanent retirement in the attic after centuries of loyal service.[30] Extra and unseasonable wearing apparel had previously been stowed away inside chests underneath yard goods, table linens, or whatever else was piled on top. Chests were hard to use. A person had to crouch alongside them or paw through their contents from a stooped position overhead. Their immense popularity testifies that such inconveniences had long been tolerable to men and women who changed their clothes infrequently by later standards and, when they did, were accustomed to hang idle garments on pegs rather than fold them and lay them away flat. Chests and trunks best stored stuff that was seldom needed. Their poor design for daily use only became an inconvenience when people began wearing clothes made from thinner, lighter, linen and cotton materials and when advancing fashion required a greater assortment of such garments.[31]

In England urban aristocrats and rural gentlemen with plenty of houseroom to spare could accommodate the towering *clothespresses* that joiners began building about 1625 and were fitting with sliding shelves and drawers by midcentury. The lower, smaller chest of drawers was preferred by wealthy middle-class town dwellers who valued compactness and yet desired the convenience of drawer storage for the seasonable clothing they were putting on and taking off more frequently. Chests of drawers appeared almost simultaneously in London and New England in the late 1630s and 1640s. The earliest documented American pieces came over, the evidence suggests, in the baggage of immigrants from the metropolis. London-quality pieces were made in Boston and sold at London prices to the leading commercial families of that town by midcentury. Farther south in Maryland and Virginia they first show up in inventories in the 1660s.[32] Thereafter chests of drawers, the expensive kind as well as plainer, cheaper models, became steady sellers for town and country joiners throughout the colonies. Some conservative buyers initially combined old habits and new in a hybrid form, an old-fashioned lid-top chest with drawers underneath. But by 1760 drawer storage had become the norm almost without exception among middling householders of English descent even in the countryside.

What was stored in a chest of drawers depended on its location. In a hall it was likely to hold textiles for laying a table or making a bed. "Cases," or slipcovers, for sets of upholstered dining chairs were put away in drawers out of season in one fashionable Boston hall as early as 1658, a reminder that the proliferation of new furniture forms was partly its own spur to greater storage needs. Despite the variety of uses to which chests of drawers were put, their invention and spreading use were principally a response to people's growing attention to their personal appearance. When these new case pieces stood in chambers or parlors, the drawers were crammed with fresh linens, assorted seasonal garments, and ribbons, buttons, jewelry, and other accessories.

By the 1690s fine ladies and gentlemen were coming to regard a chest of drawers as an important component in a set of dressing furniture that included the table, box, and occasionally even *stands* on which they placed pots and basins for convenience or candles to shed light full face on their toilet preparations.[33] Sometimes *looking glasses* came en suite too. The small, hand-held mirrors of earlier times were superseded in fashionable circles by larger glasses. After 1660 they were often fitted with rings to hang them on the wall or struts to stand them on a tabletop, thereby providing fastidious users with a still reflection and giving beauticians use of both hands. Upright rectangular looking glasses joined the kit of dressing chamber paraphernalia as English mirror glass manufacturers (holding patents since 1663) found ways just before 1700 to elongate the squarish face glass into a three-quarter-length living portrait of face and figure fashionably united. Never before in human history had people seen themselves "from top to toe," as one delighted English woman described the first experience of seeing her reflection at full length.[34]

Silvered reflections and painted "effigies" were the quintessential expression of the personal identity that men and women concocted with the things they kept in drawers and dressing boxes to create the artificial self-images that they then saw mirrored back at them from looking glasses in the parlor chamber and from oil canvases on the parlor wall. *Painted portraits* were yet another new addition to the furnishings of prosperous American homes in the second half of the seventeenth century.[35] As such they appropriated and domesticated a category of artifacts that earlier ages had reserved for church and state officials and others of great estate. Portrait painters, including miniaturists, worked in the prevailing mannerist idiom. Mannerist art theory held that the purpose of "pikture-making" was to "record and perpetuate the Effigies of Famous Men."[36] That justification was widely accepted by Americans in the seventeenth century, a point that Samuel Sewell was making when he recorded in his diary in 1685 that "Govr. Bradstreet's Effigies [are] hung up in his best Room."[37] The earliest pictures painted abroad and imported into the colonies were often portraits of religious leaders and civilian officials, like the "judge Richardson to the wast in a picture" inventoried in 1660 among the possessions of a Virginia planter who appears to have been no relation to the judge.[38]

Soon the likenesses of unexceptional householders were added to the gallery of famous men. For the living, portraits advertised an individual's place in society. Men often held gloves, canes, books, documents, and other recognized badges of office; gentlewomen posed with fans, Bibles, and bouquets of flowers.[39] Not a few portraits spelled out the subject's name or initials or inserted the family's crest so that viewers could not fail to make the right connections and be duly impressed. An oval format popular by the end of the century signaled superior breeding by reference to the roundel heads of ancient patricians (fig. 12). After death, portraits honored the memory of the sitter and celebrated the family's genealogy no less than funerary monuments immortalized its reputation in the churchyard.

FIGURE 12

Portraits with an early Maryland history. Both Wetenhall portraits, his and hers, were passed down in a Maryland family said to be descended from Colonel Henry Coursey. He and two brothers came to the American colonies in 1649. These two waist-length pictures and four others appear to have followed the Courseys to Maryland by 1707, enduring reminders in a faraway place of the family's European lineage. A coat of arms vouched for the two sitters' pedigree, and Sir Thomas's fancy dress armor was an old-fashioned badge of office and ancestry. By contrast Lady Wetenhall's likeness asserts her gentility not with the painter's props that traditionally accompanied gentlewomen in seventeenth-century portraits—fans, Bibles, or bouquets of flowers. Instead she relied entirely on her a la mode court dress and high-style coiffure.

Sir Thomas Wetenhall, oil on canvas, artist unidentified, probably English, before 1665.

Lady Elizabeth (?) Wetenhall, oil on canvas, possibly Sir Peter Lely or a follower, before 1665.

The medium lived on to enjoy even greater popularity in the baroque-style portraiture introduced into the colonies after the turn of the century by John Smibert, Peter Pelham, Gustavus Hesselius, and Charles Bridges.[40] Their mastery of the Italian chiaroscuro technique of modeling light and shade relied less on explicit signs and symbols to indicate social standing. Instead it revealed the inner refinements of a genteel character through an integrated composition of costume, carriage, and complexion. By the 1730s or so, the portrait habit had been thoroughly ingrained. Painted faces conferred respectability on their subjects by proxy. Framed portraits bore witness to the good taste and well-deserved reputations of those whose walls they adorned.[41]

It is not inaccurate to see in this related group of seventeenth-century household artifacts associated with the activities of dressing, grooming, and image-making a continuation of a venerable and nearly universal preoccupation with self-adornment as an individual's most explicit expression of social eminence. There was little new in that. It can even be argued that the mannerist ornament that embellished these otherwise utilitarian objects merely corrupted classical motifs into a superficial decorator style whose separate elements imitated in baser materials the rare gems and precious baubles that had always encrusted sacred and ceremonial objects, including the sumptuous garments that men and women of great estate had long bespangled with ruffles, jewels, and filigree. The ambition was an old one—to look the part.

Notwithstanding, there is also something new and different to be observed in these pieces of dressing furniture, articles of clothing, cosmetics, and artificial likenesses. First, it was all equipment necessary to achieve a calculated effect. The results—fresh-smelling clothes, a pretty face, a fashionable figure—were unattainable without the gear. Its use required learned skills and careful practice. Of course that much may be said about tools of any kind. The difference worth noting is the sheer number of new tools invented or popularized in the second half of the seventeenth century to perform basic everyday chores. Washing, dressing, and making oneself presentable all reached new heights of elaboration and refinement by 1700.[42] Second, it should not be overlooked that the act of using the new equipment, the preparations themselves, assumed an importance it had never had before in bourgeois circles. The rich ornament and fine workmanship lavished on lowly toilet kits and storage boxes are one indication. So are the many popular depictions of ladies and gentlemen ensconced in their dressing chambers and busy at their toilet seen in prints, performed in comedies, and described in light literature of the period. Such scenes illustrate one final observation to be drawn from examination of dressing furniture and corroborated by probate inventories. The equipment needed for dressing and grooming was increasingly regarded as a suite of furnishings to be encountered in a specific place within the house. Inventory takers in Boston began using the verbal formula "chest of drawers, table, and dressing box" with great frequency after 1690. By the 1710s they confirm what we see with our own eyes in museum collections, that separate pieces in these sets were made to match: one chest of drawers of "black walnut, 1 table . . . , 1 black frame looking glass, . . . [and] 2 Black sconces" all worth £14 in 1711 or the "black Japand [gilded gesso] Chest of Drawers £2:10:00; ditto Table and dressing boxes, £1:5:00" that belonged to another Bostonian in 1716.[43] Although these were objects intended for personal use and the storage of personal possessions, they nevertheless joined a growing list of domestic goods that genteel householders everywhere regarded as pieces belonging to sets that users could expect to find in public rooms reserved for the activities in which they assisted. It was another step in the process of converting the many folkways that had governed people's private ablutions and informal dressing habits into a standardized system of polite public behavior. Where fashion could coerce a man at his washstand, there was no telling how it would refurnish the rooms of his house where he displayed all his resplendence to neighbors and strangers.

These numerous self-centering artifacts, however prosaic and traditional their uses, are central to understanding the argument about geographical mobility advanced in the fifth proposition—that is to say, that migrants and travelers needed a common visual language to make themselves understood in faraway places. The new accessories contributed to overhauling and standardizing people's personal appearance. No longer was it enough to be expensively dressed. To cut a respectable figure abroad, or to command respect at home from those with experience abroad, it was increasingly necessary to dress according to an acknowledged formula. Gentility put on a uniform; it wore a stock expression; it prescribed universal good manners. Drawers and dressing boxes contained the essential costumes and makeup. Mirrors imaged rehearsals. Prints popularized role models, and portraits immortalized successful performers. Bedchambers became actors' and actresses' dressing rooms, and parlors and public spaces the stages on which they performed. The analogy was one that these new moderns themselves already acknowledged and used. A gentleman's house, they heard it said, was "the Theater of his Hospitality, the Seate of Self-fruition, the Comfortablest part of his own Life, [and] the noblest of his Sons Inheritance." It was, in a word, "an epitome of the whole world," epitome both as a perfect example of every gentleman's world abroad and as its miniature model back home.[44]

4

⟫⟫⟫✦⟪⟪⟪

FASHION PERFORMED

The domestic preparations described in the preceding chapters cul-
minated in formal performances that began now to reshape fundamentally the daily routines of quite ordinary people. Burghers and a few country gentlemen were usually first, but others followed soon enough. These
were social events by definition, occasions when men and women consorted together in activities that, whatever their outward purposes, served
deep down to reaffirm and regulate the established social order. Being departures from age-old custom, they required special equipment—special
props—that warrant our attention because they worked in a new way.
The actual physical forms these newfangled objects took—the shapes,
weights, and materials that gave them their modern look and feel—not
only signified who were players and who were not in the usual old-
fashioned way; now more than ever the very anatomy of newly invented
objects modeled the users' movements and choreographed their performances. Form and function became symbiotic. Historians seldom look
for clues to people's behavior in the way three-dimensional things worked
for their users. We must. There is information to be collected from the
careful study of inventions and innovations that will be useful when we
return to consider their functions as mediums of visual communications
in the following chapter.

People everywhere have always engaged in shared practices that
reinforce their community's social categories, whether they live in traditional societies or modern ones. Sometimes the sorting mechanisms

take the form of ceremonies and rituals, other times contests. The social behavior that fashion-conscious ladies and gentlemen began to exhibit in the seventeenth century is more accurately understood as *performance* than as ritual, because it involved real win-or-lose tests of social skills, not merely the repetition of prescribed formulas. If the performer met the prevailing standard of behavior in the judgment of peers, he or she was entitled to their company, however slightly acquainted they may have been beforehand.

The occasions when such formalities were observed were frequently events that brought together people from outside the immediate family. These could be friends, neighbors, or business associates. Often they were complete strangers. Because such displays of hospitality had traditionally involved the sharing of food and drink, it is not surprising that the earliest genteel performances took place at table and radically altered the design of furniture and utensils used at mealtimes. Fashion found many other venues as the eighteenth century progressed, and it attached itself to many other artifacts later employed in these additional genteel pursuits. But our search in these pages for the origins of consumer demand in the half century before 1700 requires that we look no further than that already familiar fashion center in early American homes—the formal parlor, the forerunner of the dining room. Its furniture and other equipment used to seat, serve, feed, and entertain a householder's family and guests numbered among the earliest mass-produced consumer goods that can be called genuine inventions.

Even John Weld of Roxbury owned one such novelty despite his conservative taste. His *glass case* was an object utterly unknown to earlier generations. The form has recently been identified as a small case piece used to store drinking glasses, galley pots, and other refined table garnitures, which, when not in use, were exhibited behind an open grillwork of turned spindles.[1] The whole contraption was set up prominently on a cupboard or tabletop. It probably contained the English, German, Dutch, or possibly Venetian-made beer and wine glasses that archaeologists commonly find on colonial sites of the period 1670–85.[2]

Had Weld lived a few years longer, he might have added to its contents the sturdy, less expensive, lead crystal *drinking glasses* perfected by

English glassmakers after 1675 and widely marketed in the American colonies by the 1690s.[3] Their design, not just their affordability, responded to changing tastes in table manners. The earlier style table glasses, while sometimes delicate, were often studded with prunts or ringed with trailed-glass bands applied partly as decoration in the mannerist idiom and partly to give users a firm grip. The newer wines supported the bowl on an inverted baluster stem raised on a generous spreading foot (fig. 13). Not only were they intentionally one-handed vessels, they were designed to be elegantly held by pinching either the stem or the foot between the thumb and forefingers, as depicted in prints and paintings of the period.[4] That left the other hand completely free to engage in the practiced gestures that accompanied genteel conversations, which were the real substance of the dinner-table performance. Two-fisted drinkers, as imbibers from old-fashioned fuddle cups and puzzle jugs had often been, were looked upon askance by those cognizant of refined dining etiquette. A tobacco inspector in Virginia, for instance, a guest at Robert Carter's table in 1774, was dismissed as "Dull" and "unacquainted with company" when, drinking his host's health, "he held the Glass of Porter fast with both his Hands, and then gave an insignificant nod to each one at the Table, in hast, & with fear, & then drank like an Ox." In civilized company thirst quenching took second place to observing the proper forms, so that "the Good Inspector" was further faulted for being "better pleased with the Liquor than with the manner in which he was at this Time obliged to use it."[5] Such offenses against the rules of table had become embarrassing in gentry circles by the third quarter of the eighteenth century.

A hundred years earlier the nabobs themselves were only half initiated in the arts and artifacts of formal dining. When William Fitzhugh ordered a fabulous assortment of silver tablewares from England in 1688, his reasons recalled the values of an old-fashioned hoarder: "I esteem it as well politic as reputable, to furnish my self with an handsom Cupboard of plate which gives my self the present use & Credit, [and] is a sure friend at a dead lift without much loss, or is a certain portion for a Child after my decease."[6] His order included a single three-quart tankard, no doubt to be prominently displayed on the cupboard when the grandee was not wielding it himself. Otherwise his expensive new table service included all the

FIGURE 13

Containers for new beverages enjoyed by socia-
ble colonists. A wide variety of early seventeenth-
century vessel forms shows makers, importers, and
consumers alike casting about for ideal containers
for wine, tea, coffee, and eventually chocolate. By
the end of the century the experiments had narrowed down to a few standardized shapes that persisted into modern times.

a

b

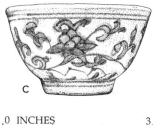

c

d

0 INCHES 3

e

Chinese porcelain wine cup (a) from an unprovenanced site at Kingsmill, Virginia. Others like it have been found at several very early sites along the James River, including
the Maine on the Governor's Land (1618–25), Wolstenholme Town (1620–22), and Causey's Care (1620s). Sgraffito-ware drinking cup (b), a top-of-the-line version of many
otherwise undecorated earthenware cups used to serve imported wine at Jamestown
tables. This and other brightly colored North Devon slipwares, stored in service rooms in
structure 112, were destroyed in a fire c. 1676. Chinese porcelain teabowl, c. 1645–65 (c)
probably used at Jamestown structure 19, one of the largest and best taverns serving
the capital from c. 1665 to the end of the century. Stem from a lead crystal goblet (d)
showing English glassmakers' modifications to a German form known as a roemer, c.
1680–90. English consumers were told in 1662 that roemers were specifically intended
for "Rhenish wine, for Sake, Claret, Beer." This one found its way into a fine Jamestown
rowhouse (structure 17) before it was broken about 1720. Early lead crystal wineglass
(e) among the household goods of Lt. Gov. Francis Nicholson, whose house in the up-
and-coming capital city of Williamsburg burned c. 1705–10. The baluster stem, raised
foot, and small bowl gave new delicacy and elegance to the wine and punch parties
where such glasses were used. English, c. 1690–1710.

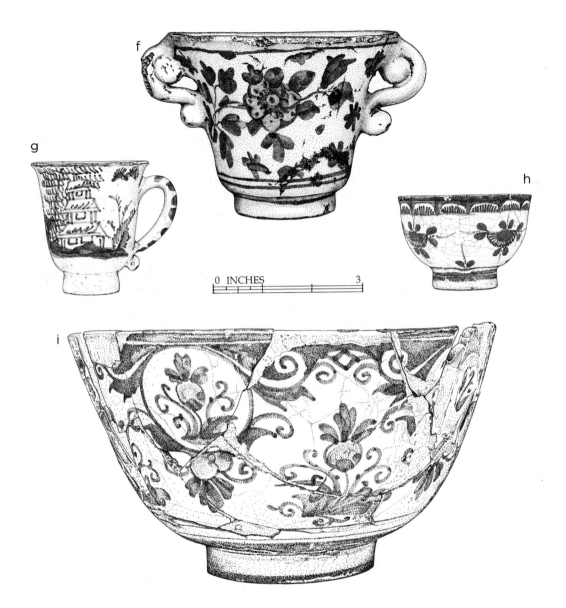

Blue-and-white faience drinking cup with two handles (*f*), known as an "ear'd coffee" in London in 1699. This one was traded to Seneca Indians and recovered from one of their village sites in western New York. Dutch, c. 1665–80. Tin-glaze drinking cup (*g*) with one handle, for coffee, cappuccino, or maybe chocolate. Presumably one of a set, this very fashionable drinking vessel belonged to John Brush, a social-climbing Williamsburg artisan, as early as the 1710s. Brush's china closet contained other specialized drink wares, including tin-glaze teabowls (*h*)—a step down from porcelain, but still very smart—and a delftware punch bowl (*i*). All his blue-and-white beverage vessels were English-made and imported soon after 1700. They were broken and discarded by c. 1717–27.

necessary place settings for a company of fashionable diners. There were knives, forks, and spoons for twelve and a dozen plates to match. A "small silver basin" may have been the same "Monteeth Bason" later recorded in Fitzhugh's will. *Monteiths* were a type of deep container said to have been invented in the year 1683.[7] Fitzhugh's must have been one of the earliest in the colonies. They were used to rinse and chill stemmed wineglasses between courses, which servants then refilled and returned to their respective users on a *salver* (Fitzhugh called his a "Salvator plate"). Salvers were another novel utensil described in 1661 as "a new fashioned peece of wrought plate . . . used in giving Beer or other liquid things, to save the [table] Carpit and Cloathes from drops."[8] Here again special equipment was desired to prevent the spills and spots that stained reputations more indelibly than clothes. Fitzhugh rounded out his new table service with a pair of candlesticks, as well as a set of sugar, pepper, and mustard casters and four serving dishes, including two "pretty large" ones "for a good joint of meat," a clear indication that these were wares sufficient to lay a formal table in two or three courses.[9] The likes of that had seldom been seen in the colonies. No wonder he instructed his purchasing agent to have "W F S & [my] coat of Arms put upon all pieces that are proper, especially the Dishes, plates, and Tankards, etc."

In their different ways Fitzhugh's invoice and Weld's inventory catch the march of table fashions at half stride. Neither the Virginia grandee nor the New England farmer had set aside all his old assumptions about tablewares and the order of company at mealtimes. Yet the one had acquired many tablewares and the other one or two that anticipated the idea that diners at the same table, although not necessarily equal in rank, were a miniature meritocracy based on each person's knowledge and practice of good manners.

Fashionable dining arbitrated even the shape of *oval tables*. Usually tables had been four-sided before, square or rectangular, large or small, but four corners had traditionally marked the metes and bounds between the head, the foot, and the two sides in between. Each was a distinct social territory. Protocol placed the most important male diner at the head or top of the table, usually located at one of the ends, otherwise midway along one side. His dependents took their places to the right and left in descending order of precedence according to gender, estate, age, and servility. Hence William Cobbett's recollection of days gone by when a typical English farmer used to "sit at the head of the oak table along with his men, say grace to them, and cut up the meat and the pudding."[10] Wives (according to prints and paintings showing upper-class dining scenes) appear to have sat next to their husbands at the head of the table or, alternatively, opposite at the foot. It is harder to say where custom assigned seats to more ordinary housewives, if indeed their traditional duties as cooks and servers gave them leisure to sit at all during mealtimes.[11]

The advent of fashionable dining changed everything, not least of all the shape of four-sided tables. They became round or oval.[12] Tables without corners made a closed circle of men and women whose shared commitment to the arts of civility outweighed any real differences in their rank. Master and mistress were replaced by host and hostess, and so thorough was the revolution in manners that husbands and wives actually traded places. The meat-carving and soup-ladling duties were reassigned to the hostess, who was ensconced in the place of honor. The host, seated at the foot, was responsible for the guests' "entertainment," that is, the company's exchange of pleasantries.[13] That, too, was said to happen more easily at round tables. "It is the custom here in England," wrote a knowledgeable housekeeper in 1758, "to eat off square or long Tables; the French in general eat on round or oval." That gave them, she said, "vastly the advantage in the disposing and placing their Entertainment." Companions seated in a circle enjoyed greater informality, which the housekeeper called "this French fashion of perfect ease.[14]

Although many a staunch Englishman was happier square than French, the Gallic-inspired oblong tables with hinged or "falling" leaves had in fact captured the fancy of some English noblemen as early as the 1630s and 1640s.[15] Their space-saving convenience and showy stylishness had recommended them to cosmopolitan London merchants by the 1650s and 1660s. Americans were no laggards either. Maryland merchant Thomas Cornwaleys owned a splendid round table by 1645, almost as early as anyone in England. "One Ovall table with bolt & catches" for the gate legs and leaves numbered among other expensive and fashionable furnishings in a Virginia hall in 1667. Another one valued at a staggering

£3 10s. furnished the first true "dyning Roome" owned by a great Boston merchant in 1669.[16] A generation later the use of such tables, often specified as walnut, was no longer confined to the advanced tastemakers. Rounded tables became increasingly commonplace in gentlemen's houses over the next half century.[17]

Mealtime performances required *matching dining chairs* whether the table was oval or not. These too made their first appearance in American parlors in the second half of the seventeenth century. Socially differentiated seating furniture had been one way that precedence-minded diners had known their place around old-fashioned tables. Where chairs had been scarce, usually they were reserved for the householder himself, sometimes his wife, and on occasion honored guests. Children, servants, hired hands, and other social inferiors had often sat on stools, forms, benches, and makeshift chests and boxes, or might even have stood. In New England where inexpensive turned chairs had been almost as common as stools in England, the "chair-man's" seat of authority was frequently distinguished by arms or "elbows," needlework cushions, extra turnings, or decorative carving. Few, however, rivaled the imposing "wainscot great chairs" that furniture historians have discovered were owned exclusively by a small number of country gentlemen, merchants, and divines.[18]

This ancient seating plan was subverted by the invention of the *upholstered back-stool* about 1615.[19] Literally joint stools with stuffed seats and backrests, they gained great popularity simultaneously in London and Boston in the 1640s and elsewhere in the ensuing half century.[20] In Virginia "Chair stooles" were owned early enough to have worn out by the 1670s, and yet some still considered them "new Fashion" in Maryland as late as 1710.[21] Two features recommended their use in polite society. First, they usually came en suite, often in sets of six or a dozen. An additional single matching "elbow chair" conferred the traditional chairman's symbolic authority on a host or hostess, but otherwise each diner was shown to an individual and identical seat.

The second feature, their coordinated upholstery, reinforced this impression of sameness and, not coincidentally, conferred on the whole assembled company the superior status long attached to rich textiles. A covering of expensive-looking fabric, trimmed with fringe and garnished with brass nails, literally clothed the new furniture form in a familiar status symbol of great antiquity. Dining chairs upholstered in Russia leather and woven Turkey work (the former imported from London to Boston by the late 1640s and the latter by 1654) are a historian's clue that back stools were not intended for the whole universe of trenchermen who had formerly bellied up to supper tables set round with communal benches and assorted stools without backs. Matching sets of dining chairs were reserved for the new breed of parlor users. They were the colonies' most prominent citizens at first, men like the councillors of New Amsterdam for whom the governor ordered from Holland in 1660 "8 Spanish chairs for the gentlemen," adding parenthetically that "at present we use only pine benches."[22] By 1700 numerous references to "Rushy leather" and "Turkie workt" chairs in American inventories give ample proof that many middle-class colonists were importing a fair share of the "5000 dozen" such chairs that were said to be produced in England every year, not to mention those they bought from American joiners and upholsterers as early as 1662.[23]

Yet even before the popularity of Turkey work and leather chairs had peaked, artisans in London developed a line of high-backed *cane chairs* that were mass produced in such astonishing numbers and enjoyed such tremendous success in the marketplace that they revolutionized the furniture industry and made genteel dining affordable to large numbers of middling consumers on both sides of the Atlantic.[24] They also took an important step away from the medieval tradition of covering sturdy oak furniture with costly textiles. These chair frames were built either of walnut or other fine woods for the gentry or, less expensively, of beech stained brown or black in imitation of walnut and ebony. What their caned bottoms and backs lacked in splendor, they more than made up for (their makers explained in 1688) by "their Durableness, Lightness, and Cleanness from Dust, Worms and Moths, which inseparably attended Turkey-work, Serge, and other Stuff-Chairs and Couches."[25] Here was clean modern furniture for the same persnickety people who turned up their noses at spotted tablecloths and ripe-smelling linens.

For everyday use it hardly mattered that cane chairs lacked coordinated upholstery, which sitters always covered up anyway. Sets of high-backed chairs had something better. Their identical carved crest rails towered above the tallest users in unobstructed affirmation of every diner's equal right to occupy one piece in the set. Crested chair frames communicated other subliminal messages as well. We have already noted the resemblance between picture frames and looking glasses of the period. Similarly, many late seventeenth-century mirrors were surmounted by fretted crests that reappeared in almost identical form atop high-backed chairs from the 1680s. Thus the correspondence was complete from model to rehearsal to performance. Ebonized high-backed chairs enframed a person's fashionable face and figure in the same image that he or she had composed it earlier at the dressing table and could further study its idealized form in the prints and portraits that lined the parlor walls. En suite meant more than chairs by the dozen or rooms decorated with color-coordinated curtains, upholstery fabrics, and paintwork; more fundamentally, it was a state of mind made manifest in a pervasive and unified aesthetic and a corresponding system of artificial good manners.

Cane chairs date and document very precisely the spread of those manners to mass markets throughout the English-speaking world. The first ones were made in London in 1664. Their popularity caught hold in provincial England and in the colonies in the early 1680s. By 1688 it was said that they were "much used in England, and sent to all parts of the World"; specifically "above Two thousand Dozens [were] yearly Transported into almost all the Hot Parts of the World" where upholstered furniture fared poorly.[26] Immigrant metropolitan chair-frame makers had set up shop in Boston by 1690 and Philadelphia by 1700. Less than ten years later Boston's craftsmen were supplying a huge export market throughout New England, New York, and farther south with a cheaper, leather-covered, high-backed chair in a "plain" turned style that sold six times faster than the carved variety. The demand for them was so great that chair makers could not manufacture them "so fast as they were bespoke."[27]

The customers for such sets of new chairs and the parties that gathered round the new walnut tables sat down to meals that were not mere "yeoman's fare." That was the term applied to the one-course menu of boiled meat, beans, or porridge, plus bread, cheese, and beer or milk, that traditionally had given "solid sufficiency" to the Englishman's midday meal.[28] Polite dining produced a more *elaborate cuisine* eaten with tools and following rules designed to sort out the initiated from the uninitiated. True dining, it was said, "was a thing lately sprung up" in Elizabethan times when "pampering of the belly began to take hold, occasioned by idleness and great abundance of riches."[29] One-course meals yielded to two, three, and more, each with more than one standing dish, that is, food that appeared on the table almost daily.

Cooks and guests alike increasingly needed special instruction not only to prepare but even to recognize the "variety of many severall Dishes, that in the former Service were neglected"—that, in the not-so-humble opinion of the first English cookery book writer (1609) to set himself up as a culinary arbiter of "the Name and Kindes of all ['Meates and Drinks' lately] disputed of."[30] *Cookbooks* published in England in the sixteenth century had been few and mostly medicinal. Starting in the 1590s recipes began to rival remedies. For the first time housewives were introduced to "proper Sauces" (1591), the "newest fashion of cutting up any Fowle" (1617), and "the orderly serving [of meat and fish dishes] to the Table" (1594).[31] One little book addressed to "all ladies and gentlewomen and others whatsoever" was the first English publication (1621) to contain engraved diagrams illustrating the preferred placement of sweets on the table.[32] By 1653 such hostess lore had become "very necessary for all Ladies and Gentlewomen," a social obligation in which cookbook writers and their printers were eager to assist.[33] Forty-six new titles and many reprints appeared in the second half of the seventeenth century (compared to sixteen in the first), and ten more were issued by 1710 before the numbers dwindled again.[34] One ingenious English publisher sold *The Genteel House-Keepers' Pastime* (1693) with "a pack of Playing Cards," which an inexperienced hostess could hide in her pocket to sneak a look at when she set the table or carved the roast.[35] A few English cookbooks found their way into American kitchens before the end of the century. Already by 1705 it was observed that the Virginia "Gentry pretend to have their Victuals drest, and serv'd up as Nicely, as at the best Tables in London."[36] The prescriptive cookbook literature neatly brackets the freshman years of this new Epicurean age.

New foods begot a bewildering array of new tablewares. Traditional "country fare" had usually been served in wooden bowls and trenchers before the sixteenth century. Thereafter, improving standards of living and rising expectations had set many farmers' tables with pewter and earthenware as well.[37] Still and all, eating and drinking vessels had been as few as need be and strictly utilitarian—bowls and deep dishes for everyday stews and pottages, a few plates and platters for roasted meats, and sundry jugs, bottles, tankards, and flagons to pass around home-brewed beverages. Cutlery had been confined to horn, wood, and base-metal spoons and to pointed knives for cutting and spearing. Hands and fingers substituted for nonexistent forks. When meat was eaten, for example, a person displaying good table manners had anchored it to the bowl or plate with one hand while cutting it into pieces with a knife held in the other. Napkins cleaned up sticky fingers afterwards. Such customs prevailed universally at polite American tables. Inventories routinely record piles of napkins and motley assortments of wood, pewter, tin, and pottery hollow wares. What later struck Dr. Alexander Hamilton as "a picture of that primitive simplicity practiced by our forefathers" (he had just witnessed a ferry keeper and his family eating their unsauced vittles from "a dirty, deep, wooden dish which they evacuated with their hands, cramming down skins, scales, and all") had not so many years before been the unremarkable custom of all diners.[38]

Those were the days (Hamilton concluded) before "the mechanic arts" had supplied men like him "with instruments for the luxury and elegance of life." Such newfangled eating tools accompanied the multiple-course meals that first appeared on fashionable dining tables after about 1650. Flatwares (that is, plates and platters) begin showing up on American archaeological sites in greater proportion to hollow ware bowls and deep dishes after the 1670s.[39] Culinary historians are still learning how such tablewares were arranged and how those arrangements assisted in the observance of the new table proprieties. A table setting for a "variety of messes" must certainly have required more numerous *large serving dishes* like the two for "a good joint of meat" that William Fitzhugh ordered in silver in 1688, or like the colorful sgraffito-decorated slipware dishes made in North Devon, traded by the hundredweight to Ireland

FIGURE 14

North Devon sgraffito-decorated slipware dishes (*a-b*) discarded c. 1695 on the site of gentleman Henry Harwood's house at Jamestown (structure 86), c. 1640–70. Italian marbleized slipware dish (*c*), possibly Pisa, excavated at Newport News, resembles shards from William Harwood's farmstead at Martin's Hundred, occupied c. 1625–50. Blue-and-white, tin-glaze, earthenware dish (*d*), probably Portuguese, excavated at Jamestown near the site of a small dwelling or workshop (structure 21) occupied in the last quarter of the seventeenth century, c. 1670.

a

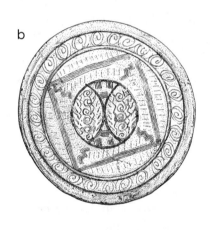

b

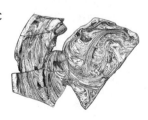

c

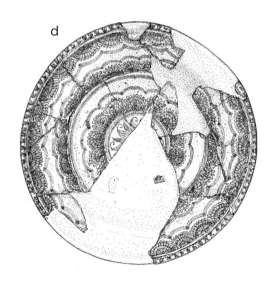

d

0 INCHES   12

and North America, and excavated at Jamestown and other Virginia and Maryland sites in contexts seldom earlier than 1670 (fig. 14). Fancy serving dishes found their way onto American tables from potteries in Britain, Germany, the Netherlands, Italy, Spain, and Portugal, including a matched pair of lobed dishes found in the ruins of Capt. Thomas Pettus's plantation house along the James.[40] Many platters were pewter. "Three large pewter dishes marked on the outside with W" set Virginia planter Richard Watkins's table in the 1660s, along with five "middling dishes" and another small one, all in pewter and all proudly monogrammed with his initial.[41]

Hostesses who followed the cookery books that came with "Pictures curiously Ingraven displaying the whole Arts" of table setting were instructed to place such platters symmetrically in the middle of the table. They might elevate the centerpiece above the lesser dishes on a *dish ring* like the one a Virginian ordered from London in 1728, describing it as "a fashionable ring to set a dish upon in the middle of the table." Less fancy "wicker rings to set under dishes" were used to display cooks' handiwork as early as 1668 in Virginia and by 1677 in Massachusetts. Everywhere their purpose was "to make the feast look full and noble."[42] The savories, sauces, and sweetmeats that accompanied the main dishes were served in accessory bowls, dishes, and porringers. All these were old standbys. Now they were joined by newly invented *sugar boxes* (earliest American reference 1638), *fruit dishes* (1667), *covered mustard pots* (1674), and even *sauce boats,* which potters were supplying in affordable delftware by the 1660s (fig. 15).[43]

An acquired taste for imported wine and a genius for concocting other beverages and palliatives using wine as an ingredient set artisans to experimenting with many special-purpose drinking vessels. The earliest were sometimes made in silver for the custom trade, but were soon copied in pewter and earthenware for wider markets. Among these, delftware and slip-decorated ceramic beverage containers are uniquely instructive to historians because numerous dated specimens record the onset of new vessel types and the periods of their greatest popularity, while potshards verify their use on American sites. The roster starts with tin-glazed earthenware *posset pots,* first dated 1631 and much in vogue from 1650 to about

FIGURE 15

Lid to a silver skillet or saucepan, hallmarked London 1638, excavated at Mathews Manor (inset plan), Denbigh, Virginia, in a c. 1650 context. The pounced initials *SSM* stand for Capt. Samuel Mathews and his second wife. Mathews was a planter-trader who earned a reputation in Virginia as a "most deserving common-wealthsman" before his final return to England in 1652. Utensils such as these were just beginning to bring new refinements to English dining tables in the 1630s. Cooks prepared candied fruits, sugared nuts, and other sweetmeats over kitchen fires in long-handled "ladle skillets," also known as "sauce pans." They must then have transferred them to these smaller covered skillets intended for table use. The short legs kept them standing upright on a warm hearth until they were carried to the table and served to guests, who not only savored their contents, but admired the precious metal containers and the engraved ornament that embellishes many surviving specimens. The wonder is that such dainties were being served in such a fashionable skillet at this Denbigh plantation almost as soon as such utensils graced London tables. The explanation: Mathews was sent back to England to stand trial for treason in 1637. Released, he returned to Virginia two years later with a new wife, a silver skillet, and a cultivated sweet tooth.

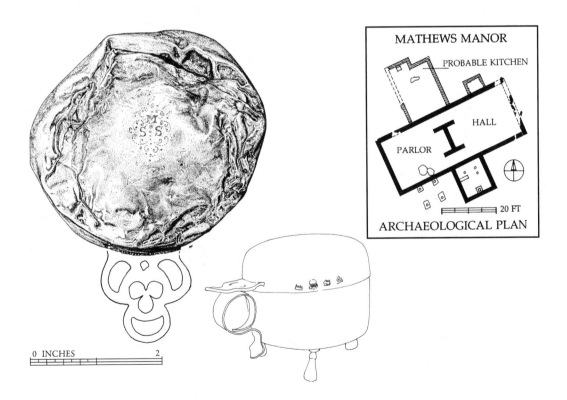

MATHEWS MANOR

PROBABLE KITCHEN

HALL

PARLOR

20 FT

ARCHAEOLOGICAL PLAN

0 INCHES 2

1710.[44] *Caudle cups,* the earliest inscribed 1645, drove delftware tankards off the market from approximately 1650 to 1680 during the same period when sgraffito-ware wine cups appeared on gentry tables in Jamestown (see *b* in fig. 13).[45]

By the 1650s potters in Southwark were marketing *goblets* for beer drinkers that mimicked communion chalices but spoke the language of the alehouse—"HE THAT HATH THIS CUP IN HAND DRINKE UP THE BEERE LET IT NOT STAND 1656."[46] Toward the end of the century these and caudle cups were more or less superseded in turn by *punch bowls,* which began their long reign around 1681 (the earliest dated delftware example) as accessories first to Venetian-style wineglasses and then to improved lead crystal stemwares after about 1690.[47] Common to all the new cups and glasses was their small size. These were individualized drinking containers, a world removed from the belching great bottles and flagons that had formerly passed from grip to grip.[48]

Tablewares in matching sets signified each diner's provisional membership in the dinner table company. At the same time they provided each individual with the personal tools that he or she needed to demonstrate the polite skills that validated claims to gentility. The kit evolved from the middle decades of the seventeenth century to include individualized dinner plates and drinking vessels and eventually forks as well as knives and spoons. One of the greatest merchant-planters of Maryland owned a whole "Boxe of Purslayn China dishes [and] two Boxes of drinkinge glasses" within the first decade of that colony's settlement.[49] *Matched plates* in sets of dozens and half dozens were also sold in pewter and earthenware at more reasonable prices. The earliest delftware set is dated 1661. An inscription painted on each identical plate advertises the host's reputation for civility (and by implication acknowledges his guests' ability to read if not spell) in the greeting "Weilcom my Freinds."[50] Here was the forerunner of "company china." Pewter plates inventoried in multiples of twelve hint at the appearance of flatware sets on a few affluent gentry tables in Virginia before 1659. Matched tin-glazed dishes were used in the capital of Maryland before 1668 if "several peeces of blew Earthen ware" were in fact dinner plates.[51] Like the dozen silver plates that came with Fitzhugh's dinner service, plates in sets were intended as accessories to the new cuisine. Sometimes that connection had to be spelled out. One inscribed set of dinner plates dated 1712 (and still "speaking" in the first-person voice of folk pottery) gave untutored users explicit versified instructions: "On me to Eat Both sauce & meat."[52]

New-style *cutlery* presented novices with other daunting challenges. The test was not simply which fork to lift first, but how to use a table fork at all. Bluffing was difficult without going hungry, because just when forks were introduced into wider social circles in the third quarter of the seventeenth century, table knives were redesigned with blunt points. Not by accident was it no longer possible to bayonet pieces of food with the same tool used to cut them up. The new-model forks and knives found their way onto American tables very slowly before the 1690s, but after that their popularity paralleled the cane chair's.[53]

Archaeologists and curators can now furnish quite accurately this seventeenth-century parlor dining scene that I have described at considerable length. Likewise, costume historians can dress authentically a fashionable company of men and women diners, and culinary historians can spread their table with a reconstructed banquet of cookbook foods and imported beverages. By contrast, social historians still have much to learn about the event itself, the dinner table performance that became the earliest fully developed and most frequently practiced form of social interaction among genteel friends and acquaintances. Slow as that scholarship has been in coming, careful attention to the material evidence presented here supports two or three observations about fine dining, which shed light on the nature of consumer culture generally. First, fashion as always was inherently exclusionary, a point that almost every writer on the subject has been quick to make. Fewer have remarked on a second equally important quality, that fashionable living was also extraordinarily accessible, not just open to the obviously qualified, but almost evangelical in the enthusiasm with which proponents extended a helping hand to promising aspirants, however rigorously they enforced the initiation rites and upheld the rules of membership afterwards.

Both observations, and a third one as well, are superbly illustrated by an unusual group of decorated tin-glazed tablewares that enjoyed great popularity in England and the colonies. Seventy years separate the first dated specimen in 1682 from the last in 1752.[54] Curators and collectors call these dinnerwares "Merryman plates" because the set of six is always inscribed with a rhyme that poses the question *What is a Merry Man?* They proceed line by line and plate by plate to instruct a would-be host "To entertain his Guests / With wine and merry Jests" (fig. 16).

Was such fun-loving crockery actually used at formal tables? Each piece in the series is always conspicuously numbered "1" through "6," probably to assist illiterate servants—increasingly a class apart—to set the plates around the table in the correct sequence. Why? Perhaps so that the educated guests could recite the verses aloud as one of their "merry Jests" in an evening's entertainment. No one knows for certain. But in that robust age when sophisticated tastes and refined table manners were still newly learned from cookbooks, crib cards, and instructions painted on the dinnerwares themselves, it was not unheard of for a Merryman and his tipsy friends to backslide into their former state of bucolic revelry. The last two plates in the series warned him and them that on those occasions that "if his wife Do frown," then "All merryment Goes Down." The verse takes a tiresome dig at scolding wives, but in fact the real butt of the joke was the relapsed Merryman, whose spouse was no mere party pooper but a new-model hostess performing her appointed duties. Less than a hundred years after Shakespeare rued that "It was never merrie worlde in England since Gentlemen came up," wives too had assumed no small share of responsibility for policing the dinner table, a portent of bigger things to come. Frowning Mistress Merryman demonstrates the point about accessibility. Women had been beneficiaries of their father's or husband's status in the Middle Ages, legally and socially. The advent of consumer culture gave them access to a social reputation that they earned themselves.

The seventy years between the first and last Merryman plates encompass the time period in which I have here set about to pull together scattered evidence from a variety of sometimes unlikely sources to create a picture of material life that is recognizably the forerunner of the fashionableness about which so much was being said and written later in the eighteenth century. I have paid very close attention to the earliest dated appearance of newfangled housewares and foodstuffs as authenticated by

FIGURE 16

Set of six "Merryman plates," English tin-glaze earthenware, 1693, probably made and monogrammed for the Arbuthnott family of Scotland. Each plate is sequentially numbered above the verse. Few knife scratches in the glaze of these and similar plates in the Winterthur Museum and Colonial Williamsburg collections bolster the suggestion that such wares were intended only for occasional use at table, and then, perhaps, as the fruit plates that are often pictured in Dutch genre paintings. Merryman plates seldom have holes in the footrings common to decorative plates hung up for display.

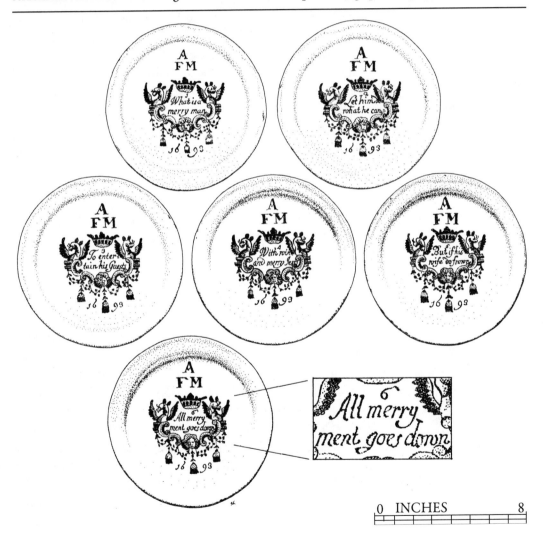

0 INCHES 8

documents, stratified archaeological assemblages, and the hallmarks and dates affixed to artifacts in museum collections. That evidence shows conclusively that the seventeenth century was a time of lively innovation. A trickle of new products in the 1630s, 1640s, and 1650s became a steady stream after the Restoration and swelled into a torrent by 1720.

As we told ourselves when we began this long cross-examination of the artifactual record, timing is one crucial factor in substantiating the central proposition of this volume. Consumer behavior was an evolving form of social interaction resorted to by people whom events had scattered far beyond their birthplaces or, alternatively, homebodies who nevertheless regularly consorted with strangers. Historians have never before demonstrated that the invention and introduction of standardized, fashion-bearing, consumer goods coincided very closely with accelerated, short-distance, inland movement among the professional classes and landed gentry in England after 1660 as well as increased long-distance migration to the colonies by a new breed of post-Restoration entrepreneur. Careful attention to dated artifacts confirms that correlation and demonstrates the well-timed utility of these household novelties.

Inception is one way to apply the time factor. Pace is the other. How rapidly did fashionable living penetrate to lower levels in English and American society? Two other variables used to test my hypothesis bear on this second measure of timing, namely, class and place. The spread of consumer demand varied appreciably from town to country and from class to class as defined by wealth and occupation. Therefore, wherever possible my account of genteel consumption in the seventeenth century has identified tastemakers and fashion centers as well as new inventions. London, Boston, New York, and early Philadelphia have recurred again and again in reference to cities and towns at the forefront of the new bourgeois taste. So have tiny Jamestown, Virginia, scraggly St. Mary's City, Maryland, and even a few rural counties on the lower Virginia peninsula where a consistently profitable sweet-scented tobacco turned industrious planters into wealthy grandees. Were comparable and reliable archaeological information available for plantations in the Caribbean, they too could probably be added to the list. The prominence of these few remote centers of fashionable consumption, along with the larger mainland seaports to the north, seems surprising until one remembers that all these places were home to the same class of rich merchants for whom the Navigation Acts opened an empire to commercial exploitation. For the thesis advanced in my fifth proposition to bear up, it has to be shown that consumer goods answered needs that these men felt first and foremost.

Great merchants were travelers and townspeople by definition. They did business with others like themselves. Their success served as a cultural model for their lesser neighbors no less displaced. Townspeople were rootless people, never more so than the citizens of the boomtowns that sprang up in North America.[55] Far more so than most country folk, urban dwellers needed a universal and portable system of social communications simply to signal to others who they were and to recognize birds of the same feather. Townspeople were therefore especially eager to learn the rules and acquire the goods that made the new system work.[56] Where they settled densely, their patronage attracted and sustained communities of luxury craftsmen, traders and retailers, and suppliers of genteel services.

Townspeople developed a distinctive lifestyle. At first it was not shared even with those nearby country gentlemen who were rich enough to join them, but having less occasion for polite intercourse among their all-too-familiar neighbors, had less need for fancy clothes, toiletries, tablewares, dining and seating furniture, and later tea sets, gaming tables, and other pieces of specialized social equipment.[57] Those were precisely the things that townspeople spent ever greater proportions of their non-capital wealth to acquire. Even artisans and tradesmen living in towns consumed luxuries that most country gentlemen had little use for initially.[58] When landed families finally succumbed to fashion, often their first destination was a county town or watering hole where they too could sample urban amenities for a whole social season and hobnob with other butterflies from round about and far away.

In cases where trade and commerce took gentlemen to such town-forsaken ends of the earth as the Chesapeake colonies, a few were careful to keep up not just appearances but imperial connections as well. The same Maryland and Virginia households in which we have already noted unusually early ownership of fashionable furnishings for grooming and dining were oftentimes also supplied with maps, charts, globes, clocks, secular books, portraits of the king and queen, and prints of London landmarks.[59] In other words, wherever the earliest new consumers were located, even on remote plantations, almost always they appear to have plugged themselves into commercial and cultural networks with links back to England and the metropolis.[60] Over and over again the earliest documented users of dressing boxes and chests of drawers, for instance, or the first importers of refined tablewares have turned out to be town-dwelling merchants, sea captains, colonial officials, and various hangers-on, or in the rural South, placemen, lawyers, and large planter-capitalists. In virtually every case but the last, they were men and their wives who were entitled to a considerable reputation but were deprived of a landholder's traditional means of showing it.

Other migrants, of course, also needed help to assimilate themselves socially into their New World homes. Why were so many not quicker to adopt the city dweller's shortcuts to respectability? Many simply could not afford goods that were still very expensive in the seventeenth century or could not spare the leisure time to learn and practice their use. For others old integrative channels still worked tolerably well.[61] Seventy percent of the farmers and rural artisans who settled in the Massachusetts Bay colony migrated in company with families, neighbors, or members of the same church. Former village elders in England often became town fathers in New England. The largest landowners in one place frequently were first in line to acquire comparable holdings in the next. The continuities between Old and New England must not be exaggerated, and, indeed, I will have something to say shortly about the discontinuities that were inherent everywhere in the American experience. Nevertheless, the fact remains that the agricultural communities that grew up in the northern colonies retained and observed many customary measures of status and reputation that helped country folk find a familiar niche. Similarly, the apprenticeship system gave immigrant artisans an immediately recognizable place in society with a master and shopmates to serve as a newcomer's ready-made social world. In another way, indentured servitude, while hardly providing traditional channels of access to the social order, nevertheless assigned status to tens of thousands of unattached men and women from Britain who landed everywhere in North America, but labored in the largest numbers in the southern colonies and on the islands.

Enslaved Africans represent a special case that deserves and repays a closer look at the part that visual things played in their assimilation (or not) into the American scene. Bondage deprived individuals of their Old World reputations totally and completely. Self-fashioning a personal appearance became for many slave men and women the first step in making a place for themselves in a world with few other choices. Even that excited fierce opposition from slaveholders. Whites took extraordinary measures to bar black people from access to mainstream American society, even free blacks. All the same, bondsmen from Africa and the islands underwent a process of assimilation over the course of the eighteenth century that resembled the experience of those European immigrants who relinquished their ancient customs in favor of hybrid habits that smoothed their acceptance into communities full of strangers.

Black Africans were strangers too, of course, not just to whites, but usually to one another as well. Although captives from West Africa were transported and settled in more coherent ethnic groups than historians once supposed, subsequent sales and relocations steadily eroded clan identities.[62] The mix was further muddled and memories of the homeland further diluted with the passing of each generation and the growth of creole communities. From scratch, Africans and then African Americans developed their own homegrown social networks. Little by little, they created indigenous material cultures. Seen notably in their wearing appeal and personal hairstyles, material culture became for them a language of visual communications no less conducive to social integration among themselves than genteel behavior and its accouterments were for European Americans.[63] Both followed parallel, simultaneous, and, though separate, often curiously overlapping lines of development from the mid-seventeenth century to the Civil War and beyond. For our purposes, the virtually independent invention of African American material cultures illustrates in microcosm how uprooted peoples initially adopted (or were forced to adopt) someone else's manner and appearance to fit themselves into their immediate surroundings. Eventually they learned to manipulate that look to ease their passage to places often far away. Like other

Americans, blacks too were a repeatedly uprooted people, either sold off, removed against their will, or driven to flight out of sheer desperation. Like other transients, appearances could be their all-important passport.

Most "saltwater Negroes" straight off boat from West Africa came with no possessions whatsoever. Slavers shipped their cargoes of men, women, and children "all Stark naked," save for some few who "had beads about their necks, arms, and Wasts, and a ragg or Piece of leather the bigness of a figg Leafe."[64] Once they were sold, their new masters garbed them in European-style clothes cut from coarse linen Osnaburg, English woolens, and other cheap "Negro cloth" imported for that purpose. Certain "country marks" were, of course, indelible. Pierced noses and ears, filed teeth, and ritual scarification recalled former tribal affiliations among African-born newcomers, but such insignia were seldom copied by their offspring.[65]

For a while hairstyles and homemade modifications to standard-issue slave clothing occasionally harked back to ethnic traditions remembered from Africa, like the runaway from a Virginia plantation who wore his hair "like a Madagascar's" or another fugitive, originally "of Angola country," who absconded with a jacket seamed "in the shape of a serpent."[66] By and large though, most enslaved men and women, being field hands, were issued work clothes that slave owners described in ads for runaways as "the usual clothing of labouring Negroes" or clothes "such as crop Negroes usually wear." They could be confident that newspaper readers would know exactly what to look for. A black man would likely be recognized by his "old white negro cloth jacket and breeches" and a female laborer by a short, loose gown and petticoat with a waistcoat-like jacket on top. Alternatively, whether by custom or necessity, some adult male field hands wore "only an Arse-Cloth," women only a wraparound skirt, and their children nothing at all.[67]

Household servants, personal manservants, and ladies' maids fared better, always of course at their masters' pleasure. A few grandees upholstered their most visible serving men in full livery replete with gold braid and brass buttons not unlike chairs and sofas. More commonly male house servants wore plainer suits styled after those worn by the gentlemen they served. Female house slaves were usually dressed in the familiar short gown, petticoat, and waistcoat of British working women generally, but made of finer fabrics than field hands were given.

All "Negro cloathes" supplied by slaveholders functioned ultimately as uniforms, sometimes even being stitched with the owner's initials. Whites enforced this dress code, though often haphazardly, to reinforce the hierarchy they imposed on the blacks under their control and to keep them in their place when individuals traveled (with or without permission) beyond the confines of the towns, farms, and plantations where they lived and worked. For whites, standard-issue clothing was the first line of defense against slaves' social and physical mobility.

Slaves themselves learned to game the system. Everyday life at the quarter involved many situations where men and women competed with each another for marriage and sexual partners, trading opportunities, leadership positions, and even creature comforts—more food, better housing, warmer clothes, extra blankets—that masters sometimes dispensed to favorites. The qualities that recommended such individuals for special treatment by their owners were often the same attributes that made them strong competitors among their peers. Consequently their superior clothing, improved diet, possession of hand-me-down household goods, and other signs of favor were signals that potential mates, allies, and rivals heeded as well.[68] Enhanced respect was every show-off's goal, such as a "very foppish" runaway from a North Carolina plantation who, it was said, thereby "assumes an air of importance among other Negroes."[69]

Some whites halfway understood what was going on and played the blacks' value system to their own further advantage. When certain black slave drivers, for instance, were observed to dress themselves "better than the other negroes," overseers were known to indulge their flamboyance so as "to maintain a pride of character before [the others], which," they noted, "was highly beneficial," meaning beneficial to management, of course. Whites seldom appreciated the further consequences of such special treatment, the fact that fancy dress also enhanced the wearer's reputation and success within his or her own community. Thereby favoritism by slaveholders undermined the very regulations they themselves created. Already by the 1770s the rules were broken so often and the infractions condoned so widely, especially among city dwellers, that one perceptive traveler to Charleston remarked that "there is scarce a new mode [of fashionable dress] which *favourite* black and mulatto *women slaves* are not immediately *enabled* to adopt."[70]

Storekeepers' account books and archaeological collections reveal that the signaling system slaves adopted to compete with one another did not wait on the favor of indulgent masters. African Americans became steady customers at stores in the Chesapeake region and elsewhere as the growth of towns and a diversified agricultural economy opened opportunities, albeit unintended, for slaves to engage in petty trade.[71] Purchases made with ready money earned from the sale of poultry, fish, baskets, brooms, and garden produce were spent on rum and molasses first and foremost, but, after those, principally on wearing apparel—hats, hose, shoes, stockings, buckles and buttons, ribbons and handkerchiefs, and yard goods much finer than plantation-issue "plains." Frequent sales of sewing tools, carding equipment, and dyes for coloring fabrics reflect a growing practice on plantations in the decades following the American Revolution to require slaves to make their own clothes. This cost-cutting economy for owners thereby had the unintended effect of broadening opportunities for African Americans to personalize and accessorize their dress even though it did assign additional burdensome tasks to enslaved women. Rules or no rules, more and more blacks began sporting clothing that whites deemed "beyond their Condition," as one South Carolina planter ruefully described them, fancy dress "too good for any of [their] Colour."[72]

Dress code violations that whites deplored were, for blacks, strategies with both costs and benefits. The costs required prudent choices for people who never owned much anyway and were chattel themselves. Careful parsing of archaeological evidence shows that enslaved men and women made quite different consumer choices and made them at different times in their lives.[73] Archaeologists excavating storage pits under slave cabins and workplaces sometimes find unusually large numbers of showy metal buttons, for instance. These concentrations seem to be associated particularly with sites where teenage boys lived and worked, such as the nailery on Mulberry Row at Thomas Jefferson's Monticello.[74] Adjacent sites have yielded significantly fewer buttons. The correlation suggests that the acquisition of buttons and their display on coats and jackets was an investment worth making for young men who were reaching the age when vying for mates and other perks could be greatly aided by being (in the timeless self-description of one ex-slave) "bout the mos' dudish nigger in them parts" (fig. 17).[75] Unattached young men also accounted for many runaways, another circumstance in which looking sharp was sound strategy. Even the buttons themselves attest to their wearers' restless eye for fashion. Silvery metal buttons worn for most the eighteenth century were (archaeologists tell us) quickly replaced by slave-quarter dandies when more expensive, gold-colored buttons become modish after about 1770.

Sites of slave households headed by women who held prominent positions in the master's house or kitchen are occasionally associated with another costly product—fine ceramics—including pearlware tea sets and dinnerwares and sometimes even pieces of Chinese porcelain. Significantly these concentrations never occur on the same sites that yield buttons in profusion. That suggests that slave consumers could seldom afford more than a single extravagance, if that. They therefore carefully picked and chose whichever one promised to send the strongest signal to their intended audiences and rivals. In the case of matriarchs who headed extended kin groups or younger women who challenged their rule, competition may have taken surprisingly European forms—namely, handed teas and plated meals, or alternatively some distinctive African American rendition of these "big-house" protocols. Surprise was certainly the reaction of one foreign visitor who inspected George Washington's slave quarter at Mount Vernon, and there "in the middle of this poverty" was astonished to find "cups and a teapot."[76]

The larger question—why enslaved men and women accepted the expense and risks inherent in the act of appropriating Europeans' consumer culture, in effect the same question we have asked about white Americans, *why demand?*—produces two familiar answers. First, among people who were denied the usual means to demonstrate achievement, material things, especially costly things, substituted as signs for socially desirable qualities—virile or fertile partners, savvy traders, wise elders, and leaders worthy of trust. That much was for home consumption at the quarter or round about the neighborhood. In addition, slave apparel

FIGURE 17

The Old Plantation, watercolor on paper by planter and slaveowner John Rose, Beaufort County, South Carolina, 1785–90. This earliest known group portrait of mainland American slaves reveals a blend of African and European cultural traditions. The men wear workaday short jackets typical of sailors and artisans, the women plain gowns and patterned kerchiefs. The head wraps and bare legs and feet betray lingering African customs, as does the dance the central figure performs to music played on a banjo, a percussion instrument, and two *shegureh* gourd rattles.

and coiffure were highly portable signaling devices, like clothing and hair-styles everywhere. A slave who traveled on business carried a pass that vouched for his errand to whites he met along the way. A runaway slave had only and literally the clothes on his or her back. For both, though, personal appearance supplied an indispensable entrée into distant African American communities where legitimate wayfarers looked for home-away-from-home companionship and runaways sought succor. For blacks no less than whites, however differently, appearances and behavior were the currency that bought social cachet at home and substituted for reputation abroad.

Haberdashery served as a medium to reinvent the self for Native Americans no less than for blacks. Indeed, sometimes it served them better in as much as whites generally approved when Indians dressed like gentlemen. European-style clothing adopted and often imaginatively reconceived by Indians not only helped them bridge cultural differences among themselves. Frock coats and ruffled shirts could also be accessories to a diplomatic language that Indians used to create a middle ground of mediation with fur traders, army officers, and treaty negotiators.

The Mohawk Valley trade route through New York became home to a notorious miscellany of uprooted Indian peoples by the second quarter of the eighteenth century. There Indian agent William Johnson and his opposite number, Mohawk leader Hendrick, made deft use of trade goods to clothe all parties in a visual idiom that everyone plainly understood (fig. 18). Social ceremonies appropriated from European practice were put to the solemn task of communicating matters of state. Tea etiquette was easier to learn than pidgin languages, and often it was more readily comprehended.[77] No surprise then that all along the Indian frontier, yard goods, clothing, and wearable trinkets outsold weapons and tools, sometimes by as much as three to one.[78] For the "other" Americans, displaced Indians and enslaved Africans alike, the purchase of European-made clothing and accessories was often the starting point for refashioning personal identities to replace those shattered by slavery and bloodshed.

At first, the pressure to invent an entirely new material culture bore less heavily on free migrants to the colonies than on bondsmen who arrived with next to nothing or on American Indians whose traditional

FIGURE 18

Print of Hendrick Theyanoguin, known to his English allies as King Hendrick, Mohawk Indian sachem, probably engraved and printed in London, c. 1740. A linchpin in Britain's defense against France along the New York frontier, Theyanoguin joined a legation to London in 1740 where King George presented him with a green satin waistcoat edged with gold lace. Hand-colored copies of the print suggest that the sachem not only wore the prized waistcoat when he sat for his portrait, but also a red jacket with blue cuffs. To eighteenth-century eyes contrasting colors in coat and cuffs were hallmarks of livery—in other words, a high-status servant's uniform. Possibly haberdashery made visible what the inscription under the print made explicit: the Chief of the Mohawk Indians was "Subject to the King of Great Britain."

The brave old Hendrick the great SACHEM or Chief of the Mohawk Indians. one of the Six Nations now in Alliance with & Subject to the King of Great Britain. Sold by Eliz. Bakewell opposite Birchin Lane in Cornhill.

cultures Europeans had thrown into disarray. As long as tried-and-true paths of access worked for most white colonists, the impetus to adopt the manners and trappings of gentility was at first felt mainly by wealthy townspeople, the same class of trendsetters that figured prominently in our survey of dated artifacts. The problem was that those traditional paths into unfamiliar social surroundings worked less and less well as the seventeenth century wore on, both in America and at home in Britain. New arrivals in English towns and cities found fewer kin to lodge with and look after them and fewer brides with family, friends, and position to bestow as dowry. Charities that once dispensed hospitality to strangers were swamped by the tide of vagrants that surged through the English provinces before 1640. In New England as well, the initial settlements were followed by innumerable dislocations and out-migrations as new towns hived off old ones, land-poor grandsons went searching for greener pastures, and individual wageworkers followed wherever opportunities beckoned. North America was seldom a one-stop final destination. "Wandering about," said one astonished English observer of Americans' peripatetic habits, "seems engrafted in their Nature."[79] Seen in the broader course of events, pulling up stakes and moving on in the New World were episodic events in the continuing resettlement of northern Europe.

The swelling volume of this ceaseless moving around by whites, slaves, and Indians becomes just as important to my argument as the continued arrival of new immigrants and bondsmen, maybe even more so.[80] Turnover migration is the hardest of all population movement to track or measure. Historians' picture of it in the colonies, fractured though it is, nevertheless suggests that these perpetual pioneers were sufficiently numerous and some of them prosperous enough (those of European descent at least) to have contributed significantly to the continued downward and outward spread of consumer culture even when the flow of overseas immigrants from northern Europe flattened out from 1650 to 1710.[81]

The raw numbers can only be approximated, and then most reliably for those empty frontiers that were just filling up. Yet even informed guesswork hints at droves of old and new settlers who were forever on the lookout for better prospects: 1,000 homesteaders in the Albemarle region of North Carolina in 1660 became 10,000 by 1700. In just half that time, the population of Pennsylvania jumped from 700 to 18,000.[82] Some of these were new arrivals. Others were drifters from the economically depressed Chesapeake colonies. Former servants and landless sharecroppers swelled the ranks of "Loose and vagrant persons, That have not any Settled Residence."[83] Like the miserable subsistence migrants who wandered through the English countryside before the Civil War, the "scumme and refuse of America" who tramped the roads in the decades before 1700 were indeed homeless, but also much too poor to spend their way to respectability by acquiring status-giving personal possessions.[84] Still they were free laborers, and work in the colonies was plentiful. Not a few got lucky eventually. In time some of them purchased the trifling "superfluities" that, modest though they were, often attracted unfavorable notice from those who condemned them as "altogether unsuitable to their poverty."[85] At the very least, able-bodied men and women in labor-scarce North America were always *potential* consumers.

Not all turnover migrants were poor. Small planters in Virginia moved whole families to the Eastern Shore of Maryland in the 1660s and 1670s and to Pennsylvania after 1680 where larger tracts of empty land could be had more cheaply in districts newly opened. Similarly, refugees from the earliest New England settlements began dispersing along the coast from Maine to Long Island and far into the interior almost from the moment of arrival in a settling-out process that never ceased in the generations that followed. Persistence rates, which measure the stability of stay-at-home populations, began to decline in New England towns in the 1730s. They never recovered. While many movers came from the lower social ranks, they were joined by significant numbers of middle- and upper-class fortune seekers as well. Except for the longer distances everyone traveled in the colonies, these more substantial migrants resembled their counterparts in Restoration England who changed addresses not so much from necessity as to improve their already favorable circumstances still further. Their optimism and readiness to act on their ambitions sometimes disposed these betterment movers to consider the advantages that might be gained by acquiring the consumer goods that could launch them into polite society. Often they brought along inherited capital or at least the labor to produce the capital needed to buy instant respectability to replace the reputations that their forefathers had earned the old-fashioned way in the towns and neighborhoods the younger generation left behind. Inventory studies of the upland counties they settled in central Massachusetts and Connecticut indicate that they made heavy investments in material goods once the hardships of homesteading were past, at the same time that the relative value of such assets was declining in the older settlements.[86]

To contemporaries blinkered by older ways of thinking, it surpassed understanding that people would voluntarily "abandon their friends and families and their ancient connections" to gamble on an unknown future.[87] "Emigration is a form of suicide," wrote one dismayed correspondent to a Bavarian newspaper, because, he said, "it separates a person from all that life gives except the material wants of simple animal existence."[88] He was right about the separation and, actually, he was not wrong in predicting that many of his emigrating countrymen would indeed lead impoverished, violent, animal-like lives on the margins of North American civilization. What he could not appreciate from his Old World vantage point, even as late as 1816 when the news story appeared, was the prospect that some emigrants could do better than that. Early nineteenth-century America had already become the proverbial "best poor man's country," where ordinary, hardworking men and women could satisfy a good deal more than simple material wants. By then inexpensive consumer goods and easygoing gentility were fast replacing severed ancient connections. They were cauterizing the wounds of separation. They were, in effect, the key to life after suicide.

The first signs of the consumer revolution appeared almost simultaneously among the freest-wheeling participants in the British and American economy in the latter half of the seventeenth century. Proving that was one reason to date precisely the earliest appearance of diagnostic consumer goods. Ownership of such things spread rapidly to other groups in provincial England and colonial America in the decades after 1690 as more and more people saw the social advantage to be gained by identifying closely with their goods. Evidence for that is everywhere scholars look. Furniture historians tell us that almost £5,000 worth of (mostly cane) chairs—more than "sixteen hundred dozen"—were shipped from

England to mainland America between 1697 and 1704.[89] Zooarchaeologists find microscopic pollen grains in early privy pits showing that up-and-coming artisans were dining on the same broccoli, parsley, and other haute cuisine vegetables in the 1720s that it was said gentlemen themselves had only "very lately tryed" ten years later.[90] Counting and cataloging ceramic shards, archaeologists also report "a marked increase of fine imported wares" in the closing decades of the seventeenth century.[91]

Most persuasive of all are the social historians who use a so-called amenities index to analyze probate inventories.[92] They can detect consumer goods in minuscule quantities—a table fork here or a teapot there—and then can add all the evidence together to reveal broad chronological trends, sorted according to regions, wealth groups, and town and country residence. There is no arguing with their conclusions. Among rural buyers, goods that indicate some degree of fashion consciousness began appearing in 10 percent or more of poorer households (those estates valued at less than £100) by the 1720s and 1730s. That seems to be the moment that economists call the "takeoff point." At least one in ten wealth holders worth less than £49 (the poorest group) owned table forks by the 1730s; one in ten was drinking tea by the 1740s and 1750s; and his one-in-ten wife was setting the table with a few pieces of refined earthenware by midcentury in some localities and from the 1760s and 1770s in others. Generally speaking, the wealthier they were, the higher and sooner rural consumers score on the amenities index. Item by item they approach the consumption levels achieved earlier, faster, and more completely by townspeople and a few prominent country gentlemen.

Quantitative historians who have developed this valuable indicator are quick to remind us that one in ten consumers still leaves nine of ten who were not. They also caution that mere possession of a table fork or a teacup is never proof positive that the owner fully embraced or even fully understood etiquette-book culture. The woman who "drank the remains of [her] tea from the spout of the tea-pot, saying 'it tasted better so,'" would receive the same score for that amenity as Norborne Berkeley, baron de Botetourt, governor of Virginia and a renowned "man of parade," who doubtless gave smashing tea parties using his "2 red china teapots" set out on a "Scollop'd claw tea table" and served in "29 bleu

& white tea cups & 64 saucers."[93] Such reminders aside, it is impossible to deny the essential truth of the quantifiers' bottom line, that "a rising standard of consumption was underway on both sides of the Atlantic" by 1770, bringing with it a lifestyle that "penetrated . . . all but perhaps the poorest levels of rural . . . society."[94]

As a matter of fact, even there, even in slave quarters on Caribbean and mainland plantations, men and women who were property themselves nevertheless sometimes managed to acquire an assortment of European wares, some brand-new surprisingly, others second-hand imports that became common enough among ordinary freeholders in the 1770s and 1780s to be cast off, bartered, bought, or pilfered.[95] Just how slaves used the unmatched plates and saucers recovered from trash pits is anyone's guess. Anthropologists remind us that people from one cultural background often make imaginative use of objects appropriated from other cultures.[96] That said, it is hard not to surmise that African American customers, like one named Will who purchased a dozen, brand-new, dinner plates from a country store in Virginia in 1807, had not bought into European dinner-table customs and dietary preferences.[97] Not only could Will or his wife set matching places at their own table, but his choice of dinner plates strongly suggests that that family and no doubt others too enjoyed a wider variety of tastier foods than slaves' standard diet of cornmeal hominy eaten from bowls. The gradual disappearance of slave- and Indian-made made pottery from antebellum plantation sites throughout the South argues that consumer values transformed folkways even there.[98]

From this picture of consumption's expanding reach, the further conclusion does not logically follow that new consumers were inspired to ape their betters by nothing more than envy. Amenity scores tell us how far consumer behavior spread and how fast, but not how come. To answer that was the second reason I examined so exhaustively the activities and artifacts of grooming, dressing, image making, and formal dining in seventeenth-century American parlors. When historians take the trouble to trace modern consumer behavior back to its origins and use the evidence of artifacts to ask how fashionable living really worked for those engaged in it, their actions appear to require a more complicated historical explanation than one that merely makes consumption a footrace between gentlefolk and a pack of impertinent social climbers nipping at their heels. When the goods that consumers consumed are used to refurnish the intimate social spaces that their users once inhabited, the effect is to magnify genteel domestic activities to a large enough scale to reveal their composition of separate elements. They start with instruction and preparation, go into rehearsal, climax in performance, garner approval or not, and win social acceptance or rejection. Those components leave little doubt that there was more to a formalized lifestyle than can be adequately explained by what sociologists and anthropologists like to call "elite group boundary maintenance." As a regulator of social interaction, gentility worked better as a maze than a wall. Increasingly those labyrinths were navigated within the four walls of a gentleman's or gentlewoman's formal residence.

5

⤜⤜⤜≪≪≪

LIVING EN SUITE

The interconnected parlor activities that I have anatomized one utensil at a time were enlarged upon and elaborated in the course of the eighteenth century until they ruled over a fashionable gentleman's entire house as completely as they ruled his whole life. Having now dated the introduction of fashion-conscious household goods to the second half of the seventeenth century, it would seem that further comment on the gentrification of American homes need only demonstrate how fashionable living became an international code of behavior observed by many of the "middling sort" and eventually known and acknowledged by virtually everyone.

Easier said than done. While it is true that dwelling houses and their furnishings became ever more standardized after 1700, regional differences not only persisted, they flourished. At the same time that carpenters and cabinetmakers in different parts of England and different colonies in America designed, built, and furnished patrons' houses in a manner that travelers and strangers recognized and approved, their work never lost its hometown look. Two such different aesthetics would seem to work at cross purposes. Not really. There are simply two stories braided together here that must be untangled before we can appreciate that the visual communications system that evolved in the eighteenth century broadcast on two frequencies simultaneously: one for outsiders and the other one for a home audience. The first bears directly on my central argument. The second complicates it.

The rise of formal domestic living can be quickly summarized to highlight those features that met so well the needs of an international community of users. The standardized architectural spaces that consumer goods turned into ubiquitous social settings derived ultimately from French interior decoration developed in the salons of Paris after about 1625. There aristocratic designers had relaxed the stiff and formal architectural aesthetic of Renaissance Italy to create interiors that were practical and comfortable by the standards of the day while giving up nothing to elegance and grandeur.[1] They employed two devices to achieve their impressive effect. First, they organized the principal rooms in a house and the dominant pieces of furniture in those rooms in hierarchies of social importance. Second, they subordinated the decoration of public rooms to single harmonious schemes of coordinated colors, forms, patterns, and materials. Variations on those two principles have shaped the history of domestic art in the West ever since.

All we need note about the planning of Parisian town houses and noble palaces are those elements—much boiled down—that eventually influenced first English and then American taste, mostly by way of the Netherlands before and soon after 1675. The salient features were the division of houses into state rooms and domestic apartments; their arrangement into suites of rooms in ascending order of importance and intimacy as one approached the owner's inner sanctum; the creation of specialized entertaining rooms for use by his family, friends, and closest associates; and the unified decoration of rooms into which this invited public was admitted.[2] Needless to say, neither London merchants nor wealthy colonists built a full complement of princely great chambers, antechambers, withdrawing chambers, and state bedchambers with adjoining private closets. That said, some were sufficiently attuned to aristocratic fashion to recognize its essential correspondence to those parallel developments in vernacular building practice that already were transforming parlors into sitting rooms and upstairs chambers into best bedrooms.

Several leading commercial families in early Boston and Salem built scaled-down versions of formal suites of rooms containing "great" and "little" parlors and corresponding greater and lesser upstairs bedchambers, all as early as the 1660s (fig. 19).[3] Their mansions (in contrast to their neighbors' dwellings) set aside special places for entertaining social equals who took meals with them in "dyning rooms," strolled through their picture "galleries," or conferred with them privately in "closets" and "studies."[4] They also may have been the first New Englanders to admit callers into entryways that had become passages to control access to other parts of the house.[5] Here again a Frenchified design element subsumed another venerable feature of vernacular house plans, the cross passage, and conflated that with a more recent innovation in folk housing, the circulation corridor. Together they created a stylish entrance hall that functioned as the first receiving room in the sequence that led to the heart of the house. Such corridor waiting rooms were planned into new gentry houses or added to old ones more and more frequently after 1690 in all the colonies.[6]

Even so, changes dictated by foreign fashion made slow headway against the weight of tradition. Innovations were usually undertaken only by the wealthiest, most worldly builders, and even they seldom embraced new ideas uncritically and without making concessions to local practice. Although a few halls were converted into dining rooms as early as the 1660s, seventy-five years later there was still confusion about whether a ground floor room reserved for public sociability was "hall or entertaining room."[7] The high gentry in Virginia only began calling "passages" by their proper Anglicized French name—saloon—after 1760 or so. Often as not, they continued using them as "summer halls" in the time-honored manner of the region, a practice that one surprised foreign traveler explained was "preferred by the family, on account of [passages] being more airy and spacious than any other [room]." Sometimes a saloon also doubled as "an occasional ball-room."[8] Consequently, some entrance halls in southern houses received a higher degree of architectural ornamentation in relation to subsequent rooms than was usually the case in comparable English and French houses.[9] Once visitors penetrated beyond these cross-ventilated entry halls in the most ambitious gentry houses built in the colonies after the middle of the eighteenth century, especially in major cities, they might very well encounter one or more pairs of high-fashion entertaining rooms: formal parlors communicating with dining rooms

FIGURE 19

Super-wealthy shipowner and merchant John Turner Sr. initially built a two-story, clapboard-covered frame house with a porch tower and two facade gables that resembled other large vernacular houses in Salem. Soon after, he added and furnished a spectacular block of downstairs and upstairs rooms that shows how formal living made its entry into the provinces. The senior Turner's innovations lasted thirty or forty years until his son reached the zenith of his own career as a merchant, magistrate, and king's councilor. John II replaced the casement windows with sash and installed smaller, more efficient fireplaces. He also employed a Boston- or London-trained joiner to repanel the lobby and entertaining rooms and build a buffet in the parlor. These alterations further refined the family's use of the apartments in accordance with international gentry practice.

Elevations and plans of John Turner House, Salem, Massachusetts. Property acquired 1668 (deed), house built soon thereafter (window cames dated 1664), enlarged with a parlor wing and kitchen ell probably by 1680 (inventory presented 1693), modernized c.1710–30, lean-to and kitchen removed 1794, Victorianized after 1858, restored 1909. The ground-floor rooms in the original structure included a fine large hall and probably a kitchen with oven, later converted to a retail shop. The new wing raised the social ante enormously by creating pairs of complementary apartments on each floor. The former "Hall" became exclusively a dining room. The brand-new adjoining "Parlor" was fitted out as a sitting room in which the family could take private meals. All beds were removed to the floors above. There a revamped "Hall Chamber" played withdrawing room to a more private "Parlor Chamber." The one was a quasi-public room furnished for socializing as well as sleeping; the other was Turner's best bedchamber, secure storeroom, and private getaway when he wanted to write at his escritoire. Architecturally, the new wing exuded gentility. The rooms were larger and higher than usual, shoulder-level wainscot covered the walls, cased beams and fully plastered ceilings were among the earliest in New England, and a color scheme of gray and white paint coordinated the new suites of rooms. Outside, Turner proclaimed his independence from the vernacular convention of clapboards by sheathing the entire parlor block (and perhaps the rest as well) with wide flush planks shadow-molded along their edges.

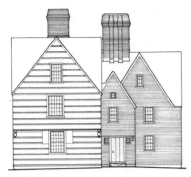

SOUTH ELEVATION

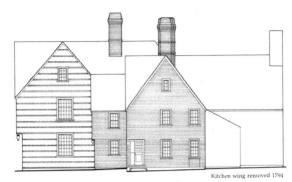

EAST ELEVATION

Kitchen wing removed 1794

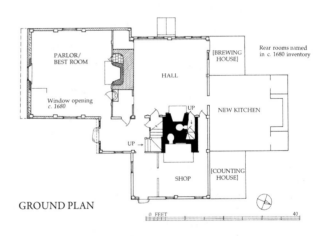

PARLOR/
BEST ROOM

Window opening
c. 1680

HALL

[BREWING
HOUSE]

Rear rooms named
in c. 1680 inventory

UP

NEW KITCHEN

UP →

SHOP

[COUNTING
HOUSE]

GROUND PLAN

0 FEET   40

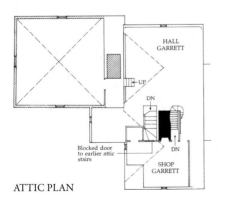

HALL
GARRETT

UP

DN

Blocked door
to earlier attic
stairs

DN

SHOP
GARRETT

ATTIC PLAN

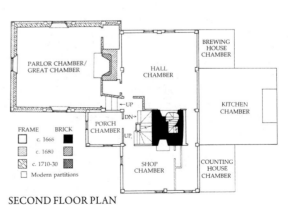

PARLOR CHAMBER/
GREAT CHAMBER

HALL
CHAMBER

BREWING
HOUSE
CHAMBER

UP

DN

PORCH
CHAMBER

UP

KITCHEN
CHAMBER

SHOP
CHAMBER

COUNTING
HOUSE
CHAMBER

FRAME   BRICK
☐ c. 1668   ■
▨ c. 1680   ■
▨ c. 1710-30 ■
☐ Modern partitions

SECOND FLOOR PLAN

FIGURE 19 (*continued*)

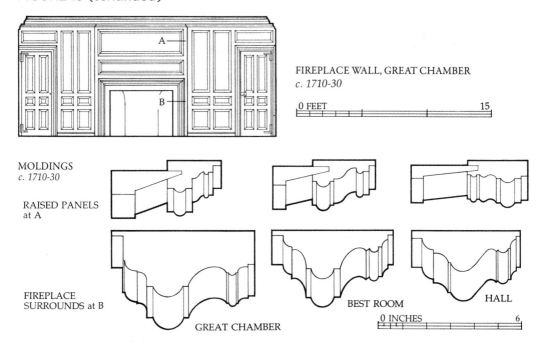

FIREPLACE WALL, GREAT CHAMBER
c. 1710-30

0 FEET   15

MOLDINGS
c. 1710-30

RAISED PANELS
at A

FIREPLACE
SURROUNDS at B

GREAT CHAMBER

BEST ROOM

HALL

0 INCHES   6

Turner House fireplace wall, moldings, and original exterior door. John Turner II's alterations in the second quarter of the eighteenth century moved formal dining and tea taking from the hall into the parlor, renamed the "Best Room." A long table and some old leather chairs stayed behind in the hall for lesser occasions. The social center of the house removed upstairs to the "Great Chamber," which, besides its lavishly appointed tester-bed, contained other fashionable gear three times more valuable than the similar bed-sitting equipment next door in the hall chamber. Conceivably at the same time a disused flue was ingeniously reconstructed as a tiny back stairs leading directly from the ground floor hall to a servants' or slaves' garret, thereby creating the secret passage that Nathaniel Hawthorne made famous in this, the House of the Seven Gables.

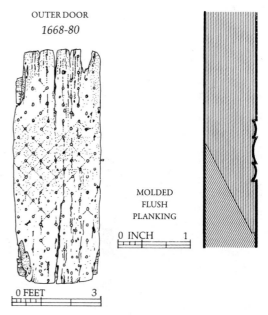

OUTER DOOR
1668-80

MOLDED
FLUSH
PLANKING

0 INCH   1

0 FEET   3

on the ground floor, drawing and withdrawing rooms upstairs, dressing rooms equipped with tea tables and replete with side chairs removed from adjacent bedchambers, and here and there even a ballroom coupled with a card or supper room. Always the architectural details and the quality of the furniture were finely calibrated to indicate to trained eyes which was the superior room where the most socially important activities took place (fig. 20).[10]

American prodigy houses containing suites of rooms that gave full play to ladies' and gentlemen's good manners were, of course, few and far between. The lesser gentry had decidedly less to show, often scarcely more than a dining room graced by a formal mantel and chimneypiece or a parlor from which the beds had recently been removed. Be that as it may, house plans began to exhibit a greater uniformity from the early eighteenth century on. Variations still abounded where patrons and builders bowed to hardy regional preferences, but upper-class houses increasingly incorporated a few of the spatial relationships and visual cues that told persons of taste that genteel behavior in some form or other was known and practiced by the owner.[11] Below the gentry level, the mass of folk housing remained impervious to the advance of fashion until the opening decades of the nineteenth century.[12] Because dwellings were usually people's largest and most valuable possessions, they were often the last to be rebuilt or replaced.

For that reason many newcomers to fashion found that it was easier and less expensive to create tasteful interiors in the new style by following Anglo-French models in the appointment and furnishing of rooms. Upholsterers and paperhangers were more affordable than carpenters and masons. Best rooms, of course, had never been utterly devoid of ornament, even in vernacular buildings. Farmers and town dwellers in England and the colonies had long brightened up halls and parlors with painted canvas hangings and with colors liberally brushed and sponged over walls and ceilings (see fig. 9).[13] What French designers introduced was the idea of architectural decoration complemented by a room's upholstered furnishings. The concept of en suite applied not just to furniture in sets but also to wall coverings color-coordinated with bed hangings, window curtains, and upholstery fabrics, all to heighten the effect of luxury and elegance.

FIGURE 20

Trackers through unfamiliar social landscapes knew where they were, what to expect, and how to behave inside well-appointed genteel buildings by using their sixth sense for the subtle indicators of status that were provided by architectural fittings and furnishings in public rooms. Even architraves around window jambs and door openings could communicate subtle social messages by their various combinations of moldings, carving, materials, and paintwork. The code was also embedded in single elements. Architraves around the windows at the Miles Brewton House in Charleston, South Carolina, perfectly calibrated the pecking order among the publicly important front rooms on each floor. Ladies and gentlemen developed a keen eye for such meaningful details in the eighteenth century. Josiah Quincy dined with Miles Brewton in 1773 and afterward made careful notes on the appearance of the drawing room: "The grandest hall I ever beheld, azure blue satin window curtains, a rich blue paper with gilt maschee borders, most elegant pictures, excessive grand and costly looking glasses, &c." His host's new house was finer than any Quincy had seen before, but his discerning eye had been honed in lesser gentlemen's houses built along similar lines.

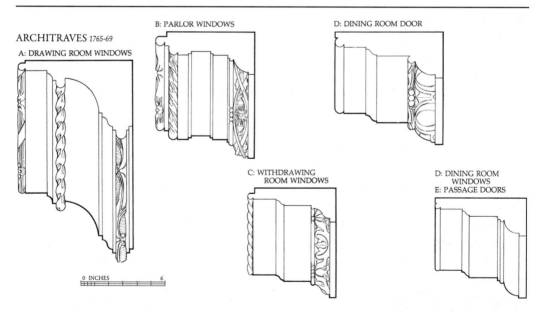

ARCHITRAVES *1765-69*

A: DRAWING ROOM WINDOWS

B: PARLOR WINDOWS

C: WITHDRAWING ROOM WINDOWS

D: DINING ROOM DOOR

D: DINING ROOM WINDOWS
E: PASSAGE DOORS

0 INCHES 6

Decorative elements, Miles Brewton House, 1765–69. Few eighteenth-century buildings employed a more sophisticated lexicon than the Miles Brewton's exceptionally lavish Palladian town house. Outside it announced its prominence by its splendid wrought-iron gates and two-story portico. Inside visitors encountered suites of rooms on each floor. The relative importance of each social space was a sum of its parts—pilastered, paneled, papered, or plastered walls; architraves with or without crossettes; marble or wood mantels; chair boards carved or plain; concealed or exposed hinges; and papier-mâché ceiling ornaments reserved for the best rooms.

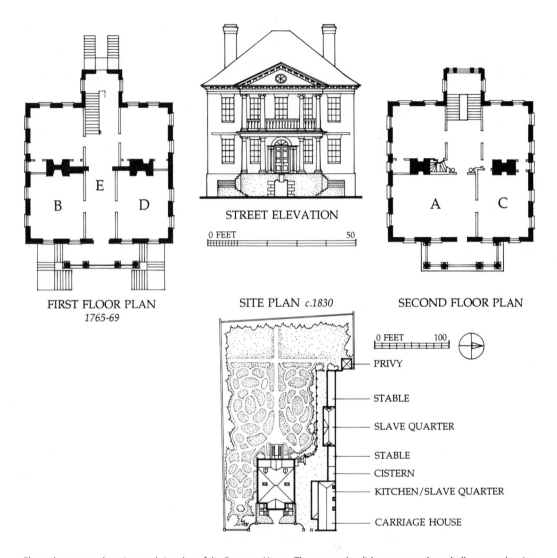

FIRST FLOOR PLAN
1765-69

STREET ELEVATION

0 FEET ⊢⊣⊢⊣⊢⊣⊢⊣⊢⊣ 50

SITE PLAN *c.1830*

SECOND FLOOR PLAN

0 FEET 100

PRIVY

STABLE

SLAVE QUARTER

STABLE

CISTERN

KITCHEN/SLAVE QUARTER

CARRIAGE HOUSE

Floor plan, street elevation, and site plan of the Brewton House. The most splendid space was a large ballroom or drawing room (A) entered from the upper passage. Its window jambs were trimmed with giant compound moldings highlighted by rococo and rope carving on the beads. Next most favored was the parlor immediately below (B). The architraves around its windows were smaller but richly embellished with more cable molding and an ovolo backband carved with flowers and frets. The withdrawing room (C) off the second-floor ballroom appears to have been slightly inferior to the parlor. Accordingly its three-part architrave lacks the parlor's elegant channel moldings but it still sports a foliated ogee backband with a bead-and-reel astragal. That separates the moldings in the withdrawing room from those used to trim window openings in the dining room downstairs (D), the only front room in which those surrounds were left uncarved. Moldings in the passage (E) are a simplified variant of the dining room architraves, and those in the back rooms simpler still.

By now it should come as no surprise to learn that merchant princes in Boston were the first Americans to remodel their sleeping apartments into the kind of penultimate public-private withdrawing rooms so sumptuously appointed that no ordinary functional room names did them justice. Instead they were called the "Green Chamber," "Red Chamber," "Purple Chamber," or just "Painted Chamber" in a telling departure from traditional room-naming practices that emphasized the new importance of decor.[14] Appearing first in inventories from the 1660s and 1670s, rooms known by the color of their coordinated textiles and wall coverings increased in popularity throughout the eighteenth century, at first, of course, with the superior class of house owners who could afford a "Paper Room" (1737) when wallpaper (another French invention) came into fashion or a "Chintz Chamber" (1774) when English printed cottons made into window and bed curtains were by all accounts "the Most Approved Manner now in Vogue."[15] Wallpaper was made in a wider range of qualities than textile wall coverings and sold at lower prices than upholstery fabrics, making "Papering as cheap as Whitewashing," according to one Philadelphia paperhanger in 1783. Where advertisers claimed that "the expense of papering a room does not amount to more than a middling set of prints," middling sorts of people were literally able to cover old walls with a paper-thin veneer of spanking-new imported elegance (fig. 21). It was observed after the Revolution that houses in Philadelphia were "seldom without paper tapestries, the vestibule especially being so treated." In truth, if one believes paperhangers' advertisements, there was not an entertaining room imaginable for which an appropriate fashionable paper could not be purchased for pennies a roll.[16]

Other architectural features that became standard components in eighteenth-century interiors underwent the same transformation from high-style French to middle-brow English and American. Everywhere the same effects were sought: to achieve greater comfort and convenience, to heighten pomp and ceremony, and to accomplish all by employing a design idiom that was universally recognized and acclaimed. Wall surfaces not covered with real or "mock" paper tapestries were likely to be "wainscotted," not with the small oak panels common to earlier interiors, but with large raised panels set in a framework of stiles and rails and trimmed around with classical moldings. Those and many other architectural elements borrowed from antiquity were concentrated on chimneypieces, ceilings, and the architraves around windows and doors. Often they were brightly colored. Not just the chimney breast received decoration, but the firebox too. Now made smaller and more efficient, it acquired a bolection molded frame (see fig. 21), sometimes a mantel shelf to display garniture, and a fascia set with painted tiles that resembled oriental porcelain and were easy to keep clean.

Buffets were pulled in behind dining room walls to become built-in cupboards fitted with glass doors to store and show off expensive tablewares. Having so many things worth seeing required more light than unglazed and shuttered openings or casement windows had admitted into late medieval rooms. Hence, engravings of the 1630s and early 1640s show daylight streaming into Parisian interiors through the earliest known double-hung, sliding-sash windows.[17] After dark, the splendors of French court life were reflected from wall sconces, pier glasses, and mirror plate set into chimney breasts, these too being elements that soon found their way onto the international cultural scene.

To describe this ensemble is to describe the appearance of houses that sprang up in every eighteenth-century English market town and every colonial seaport. The point is that these stock elements were already coming together in France by 1650, and soon after they were multiplied a thousand times in Amsterdam, London, Boston, and wherever else fashion traveled. "A Gentleman from London," according to one who was, "would almost think himself at home in Boston, when he observes the numbers of people, their houses, their furniture, their Tables, their dress and conversation." A Bostonian's display of fashion, he said, was "as splendid and showy as that of the most considerable Tradesman in London."[18] That level of perfection had been achieved by 1720, but only just.

Earlier the elements of the unifying French-Dutch-London aesthetic had still been works in progress. Innkeepers in Maryland's capital village of St. Mary's City used decorative tiles to face fireplaces in new and remodeled taverns starting in the 1670s.[19] A speculator at Jamestown lavishly refurbished a large brick edifice a few years before 1682, including a domestic parlor with a fourteen-foot ceiling and a highly sophisticated,

FIGURE 21

Before the end of the seventeenth century the largest houses on Bermuda resembled one owned by Capt. and Governor William Sayle (see inset on right). His 1671 inventory describes an old-fashioned dwelling that bears instructive comparison with the high-gentry mansion that John Dickenson built to replace it before 1714. Both were two stories high. Both had about the same number of rooms on each floor. Both called three main entertaining rooms by the same names—hall, parlor, and dining room. The differences lay in the fashionableness, formality, organization of living space, and genteel amenities afforded by the house newly built by Dickinson, a merchant and man of affairs. From the front, it represented a balanced composition of door and window openings surmounted not by the monitor roof of today but probably a pair of pitched roofs over the inhabited garret. Work buildings—a kitchen, buttery, storerooms and cellars, "Servants Lodgings," and a "Cabbin," perhaps for Dickinson's house slaves—were grouped together around back, out of sight. Dickinson's granddaughter and her husband, a prominent customs collector, modernized and redecorated the house in a still newer mode c. 1760.

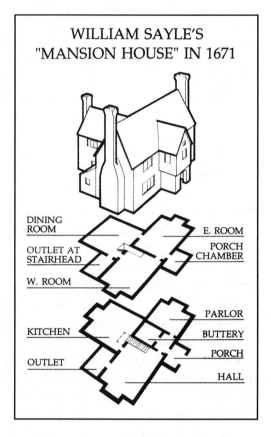

WILLIAM SAYLE'S "MANSION HOUSE" IN 1671

DINING ROOM

E. ROOM

OUTLET AT STAIRHEAD

PORCH CHAMBER

W. ROOM

KITCHEN

PARLOR

BUTTERY

OUTLET

PORCH

HALL

Elevation and plans, Verdmont, Smith's Parish, Bermuda. House c. 1700–1714 (inventory), remodeled c. 1760–82 (inventory) and retrimmed c. 1790–1820, kitchen–storeroom–slave quarter eighteenth century (maybe the 1714 "Outt Houses") with nineteenth-century improvements. Dickenson's house resembled Sayle's only in that the front entrance still opened directly into the hall, not into a center passage. Otherwise everything about the new house conformed to the dicta of international taste at the turn of the century: the double-pile plan, the hall turned into a formal sitting room and picture gallery (Sayle's hall had still been an eating room), the parlor bedchamber moved upstairs into a dressing and reception room, convenient access to all rooms from a generous half passage and staircase, and sumptuous Renaissance moldings used to trim mantels and stairs.

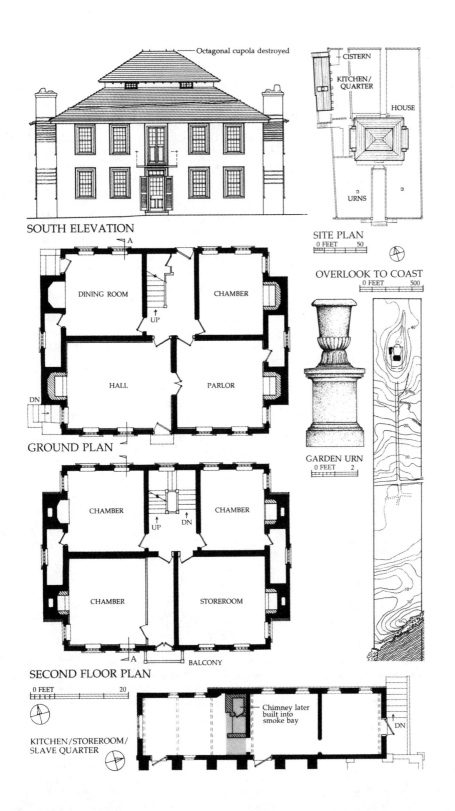

Octagonal cupola destroyed

SOUTH ELEVATION

SITE PLAN
0 FEET 50

CISTERN

KITCHEN/
QUARTER

HOUSE

URNS

OVERLOOK TO COAST
0 FEET 500

A

DINING ROOM

CHAMBER

UP

HALL

PARLOR

DN

GROUND PLAN

GARDEN URN
0 FEET 2

CHAMBER

CHAMBER

UP DN

CHAMBER

STOREROOM

A

BALCONY

SECOND FLOOR PLAN

0 FEET 20

**KITCHEN/STOREROOM/
SLAVE QUARTER**

Chimney later
built into
smoke bay

DN

FIGURE 21 (*continued*)

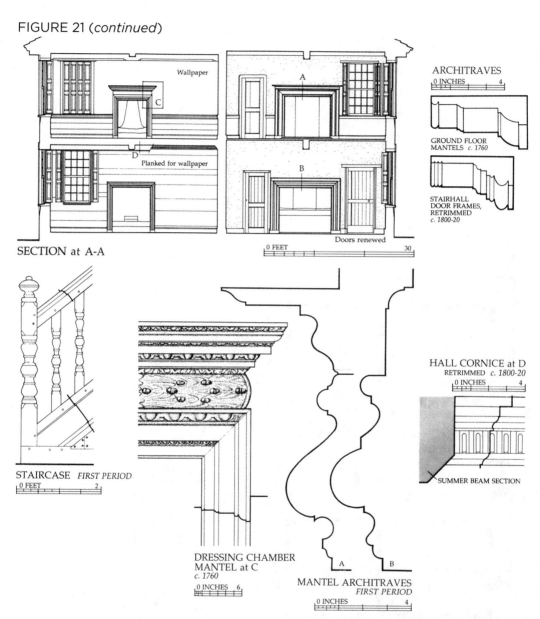

Wallpaper

C

SECTION at A-A

Planked for wallpaper

D

A

B

Doors renewed

0 FEET   30

ARCHITRAVES

0 INCHES   4

GROUND FLOOR
MANTELS *c. 1760*

STAIRHALL
DOOR FRAMES,
RETRIMMED
c. 1800-20

STAIRCASE   *FIRST PERIOD*

0 FEET   2

HALL CORNICE at D
RETRIMMED   *c. 1800-20*

0 INCHES   4

SUMMER BEAM SECTION

DRESSING CHAMBER
MANTEL at C
c. 1760

0 INCHES   6

A   B

MANTEL ARCHITRAVES
FIRST PERIOD

0 INCHES   4

Changes made to Verdmont, c. 1760: casement windows replaced with sashes and interior shutters, three front rooms wallpapered, and the fireplaces reduced in size and retrimmed, lavishly in the dressing chamber. An upstairs passage leading to a balcony was also added and the front rooms downstairs were converted into double parlors for tea, cards, and music. These improvements, topped up with a few neoclassical cornice moldings and architraves a generation later, refitted Verdmont for fashionable living well into the nineteenth century.

London-quality molded plaster chimneypiece with baroque polychrome decoration incorporating half-sized figures sculptured in high relief.[20] A Boston merchant, Thomas Banister, wrote to his London agent that sliding-sash windows were "the newest Fashion" in that city in the spring of 1701. He had seen "some curious clear glass," which someone told him was called "crown glass." One of his neighbors had "glazed the front of his house with it," and, Banister had to admit, it looked "exceeding well." So well that he too had "a great mind to have one room or two glazed with that glass" (fig. 22).[21] A few years later carpenters hired to build a house for a minister who had recently moved from Boston to the north parish of Andover, Massachusetts, were stumped by his request for new-fashioned wainscoting in the parlor and parlor chamber. They were unacquainted with the technique of slotting raised panels into grooved stiles and rails. So they boarded the wall in the usual way and simply nailed up mitered moldings like picture frames to simulate fielded panels.[22]

Elsewhere some builders were better informed. Carpenters whom Samuel Harrison employed to add a posh new wing to a plantation house south of Annapolis in the 1720s knew all about the new paneling. When they had finished installing several rooms with it for Harrison, he employed skilled painters to marbleize the walls in hues of green, red, and yellow. They were even sufficiently up-to-date to execute French-style overmantel landscapes and the fanciful *dessus-de-porte* paintings that took their name from their location above interior doors.[23] In his new dining room Harrison installed a very early built-in buffet. Its use was almost as foreign as its name was unpronounceable. Among southern inventory takers it often came out "Boofott" or "Beaufett" or (was it?) "Bow-Fatt."[24] Never mind. Owning one was all that counted.

Thus, little by little and piece by piece the standardized formal interior took shape in the American colonies. Its elaborately staged design scheme was considered necessary and appropriate principally for those rooms where important social transactions were expected to take place. The "decoration . . . is only to be found in the rooms which a visitor is likely to see," wrote a Frenchman about houses in Philadelphia in 1798. "Everything else can get along in any old way." Likewise, all that Virginians wanted in a house, it was said, was "a bed, a dining room, and

FIGURE 22

Ebonized chest-on-frame (perhaps originally a chest of drawers, opposite), Essex County, Massachusetts, maker unknown, 1700–1725, collection North Andover Historical Society, Massachusetts. The detail below on the left (*a*) shows an idealized "modern" house still fitted with traditional leaded casement windows, while the one on the right (*b*) features new-model sliding sash windows that updated a very similar town house painted on another chest of drawers possibly by the same unknown maker (Essex County, Massachusetts, 1700–1725, collection Shelburne Museum, Shelburne, Vermont). Function, form, finish, and decoration combined to make these flamboyant pieces of case furniture absolutely up to the minute c. 1700–1710. Providing drawer storage, each chest was ebonized and painted to mimic fashionable Japanned furniture. The whimsical scenery on the drawer fronts includes paired portraits of formal red brick houses that are almost identical except for the different window treatments. By the time the Shelburne Museum chest was made, the cabinetmaker or his painter had learned that sash frames glazed with crown glass were now the newest fashion.

a   b

a drawing room for company."[25] House architecture responded to changing routines in house life as more and more everyday activities assumed social significance and were played before audiences of discriminating spectators. The seventeenth-century grooming and dining performances that I described earlier had taken place mostly in undifferentiated parlors. Eventually these became "dining parlors" when bedsteads removed to separate bedchambers, and, sometime after that (by the 1760s in rural New England), when formal dining repossessed the hall, leftover parlors were known as "setting parlors" in recognition of their sole remaining use.

Houses and their furnishings became accessories to their inmates' sociability as the beau ideal civilized all manner of formerly mundane household activities and added new ones as well. While no Americans, however self-important, are known to have held levees, gentility attached no little significance to the proprieties of rising, dressing, and breakfasting, all before a day was scarcely begun. Consequently, expensive and fashionable furniture came to be located in best bedchambers, habitable closets, and dressing rooms. Beds themselves retained their age-old eminence, dignified occasionally by canopies and commonly by curtains and valances.[26] They were attended increasingly by a swarm of side chairs, high and low stools, couches, and daybeds, often in matching upholstery and perhaps still faintly echoing the status distinctions that the same pieces of chamber furniture had signified in France and the Low Countries. Furniture historians believe that they were used to seat companions who had leisure hours to spend lolling about on the overstuffed mattresses and cushions that padded late seventeenth-century seating furniture and that later became an integral part of upholstered sofas and easy chairs.[27]

Leisure was, of course, an indispensable condition of gentility. Many of the new social activities by which ladies and gentlemen earned their reputations were forms of entertainment and play devised to keep them busy without actually working. These obligatory diversions required still more specialized utensils. Cupboards full of paraphernalia were needed, for instance, just to prepare, serve, and consume the exotic beverages that were now taken at set times throughout the day—tea notably, but coffee, chocolate, punch, and probably posset as well (see fig. 13).[28] As good manners invaded room after room in the eighteenth century, special-purpose furniture fine-tuned architectural spaces in readiness for the gentlefolk whose social lives were unimaginable without them (fig. 23). Formal behavior spawned the progeny of armchairs, easy chairs, elbow chairs, smoking chairs, and lolling chairs that appear for the first time in eighteenth-century inventories, mostly after 1750. Similarly, among tables, a host of upstart forms were designed specifically for dining, tea, breakfast, cards, dressing, sewing, gaming, drinking, mixing, shaving—in short, every conceivable activity for which a flat surface was desirable. Gone were the days when convenience alone fixed the customary locations of versatile, convertible furniture. Formal living required formal settings. The stage required props in places where the actors could count on finding them from one performance to another (fig. 24). So ensued those furniture forms known only by their place-names—corner chairs and corner tables, end tables, sideboards, side tables, and side chairs.[29]

While tea and calico were remembered as "the chief initiating articles" that introduced ordinary people to consumer goods "by imperceptible degrees" after 1750, the famous Philadelphia antiquary John Fanning Watson believed that it was principally household furniture, greatly "added to both in quantity and kind," that "began the marked distinction between rich and poor, or rather between new-fashioned and old-fashioned."[30] Daniel Defoe had made a similar observation about the march of fashion in Britain a generation earlier. Fashionable clothing had always been faddish, he noted, "but it never went such a length in other things as it does now." Recently fashion had begun altering "more durable kinds of things, such as Furniture of Houses, Equipages, Coaches, nay even of Houses themselves."[31] Three decades later in Philadelphia Watson had even more reason to draw a distinction between affluence and fashion. Consumption was no longer a prerogative of wealth. By midcentury people of fairly modest means were becoming consumers too, and their purchases were not confined to small comforts and trifling conveniences. Like their betters, they too increasingly resorted to fashion to define their social relationships. To entertain stylishly, even on a limited budget, a householder required absolutely a few appropriate pieces of furniture. Their specialized forms, standardized ornament, and assigned places provided the essential visual signals needed to cue the newfangled

FIGURE 23

Mr. Peter Manigault and His Friends, ink and wash drawing by George Roupell, Charleston, South Carolina, c. 1750. The host (on the left, addressing "Howarth") and seven officers and gentlemen friends exchange toasts and show off their clubical manners at a punch party held "at the House of Mr. Manigault," either his town house or "Steepbrook" at Goose Creek. Eighteenth-century American scenes seldom depict so comprehensively all the elements attendant on the kind of genteel performance shown in this drawing, notably the setting, props, costumes (including the enslaved waiter's livery), and gestures. Even the performers' lines—"Pray, less noise Gentlemen" and "Squire Isaac your Wig, you Dog!"—had been scripted by the participants' long instruction in the arts of civility and rehearsed over a lifetime of similar encounters with social equals.

FIGURE 24

Diagram of tea drinkers fashionably deployed in the parlor of Dr. William Shippen's Philadelphia town house, 1780, sketched by one of Nancy Shippen's suitors, who happened to be passing by on a Sunday evening about 8 o'clock. "I peep'd through the window and saw a considerable Tea Company," he wrote to her later the same evening. "You will see the plan of this Company upon the next page." The diagram shows the location of chairs and a rectangular tea table pulled out from the walls and set up for use. The family and guests are positioned accordingly: an aged grandfather (A) "sitting before the Chimney meditating," an uncle (B) "walking up and down" and entertaining the guests (E, F, G) with "his agreeable conversation," Nancy herself (C) in charge of the tea table, at which her mother (D) was also seated, and Cyrus, the Negro butler, "standing in the middle of the room—half asleep" (H). This occasion was not the first or last time that the amorous "Spy" (I) and presumably other passersby on South Fourth Street observed the Shippens' mannerly parlor activities through the large, uncurtained, street-level windows. Big cities afforded countless instructional opportunities to attentive window shoppers.

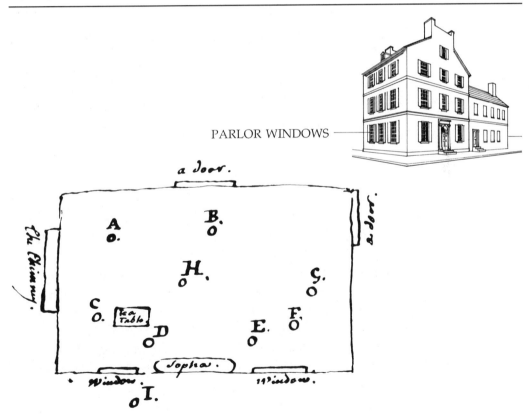

good manners that Watson's "genuine old-fashioned sort of people" were increasingly at pains to learn.

The whole history of Western art can scarcely produce another earlier example of ideas that spread so rapidly and widely from court to countryside. Domestic architectural spaces planned, decorated, and furnished en suite refashioned drawing rooms and parlors around the world little more than a century after their invention in early seventeenth-century Paris. The scale was much reduced, the splendor diminished, the lines simplified, and the materials cheapened. Yet one idea endured. That was the notion that virtually anyone could hold court in his or her own house by carefully observing prescribed conventions and correctly using a few pieces of standardized equipment. The goods could be purchased at popular prices and the manners learned from plays, prints, and penny publications galore (fig. 25).

Instruction in the genteel arts has sometimes been attributed to a tremendous supply-side growth in the etiquette- and design-book trade. The spread of fashionable living undeniably created worldwide markets for authors and publishers of pattern books, self-improvement manuals, and fashion-plate prints. We have seen already how a new cuisine rewrote cookbooks. Likewise, handbooks for builders began rolling off the presses from the middle of the seventeenth century. A hundred years later makers of many other fashionable goods had also fallen prey to entrepreneurial printers and booksellers.[32] Cabinetmakers, carvers, silversmiths, and upholsterers became targets for pattern books with hard-sell titles like *Household Furniture in the Genteel Taste for the Year 1760*, with their implication that today's fashions would be gone tomorrow. Some were practical treatises, but many were stylebooks like Thomas Chippendale's *Gentleman and Cabinet-maker's Director* that were aimed at patrons as much as at craftsmen. Consumers represented a huge market for these writers. Hence it was to their aspirations and anxieties that publishers directed an avalanche of betterment books on every conceivable subject where fashion held sway—on deportment, dressing, dancing, conversing, letter writing, game playing, traveling, gardening, collecting, and, of course, ultimately and inexhaustibly, on etiquette itself (fig. 26).[33]

FIGURE 25

Storekeeper's broadside, Tarpley, Thompson & Company, Williamsburg, Virginia, engraved and printed in London or Bristol, 1760–63. Like a display window, the elegant rococo frame around James Tarpley's broadside is tricked out with a profusion of mouth-watering imports—teacups, coffeepots, candlesticks, wallpaper, shoes, stockings, and ladies' hats trimmed with ribbons. His Williamsburg storehouse on the Duke of Gloucester Street sold those too. But his principal stock-in-trade was textiles by the yard. The broadside touts "A very large curious & compleat Assortment of EUROPEAN and INDIA GOODS." High-fashion fabrics in "the newest Taste" included striped and spotted lutestrings and brocaded tissues for women's gowns and flowered velvets for men's suitings. Some India goods, notably India chintzes, while outlawed in England, were legally sold to buyers in the colonies. Tarpley's inventory looks American in still another respect. His stock of osnaburg and "white & colour'd Plains" supplied the coarse linen and woolen yard goods used to make slave clothing.

FIGURE 26

How-to-do-it instruction by small multiples and dance lessons in time and space. Purveyors of store-bought culture first had to invent entirely new visual languages to convey with books the knowledge and skills that had formerly always been handed down person to person from masters to apprentices, tutors to pupils, and parents to children. Never before had education required that learners first be able to envisage information presented in two-dimensional formats and then translate that book knowledge into practice. Some early illustrations instructed through pictures alone. More ambitious authors experimented with graphics that demonstrated the steps involved in achieving the desired results. Step-by-step instructions books illustrated the subtleties of human movement only imperfectly. Ingenious engravers tried many different ways to represent the continuous motion of three-dimensional bodies through space and time. The graceful arts of dancing and deportment posed the greatest challenges to their talents.

a

b

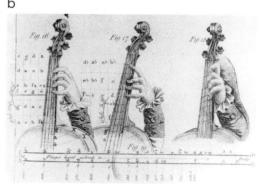

The English translator of Willem Goeree's *An Introduction to the General Art of Drawing* (London, 1674) promised readers that the author had simplified "the secret Mysteries, Power and Propertie of the Art of Painting" to "one easie and rational Method" using a set of reduction grids. An accompanying plate (*a*) showed the work in three stages of completion. Illustrators soon discovered how to apply the graphics design concept of "small multiples" to help viewers make visual comparisons that showed variations in data from frame to frame, as in John Gunn's *The Theory and Practice of Fingering the Violoncello* (London, 1789) (*b*). The diagrams in this and other play-by-the-numbers instruction manuals also made innovative combinations of pictures and standard musical notation.

c

d

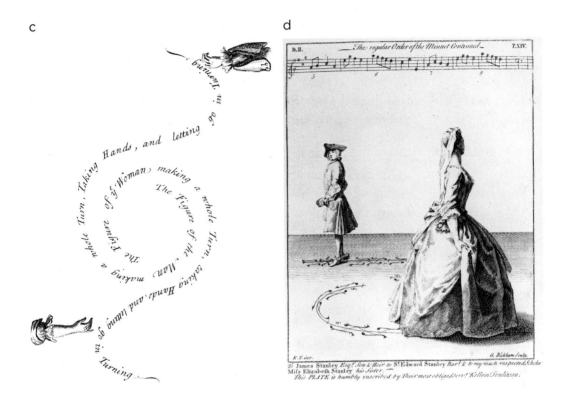

The Dancing-Master; or, The Art of Dancing Explained (London, 1744), an English edition of Pierre Rameau's famous work (Paris, 1734), used the engraved text itself to trace the synchronous movements of male and female dancers across the ballroom floor (c). By this "new and familiar Method," the English publisher advertised, "the Manner of Performing all Steps in Ball Dancing is made easy." But self-taught dancers were still confined to the flat plane of the printed page in most books. Less so the readers of Kellom Tomlinson's The Art of Dancing, Explained by Reading and Figures (London, 1735). His engraver made sophisticated use of architectural perspective and fully modeled figures to create the illusion of three-dimensional interior space (d). He covered the floor in the foreground and receding middle distance with the shorthand symbols of Tomlinson's dance notation system. The pace was regulated by sequential numbers that not only coordinated the dance partners' separate movements but keyed their progress to a musical score printed overhead. Thus, an entire dance routine—steps, gestures, melody, and tempo combined—was recorded in a single set of "cuts." Three centuries earlier the Gutenberg letterpress, movable type, and oil-based printing inks had provided the fundamental technology for print culture. Scarcely less important advances in the arts of illustration in the seventeenth and eighteenth centuries greatly expanded the number of subjects that could be effectively disseminated in books and opened communications with a vastly larger reading public.

Did such handbooks really bring the light of civilization to the outer edges of empire and illuminate benighted byways in the English provinces? They were supposed to. Architectural writers like William Pain and Thomas Rawlins explicitly addressed readers who lived in "remote Parts of the Country, where little or no Assistance for Designs is to be Procured."[34] Colonial newspaper advertisements, booksellers' accounts, and library lists tell us that design books and manners manuals were indeed imported into North America, where the conduct books sold in quantities that required numerous reprintings, new editions, collections, abridgments, and eventually American knock-offs.[35] Historians can even point to some evidence that they were read. Parents are known to have urged sons and daughters to consult the likes of *The Lady's Library and The Whole Duty of Man* "over and over again" (in Benjamin Franklin's words) whether or not children actually took the advice.[36] As for the parents, not a few willingly sat for portrait painters who bestowed on American wannabes the finery, airs, and even the idealized faces of English lords and ladies copied from inexpensive mezzotints (fig. 27).[37]

So, can it be said that the revolution in manners was chiefly disseminated in the pages of popular social guides, prints, and illustrated pattern books? Was the penny press responsible for teaching craftsmen and their customers the classical orders, the line of beauty, and the rules of etiquette? Recently historians have decided not, not directly. The courtesy books may or may not have been an exception. How effectively they reformed behavior is a hard thing to gauge. Nonetheless, scholars are quite sure that the direct influence of stylebooks on art and architecture was negligible. While they may have been a source of ideas and inspiration, sometimes a ready reference for proportions, and very occasionally an easy steal for decorative details, almost never were entire buildings or whole pieces of furniture copied cold from English designs. More often new fashions were imported as manufactured goods or were introduced by immigrant craftsmen, who advertised themselves as "late from London." Otherwise, tasteful people were busy keeping an eye on one another. Hosts gave dinner guests informal house tours in Boston by the 1760s. John Adams "went over the House to view the Furniture" after dining with Nicholas Boyleston and pronounced it "the most magnificent of any Thing I have ever seen."[38] Emulation among the already fashionable was very much the order of the day. A cabinetmaker with "carved Chairs in the newest fashion" to sell in Charleston knew that their acceptability was vouched for by advertising that they were "the same Pattern as those imported by Peter Manigault, Esq.," the city's society lion (see fig. 23).[39]

Nor did those who wanted to improve their social graces necessarily reach first for *The Friendly Instructor*. For many, dime novels became the models of choice by the end of the eighteenth century. They went one better than instruction books because, as one British traveler in the American colonies observed, novelists "attended to the personal circumstances and substance of their Characters." In short, novels were "pictures of real life." As such, he said, "they settle every etiquette of visits, balls, and tea parties," with the manifest result that "the manners of the Country are daily gaining more and more of the English character."[40]

Of course, living paragons could outshine even literary pictures of real life. Often they were the most compelling exemplars of all. Such a man was Col. William Moseley of Norfolk, Virginia. One impressionable resident of that city remembered that Moseley "was reckoned the finest gentleman we had" and on special occasions was sent for "express . . . to come to town with his famous wig and shining buckles, to dance the minuet."[41] Young men who were "utterly ignorant of the Ceremony of the Tea-Table" might find some help in books, but their best advice was to employ a knowledgeable hostess "to teach them the Laws, Rules, Customs, Phrases and Names of the Tea Utensils."[42]

Laws, rules, and terminology were the stuff of books. A Beau Nash or an accomplished gentlewoman taught something else besides. Their kind was acquainted with the prevailing customs that the rule books left out. Custom naturalized etiquette and thus produced the indefinable art of gentility that careful instruction and trial and error taught better than book learning. To understand how good manners spread so far and fast in eighteenth-century America, historians must accept the paradox that etiquette was at once a set of rules and a body of inspired improvisation. That quality of spontaneity, bounded but not hobbled by convention, was the spark that ignited fashion's infinite creativity. Cabinetmakers, the avant-garde among taste-making artisans after 1700, were known to

FIGURE 27

Fashionable lookalikes. Portraits of several Charleston gentlewomen borrowed freely from a popular mezzotint of the Duchess of Hamilton, engraved in London in 1751. The painter was Swiss-born Jeremiah Theüs (1716–1774) who launched his long and successful career as Charleston's resident portraitist by 1740. He painted his patrons' faces from life, often at home in the city or "at their respective Plantations" if more convenient. Later in his studio he added the dazzling draperies, lace, ribbons, flowers, and jewelry that were inspired—here all but plagiarized—from British print sources. Easel artists endeavored to achieve a balance between sitters' likenesses and their demeanor, finery, and settings. Theüs's passion for splendiferous costuming and his one-face-fits-all treatment of individuals suggest that for some Charleston women resembling a duchess was good enough.

Mezzotint of the Duchess of Hamilton, engraved in London in 1751.

Elizabeth Allston Lynch (Mrs. Thomas Lynch), oil on canvas by Jeremiah Theüs, Charleston, 1755. Courtesy of Reynolda House Museum of American Art, Winston-Salem, North Carolina (1972.2.1).

have a "lighter Hand and quicker Eye" than those old dogs, the joiners, and "upon this," it was said, "depends the Invention of new Fashions." It was a byword among cabinetmakers that "he that must always wait for a new Fashion till it comes from Paris, or is hit upon by his Neighbour, is never likely to grow rich or eminent."[43] Consumers as well were disinclined merely to borrow fashions unaltered. They generally held that novelties should attract attention, but not appear outlandish. Thus, the gentle arts are everywhere observed to have allowed sufficient latitude in their performance and variation in their accessories to include virtually anyone who respected the essential formalities of standardized design and polite behavior.

Susannah Holmes, oil on canvas by Jeremiah Theüs, Charleston, 1757.

Sarah Parker Lowndes (Mrs. Charles Lowndes), oil on canvas by Jeremiah Theüs, Charleston, ca. 1758. Image courtesy of the Gibbes Museum of Art/Carolina Art Association (1915.003.0001).

There arose, as a result, a new kind of regionalism throughout the beau monde, not to be confused with the parochialisms of folk cultures.[44] Yet it was not entirely dissimilar either, at least not in one vital respect. Gentility, for all its worldly ways, was a respecter of ordinary people's stubborn fondness for things reassuringly familiar. It demanded compliance with a few cardinal rules and standards observed and practiced everywhere. At the same time it also tolerated an older form of conformity to local customs and appearances. In a process reminiscent of creolization, gentility absorbed, accepted, and to a certain extent bowed to regional customs. Foreign travelers in eighteenth-century America frequently recorded how the rules were bent one way in this or that city, another way in the countryside, and differently still from colony to colony. Nevertheless, virtually everywhere they went they were usually received politely and shown courtesies they understood. Thus the new system of manners that spurred the consumption of fashionable goods solved major problems of social communications in an age of rapid expansion precisely because it was ecumenical in both senses of that word. To those abroad in the world it offered a universal code of behavior to smooth their reception in faraway places. To those homebodies, who nevertheless had their own reasons to want to appear presentable to outsiders, a tolerant ecumenical gentility was agreeably forgiving of trifling differences.

Variations in the practice of the gentle arts and localism in the design of American-made artifacts should therefore not be taken as evidence of fashion's impeded progress, as so often they have been.[45] On the contrary, they were the essential conditions that hastened its spread where otherwise it never would have gone. Benjamin Rush was addressing the creole side of etiquette when he implored young women in Philadelphia to "awake from this servility [to British manners]—to study our own character—to examine the age of our country—and to adopt manners in every thing, that shall be accommodated to our state of society, and to the forms of our government."[46]

In point of fact, polite behavior among Americans was already displaying notable republican deviations from European norms. Alexis de Tocqueville was not the first to observe that American manners were "neither so tutored nor so uniform" as in France.[47] Were they inferior?

Had Americans by insisting on their own preferences seceded from the international community of civilized ladies and gentlemen? Tocqueville thought not. American manners were "frequently more sincere," he believed. His good opinion was echoed a few years later by a Polish traveler, a nobleman's son, who explained that "good breeding prevails, and hearty, intentional politeness marks [Americans'] address and intercourse" despite their inattention to the "minute details and rites of courtesy."[48] Gentility went abroad in the new United States attired in formal clothes, but never a straightjacket. Its widespread appeal lay in its uniform standards, and its widespread acceptance in their lenient application.

The refinement of manners and the consumption of fashionable goods that mid-nineteenth-century observers held up as evidence of a "truly American and republican school of politeness" had been set in motion all of two centuries earlier and already were well advanced before the country won independence and founded a republic.[49] We began our search for this emergent American gentleman in John Weld's farmhouse in Roxbury, Massachusetts, and specifically the parlor that his neighbors inventoried in 1691. There can be no more striking measure of fashion's progress among ordinary Americans in the years following Weld's death than to peer in at another doorway in the same village eighty years later.

Stephen Brewer died in 1770 leaving an inventoried estate only slightly larger than Weld's had been.[50] Yet by then Brewer had reason to be called a "Gentleman" despite his occupation as a sometime blacksmith and barber. His neighbors knew why. Fully half the rooms in his house—no larger than Weld's—were furnished with an eye to their fashionable appearance. Guests who called on Brewer were admitted into an "Entry" lined with thirteen chairs, three tables, and a desk and bookcase. The walls were hung with pictures and a looking glass. Callers who passed muster could then be shown into the principal ground floor entertaining room where nary a bed nor old-fashioned chest was anywhere in sight. This room was reserved exclusively for formal meal taking—for dining at an oval table set with an assortment of pewter plates, glasses, and delftware and also for tea and coffee drinking. For that a special tea table was provided with the requisite pot, salvers, and sugar canister. An expensive clock chimed the dinner hour and signaled teatime in Brewer's formally regulated household. Another looking glass in this room gave invited company a second chance to adjust a wig or straighten a collar to please the barber gentleman. The third room fashionable enough to warrant yet another looking glass was Brewer's bedchamber upstairs. He not only slept there and stored his clothes in a "Case [of] Draws" (hear the inventory taker's Roxbury drawl!), but he and family or friends also used it as their withdrawing room. It was furnished with parlor-quality chairs, including an easy chair, and decorated with two large pictures and seven smaller ones hung on the walls.

Brewer's possessions totaled only a few pounds more than the appraised value of Weld's household goods. The real difference was the importance Brewer attached to his furnishings and the ways he put them to use. Weld's greatest treasures had been the dozens and dozens of fine napkins, sheets, pillow-beres, and uncut yard goods locked away in his kitchen chamber. Rarely seen and never all at once, they figured less conspicuously than his cows and oxen in making his reputation as a substantial farmer in the neighborhood. Eighty years later Roxbury residents were spending roughly the same sums to furnish their houses, or even somewhat less, but they were buying many more things, paying less for them, and getting more bang for their bucks besides. Stephen Brewer's teakettle was worth only 21 shillings, but a blacksmith who owned one and used it properly could reasonably expect to be called a "Gentleman" at home and abroad.[51]

Not that Brewer traveled abroad frequently or far. He did not have to. The world had come to Roxbury by 1770. It came in books, newspapers, store-bought goods, and cabinetmakers' work. More important, it came in person. Travelers of all sorts crisscrossed the land. Everywhere they went they sought out and consorted with local gentlefolk whose qualifications were certified by their fashionable possessions and refined manners. Historians know that for a fact because travelers said so explicitly in the diaries they kept of their journeys. Travel journals became an immense literature in the eighteenth century and now are an immensely valuable primary source for historians who want proof that international-style consumer goods and etiquette-book manners were indispensable prerequisites to people's moving around.

Diaries have often been used to document the appearance of luxuries in this place or that. Many record just as faithfully travelers' own use of fashionable things to find their social bearings where other indicators were less easily deciphered. Because the power of artifacts to communicate such information over great distances is central to understanding the nature of modern consumer culture, excerpts from a typical traveler's journal are ultimately the most apposite illustrations I can offer in support of my answer to the question that began this inquiry: Why the tremendous demand for genteel goods and services in the eighteenth century? *Some Cursory Remarks Made by James Birket in His Voyage to North America* shows us why, page after page.[52]

Birket was a merchant from Antigua. He made an overland trip from Portsmouth, New Hampshire, to Philadelphia in 1750, incidentally passing within a few miles of Roxbury on his way south from Boston. His notes are indeed cursory and wholly devoid of intentional insights. In most of the towns and villages he rode through, he tallied up the number of houses that were "of Modern Architecture" or "built after the modern taste which make a very good Apearance" or simply those he called "neat and Genteel." His list had a practical application for him. Invariably these houses were owned by the business associates he called on or those gentlemen to whom he was later introduced and with whom his diary records he then often dined. Invited into their homes, he found "many of the rooms . . . hung with printed Canvas and paper etc. which looks very neat." Others were "well wainscoted and painted," worthy of note not because they were remarkable but precisely the opposite, because they were finished "as in other places." Birket was a man who knew what to look for and was gratified when his expectations were met. That applied to people's behavior as well. A new acquaintance could receive no higher accolade in his diary than that he "treated us very kindly And in a very Genteel manner."

Birket divided American society into two parts only. There were the "Country people," whom he characterized as "the rude lazy drones of this Part of the world." They lived in "old," "sorry," and "indifferent" houses. "The better sort of People" were the go-ahead crowd that the traveler recognized by their highly visual lifestyle, to which he attached three adjectives interchangeably—"new," "genteel," and "neat." Those qualities rather than any bankable assets were Birket's guide to sizing up a gentleman's reputation. It was a fine line, which mere spendthrifts could overstep. For instance, some of the leading merchants of Boston furnished their houses "in an Elegant manner" and "Their dress [was] very genteel." But the Antiguan confided to his diary that "In my Opinion both men & Women are too Expensive in that respect."

Sometimes tastefulness was missed by inches and the offender's reputation diminished accordingly. Birket was taken to see the country house of Capt. Godfrey Malbone outside Newport, Rhode Island. He thought it made "a good Appearance at a distance," but then found that "when you came to Survay it nearer it does not Answer your expectation." His reason is quite astonishing. He found no fault with the "Hewn Stone and all the Corners and Sides of the windows . . . painted to represent Marble." Or with the "large flight of Steps into the first Story which is very Grand." Or with the "Handsome Garden" walled around the front of the house. All those were splendid and deservedly earned the house and garden's reputation as "the wonder of that part of the Country." No, the terrible problem was something else. It was a matter of a few critical inches. Upon returning from his visit, Birket carefully entered in his journal that "the upper Story is Neither . . . proportionable in the height of the rooms nor Size of the Windows." On further reflection he decided the house also suffered for having no true basement.

Poor Captain Malbone! No amount of elegance, no outlay of wealth could spare him the scorn of this traveling West Indian cognoscente! Can anyone deny that a revolution in cultural values had surely occurred when a man's property, his herds, his ships, his offices, his gold and silver, even his ancient lineage were betrayed by an ignorance of proportion? Birket was no petty one-upsman. On the contrary, he was eager to befriend people of good taste. That was just the point. There had to be rules and standards to tell the genuine article from the counterfeit.[53] What another traveler said of Virginians was true everywhere: people looked "More at a Man's Outside than his Inside."[54] Men and women had few other alternatives in the rapidly expanding world of eighteenth-century England and its colonies. Their lives were crowded with too many strangers and recent acquaintances to apply the traditional measures of respect. Instead gentility assigned a face value to the commonplace artifacts and everyday activities that knowledgeable travelers expected to encounter anywhere worth going.

At home as well as abroad their genteel manners served to distinguish and dignify the "better sort of People" from the country drones. Birket's dinner companions were often men who clearly clubbed together regularly. Sea captains, merchants, slave traders, and other men of the world brought back home the shared experiences and international outlook they had acquired in their foreign travels. They also brought home new wealth, not the only wealth in the region, but the "Opulant fortunes" that Birket said created "great Reputation." It was hard to argue with conspicuous success even if it did put on haughty airs and funny clothes. So little by little other locals less worldly-wise discovered good reasons of their own to leave off the older customs of their station and place in favor of borrowed foreign fashions that garnered for them a little of their neighbors' reflected splendor and sometimes more than a little of the prosperity that followed the carriage trade. Birket's diary gives honorable mention, for instance, to an innkeeper in New London, Connecticut, who parlayed his "great Politeness & Good Manners to his Guests" into a thriving business aimed at discriminating travelers like those in the merchant's party.

It was no great step down the social ladder from hostellers and others whose services put them directly in touch with outsiders to men like "Gentleman" Stephen Brewer, the barber-blacksmith of Roxbury. Full of get-up-and-go, he may actually never have gone farther than Boston. His customers may only have known fashionable foreigners by second- or third-hand acquaintance, through the tavern keepers who entertained the local gentry who in turn hosted celebrities from far away. Nevertheless, by 1770 many thoroughly ordinary men and women no better than Brewer saw real gains to be made by learning the rudiments of gentility and purchasing the accessories to fashion. To such an extent had "magnificence in the matter of teapots" challenged the old order and meaning of material things that even people who seldom ventured beyond the village boundaries eagerly acquired from their neighborhood storekeepers the goods that conferred social respectability in an increasingly class-conscious society.[55]

So it was wherever travelers encountered strangers, whomever they might be. Face value had currency even in cross-cultural exchanges between peoples from profoundly different backgrounds. Indeed it was crucial in those situations. While Birket traveled easily among Englishmen of his own ilk, British officials and Indian emissaries along the marchlands of Virginia and Pennsylvania and in the Mohawk Valley of New York scrupulously adopted trappings from each other's culture to create a visual vocabulary that both understood. Cherokees visiting the capital at Williamsburg wore the native breastplates, body paint, beads, feathers, and wampum that signaled their rank to one another. For that matter, whites too may have regarded this exotic ethnic apparel as a marker of the emissaries' Indianness. Notwithstanding, the headmen asked for and received English-style clothes "proper for people in their Station," as they themselves phrased it. Their request recalls the care with which Indian agent William Johnson bestowed gifts on his Mohawk hosts: shirts and body paint for warriors, and hats, coats, and shirts in "the English Mode" for the sachems. This mix-and-match haberdashery shows that Indians did not seek to pass for English, but only to demonstrate their conversance with the Englishman's rules of conduct (see fig. 18). Thereby they earned the kind of acceptance that was implied by the *Virginia Gazette*'s description of one large legation as "Forty Gentlemen and Ladies of the Cherokee nation."

Be that as it may, among Indians themselves, genteel accessories had insidious repercussions in the native villages to which warriors returned. Indian dress became "very much like the European," one British agent observed in 1762, "and indeed that of the men is greatly altered." Indians males wearing "ruffled shirts" and "double Breasted Coats" corresponded to "the better sort" in Birket's parlance. Their opposites were the Indian version of his "lazy old drones." "Old people still remember and praise the ancient days," the agent continued, "before they were acquainted with the whites, when they had but little dress."[56] Gentility forced hard cultural choices on North Americans everywhere, tradition and ethnicity notwithstanding.

The great movement of European peoples, and the dislocation of Africans and Native Americans thereby set in motion, achieved a momentum in the eighteenth century that rolls forward into our own times. It was the definitive force that shaped modern consumer culture eventually for everyone, whether migrant or not. The travelers themselves were first "to obtain the Reputation of being Men of Vertu and of an elegant Taste." They most urgently had need "to acquire foreign Airs and adorn their . . . Persons with fine Cloaths and new Fashions and their Conversation with new Phrases." They led the way, but their wake washed back on the shores they passed by and left behind. The influence of their example worked inexorably "to rub off local Prejudices" even among the firmly settled. Thus, vicariously, homebodies as well as travelers gradually acquired some measure of "that enlarged and impartial View of Men and Things, which no one single Country can afford."[57] Then as now—for indeed then *is* now— space travel opened a new view of the world at large and spun off a wealth of new consumer goods that altered the lives of Earthlings everywhere.

6

❯❯❯✕❮❮❮

AMERICAN À LA MODE

The argument thus far advanced has kept Britain's North American colonies front and center, but as only one of many regions throughout the Atlantic world where migration and resettlement brought new, widely shared, cultural forces to bear on people's social relations. It remains to ask what circumstances peculiar to mainland North America account for the rampant materialism for which Americans were singled out and praised or damned starting as long ago as the early nineteenth century.

Several characteristics of American society encouraged the remarkably rapid spread of consumer habits among ordinary people after 1800. These elements bear looking at in a final summing up of the case for consumption as a medium of social communications because they appear to explain Americans' exceptional need for consumer goods in American terms. As we have already seen, fashionable living in the late colonial and early republican years was a mixed blessing. It opened doors to countless thousands on one hand while, on another, it barred them to countless others. Taking special account of the American evidence leads to two corollary observations—one positive and one negative—to add to the five preceding statements that together encompass my interpretation of this central theme in the nation's cultural history.

Many a commentator on the American scene presumed a connection between the physical mobility of the country's "promiscuous masses" and their eagerness to acquire the trappings of success. Catharine Beecher, writing in 1841 but remembering as far back as the turn of the century, observed that "reverses of fortune are, in this land, so frequent and sudden, and the habits of people so migratory, that there are strangers in every part of the country, many of whom have been suddenly bereft of wonted comforts."[1] There was irony in the way that moving house broke up a family's accumulated possessions and then, shortly afterwards, landed the new arrivals in circumstances that placed a premium on material things that could give some clue to their personal identity and social standing. The man who boasted in 1744 that "his little woman att home drank tea twice a day" might have found sympathy from pioneer housekeepers in Kentucky fifty years later, almost every one of whom, it was said, "had some bowl or dish she brought from the old states . . . as proof of her primitive gentility."[2]

The great movement of peoples to and through the colonies in the first century and a half only increased in speed and volume as the new nation spilled over the mountains and flooded across the interior after the Revolution. "Every thing is moving and changing," Beecher later wrote in description of "this migratory and business Nation." Fortune-seeking sons left "the rich mansions of their fathers to dwell in the log cabins of the forest," and they took "the daughters of ease and refinement" with them "to share the privations of a new settlement." Extreme geographical mobility eroded familiar social distinctions. Poor people struck it rich, wealthy ones lost everything. Tocqueville reported that "wealth circulates . . . with incredible rapidity, and experience shows that two successive generations seldom enjoy its favors." A perception grew up that there were "no distinct classes, as in aristocratic lands," no "impassable lines." Even in "the more stationary portions of the community" observers remarked on "a mingling of all grades of wealth, intellect, and education."[3] American storekeepers had long heeded a piece of very un-English advice, to behave "in the same manner to every person altho of different stations in life" and, of course, to sell the same goods to anyone with ready money or sound credit.[4] A yeastier environment for the germination of materialistic values is hard to imagine. Historians therefore should not be surprised to hear an English traveler declare in 1807 that "pride of wealth is as ostentatious in this country as ever the pride of birth has been elsewhere."[5]

American society was exceptionally mobile and fluid, and it became ever more so. Both traits exaggerated people's need for affordable, portable, interchangeable status signifiers. So did another American characteristic. The country's social structure encouraged emulative consumption by its flatness as well. If England's densely layered classes bred competition and made social climbing easy, a foreshortened social hierarchy in the colonies placed an even heavier burden on appearances to define people's differences. Although hardly classless in reality, among free whites American society lacked the extremes of wealth and poverty found in Britain and Europe. Its reputation as "a best poor man's country" was deserved. More important, it was believed. Richard Montgomery, a disappointed placeman in his native England, complained in 1772 that "a man with little money cuts a bad figure in this country among Peers, Nabobs, etc., etc." Emigration was his only out. "I have cast my eye on America," he wrote, "where my pride and poverty will be much more at their ease."[6] A man of his breeding did not expect to forsake fashion in the colonies. He simply looked forward to paying less for it. It was well known that the excessive "luxuries, elegancies & refinements . . . attainable in England . . . no money [could] procure in this country."[7] Having "never known such," Americans were "undoubtedly as happy without." Ignorance was bliss. The new United States was "a glorious country for persons of industrious habits and moderate means," and "the mass of the white population," being a larger proportion of the whole here than elsewhere, was reckoned by those who had traveled or lived on both sides of the Atlantic to "enjoy here decidedly more comfort than in England." Increasingly those comforts were supplied by purveyors of attractive, inexpensive, store-bought goods.

Consumers of British-made wares sold to mass markets in the colonies came to include significant numbers of freeholders by the third quarter of the eighteenth century. Timothy Breen argues that buying and using "the Baubles of Britain" had become so widespread by the 1760s that consumption of durables and semi-durables was the principal shared experience that overcame sectional differences and made co-conspirators of merchants, planters, farmers, and artisans when the call went out to boycott British manufactures in protest to parliamentary taxation.[8] The conflict with Britain was not essentially a dispute over imports. But consumer goods became the instruments, Breen says, that mobilized a populace and linked abstract ideas to everyday experiences common to a multitude of men and women throughout the colonies. All of a sudden, this newfangled social networking medium—fashionable imports from Great Britain—acquired serious political overtones as the standoff with Whitehall developed.

The messages sent were variously interpreted. It was widely believed, for instance, that British army officers who served in North America during the Seven Years' War had, on returning home, spread wicked falsehoods that the colonies were wallowing in wealth and luxury. The political implication was that high-living Americans deserved to be taxed. Alternatively many colonists came round to the view that their consumption of British luxuries had rendered them unwitting slaves to foreign shopkeepers and thereby encouraged misrule by tyrannical officials. The solution was an organized campaign of voluntary non-importation of those same British-made goods, thereby sending a powerful message of protest to their oppressors (fig. 28).[9]

The successful boycotts against the Stamp Act, the Townshend duties, and finally the Tea Act of 1773 were dramatic episodes in American political history that provide another measure of the colonists' ever deeper involvement in consumer culture by midcentury. Revealing in another way were the colony-by-colony non-importation agreements that led to the Articles of Association in 1774. They prohibited trade with Britain generally and, for good measure, banned horse racing, cockfighting, and theatergoing throughout the colonies. There is no question that the boycotts were a new form of protest, but sometimes they were also a throwback to an older form of moral reform. Both demonstrate how deeply the American Revolution became entangled in the marketplace and how torn many American colonists were between patriotism and their passion for store-bought goods.

But did consumer politics create the united front of thirteen colonies that successfully fought the war for independence, as Breen contends? As he would have it, widespread consumption of self-fashioning goods, imports by and large, was one of the few experiences that ordinary men and women throughout the colonies shared. By denying themselves

FIGURE 28

A Society of Patriotic Ladies at Edenton in North Carolina, print attributed to Philip Dawe, London, dated March 25, 1775. The non-consumption movement gave women in the colonies a rare opportunity to make their voices heard in the political arena. That qualified them as targets for ridicule by this London printmaker. He pokes fun at a group of fashionable American women who have gathered to sign a loyalty oath and renounce "that Pernicious Custom of Drinking Tea." Mockery abounds: toddy drunk straight from a punch bowl substitutes for the banished tea. High-fashion wigs and bonnets belie the ladies' pledge not to wear "any Manufacture from England." Even the quill and inkwell used to sign a document that decries "all Acts which tend to Enslave this our Native country" is stoically borne by an enslaved house servant.

A SOCIETY of PATRIOTIC LADIES,
AT
EDENTON in NORTH CAROLINA.

Plate V.

London, Printed for R. Sayer & J.Bennett, N.º 53 in Fleet Street, as the Act directs 25 March 1775.

the pleasures of shopping, patriots who joined the boycotts not only learned the political effectiveness of self-sacrifice. Their joint action created an intercolonial public sphere. In turn solidarity gave rise to an imagined national community, an idea that prefigured and modeled an independent nation that was worth waging war to achieve. In short, consumer politics borne of the boycotts inspired trust, trust built alliances, and the resulting common cause among thirteen otherwise diverse colonies sustained the revolution.

Be that as it may, and despite his critics' skepticism, Breen's account of the embargos and the non-consumption movement is useful here in assessing the extent to which Americans were wholehearted participants in the consumer marketplace by the 1760s and 1770s. The boycotts do shed light on the rapid spread of consumption to towns and villages and other dark corners where otherwise evidence is absent. Such exceptional events also reveal the sophistication that consumer culture had already attained as a medium of nonverbal communications.

Breen insists that Americans only became fully fluent in this visual language in the course of their protest because that timetable alone serves his explanation about the real impetus to revolution. That part of his interpretation is least convincing and least supported in the historical record. Little wonder, for as we have seen, the weight of evidence clearly shows that large numbers of even quite ordinary people had been learning to send and receive complicated visual messages for more than half a century. The boycotts put those literacy skills to use. The embargoed goods themselves were simply tools that protestors employed to tighten the screws on British suppliers and pressure Parliament. Evidence is scant that by doing so the boycotters came to regard themselves as some kind of recognizable modern consumer community. That fiction misses the point that the boycotts demonstrate something else that really was modern. They are snapshots of men and women who had long since mastered and were now putting to political use a broadband communications system capable of carrying a greater volume of complex information than ever before.

Hard numbers are elusive in these years of protest, rebellion, warfare, and revolution. Yet historians can get some sense of how many Americans were swept up in the consumer economy in the decades immediately following independence by extrapolating backward from data collected in 1815 for a new tax on luxury goods.[10] This levy imposed duties on a long list of household furniture, excluding only beds, kitchenwares, family portraits, and things homemade. All households without exception were subject to assessment; those with furniture worth less than $200 were exempt from payment. Thus, by ranking the estimated total of 800,000 freeborn American families in 1815 by the value of their domestic possessions, the lawmakers created an index that historians can use to measure the progress of consumer spending shortly after the turn of the century.

Surprisingly, the number of exempt households—those least well furnished—was put at only 259,000. Less than a third of all householders fell below what might be called the poverty level of genteel furnishings. Fully half the number of families in the country, 400,000, owned luxury goods worth $200 to $600. Forty-five thousand more were assessed for clothespresses, dining and tea tables, settees, prints, pianofortes, coffee urns and teapots, chandeliers, epergnes, and other nice things valued up to $1,000. That left a top layer of no more than 76,000 affluent families who furnished their houses five times more expensively than the exempted households.

In short, consumer wealth bulked broadly in the middle ranks of American society by 1815. Moreover, much of it was invested in articles that clearly indicate that the middle classes had joined enthusiastically in the practice of the gentle arts. The great architectural rebuilding that replaced so many colonial structures on the American landscape in the 1810s, 1820s, and 1830s was obviously accompanied, maybe slightly led, by a no less thorough refurnishing and refashioning of middling Americans' homes, notably among city dwellers and farmers able to employ hired hands or slaves. Probate inventories, the 1815 property tax, and archaeological excavations on early nineteenth-century domestic sites corroborate the view that the wealth of goods was already widely shared.[11]

Soon it would expand exponentially as Jacksonian democracy championed the ascendancy of the "common man" and as new products and new ways to advertise and sell them propelled the "common woman" into the marketplace as never before. Free white women have figured significantly throughout my account, oftentimes as earners of the critical surplus income needed to purchase store-bought amenities and sometimes as collaborators with their gentlemen husbands in the performance of the refined entertainments that those amenities made possible. For decades housewives' unpaid employment had included everyday shopping for provisions needed to stock a well-run household.[12] Still other times, women who had once prized fashion made a virtue of necessity by brandishing homespun to add their protest to the clamor against British tyranny. Likewise, but in altogether different circumstances, we have seen how enslaved black women who headed extended kin groups used precious consumer goods to validate their rule over the quarter or neighborhood or, for would-be competitors, to challenge a reigning matriarch's suzerainty. Women were never less accomplished than men, and often more so, in using the language of objects, images, and fashion to communicate and understand their relationships with others.

In Jacksonian America they became consumer decision-makers to a degree that men had monopolized previously. Women and girls came into their own as active shoppers from 1820 onward.[13] They were responding to new technologies in part and also to innovative sales strategies. Printers began putting lithography to commercial use to produce a flood of broadsides, lifelike fashion plates, and other forms of pictorial advertising. Newspapers and magazines pitched to female readers illustrated the latest fashions and demonstrated their use. New print media crammed with classified ads crossed the new nation more rapidly than ever before on steamboats and eventually on trains. Home delivery meant they came into women's hands directly. So did the goods themselves. An estimated 10,000 peddlers crisscrossed the country by 1850. Their packs and wagons were stocked with "Yankee notions" both useful and flattering to women: kitchen utensils, painted tinware, jewelry, yard goods, and patent medicines.[14] In larger towns and cities a younger generation of women could venture into the public marketplace themselves and expect to find an assortment of retail outlets unknown to their mothers and grandmothers, not just dry goods stores, but specialty shops, auction houses, pawnshops, and second-hand retailers. All in all, women added to a universe of customers in Jacksonian America that grew rapidly in numbers, in extent as more and more people pushed into newly opened western territories, and in its preoccupation with what one historian has called "the sovereign self."[15] Just as a heightened respect for personal property had been fundamental to the development of a market economy one hundred and fifty years earlier, an exalted sense of everyman's (and everywoman's) individual prerogative spurred on the acquisition of personal property in the first half of the nineteenth century.[16]

This picture of rampant consumption and a cornucopia of goods can be overdrawn, of course. Travelers in the new United States still encountered rustics who substituted blanket chests for chairs and tables and slept all in one bed like a pile of puppies. The accounts suggest that the most primitive living conditions among whites were to be found in frontier settlements.[17] But even there pack trains, canal boats, and peddlers' wagons caught up with homesteaders remarkably quickly, especially after the first quarter of the nineteenth century.[18] Back East the flow of manufactures coursed along the nation's growing network of commercial arteries and branched off into the tiniest capillaries of trade to reach remote backcountry hamlets and farmsteads. Ralph Waldo Emerson observed from his own window an "endless procession of wagons loaded with the wealth of all the regions of England, of China, of Turkey, of the Indies which from Boston creep by my gate to all the towns of New Hampshire and Vermont." Summer and winter "the train goes forward at all hours, bearing this cargo of inexhaustible comfort and luxury to every cabin in the hills."[19]

Emerson exaggerated for literary effect, but his words condense on a kernel of truth large enough to substantiate the first of the corollary statements about American consumer culture that refines and extends the general propositions already advanced. I have made a case here for a causal connection between the great European migrations after 1600 and a fundamental alteration in the meaning that people gave to commonplace objects. We have already seen ample evidence of both the stimulus and the response. This much more also seems fair to say, that it was doubly difficult for such a culturally diverse and extraordinarily mobile people to establish and maintain a traditional repertory of place-centered status symbols. Consequently, Americans were exceptionally eager to adopt the international protocol of etiquette-book manners as the Esperanto of their social intercourse. Thus we can say in particular about Americans' experience of materialism that *widespread possession and use of fashion-bearing, status-giving, self-fashioning artifacts gave this nation of newcomers unusually easy access to the American social system. As the supply of factory-made goods increased and prices dropped, participation in the country's consumer culture acted as a powerful engine of democratization. Additionally, British manufactured goods and fashions often induced ethnic peoples to accommodate themselves willingly or unwillingly to the dominant English culture.*

This final sour note is a reminder that gentility was frequently a coercer. Acculturation is always a calculus of gains and losses. Historians of early America, leery of consensus history, have bothered to learn almost nothing yet about the multitude of inconspicuous non-English immigrants who lost no time acquiring standardized consumer goods to compensate for the handicaps of language and custom that otherwise excluded them from mainstream popular culture.[20] They know something about a few prominent immigrants and ethnic groups. These, they argue, conformed to English tastes under duress and mostly for show.[21]

German settlers transplanted remarkably complete and cohesive traditions from their various homelands to New York, Pennsylvania, and the southern backcountry.[22] For two or three generations, their Old World folkways remained little changed by contact with other colonists. A traveler through Pennsylvania in the early 1780s noted that even at a distance "it could be pretty certainly guessed whether [a] house was that of a German or of an English family" by the number and placement of chimneys. A single off-center stack in the middle of the house was likely to serve a common flue for a German farmer's *Küche* hearth and *Stube* stove (fig. 29). By contrast, "two chimneys, one at each gable end, [were usually an indication that] there should be fire places, after the English plan."[23] The German settler's "rough country mode of living" was commonly contrasted to the "English family used to living genteelly."[24] The difference, of course, was both one of origins and lifestyles. Germans still followed their customary folkways; "refined" Britons had become gentlefolk, recognizable as such because they declined to "work themselves and must employ servants and day laborers." Germans therefore had two hurdles to overcome to qualify as equals. They had to put aside their distinctively un-English appearances, at least those they publicly displayed, and after that, like everybody else, they had to learn leisure-class manners.

Gradually through the second half of the eighteenth century many Germans made such concessions by Anglicizing family names, learning English, drinking tea, dressing fashionably, and building houses that showed an impeccably conventional facade to passersby (fig. 30).[25] A German traveler noted with surprise in 1750 that "throughout Pennsylvania both men and women dress according to English fashion." Maybe so, but forty years later another visitor could only hope that "from clothes it will pass to house-furnishing, etc."[26] Some Pennsylvania Germans, maybe many, conformed to English ways thoroughly and enthusiastically. But scholars have conjectured that others knuckled under only where it could be seen. Behind closed doors they were slow to reorganize the traditional living spaces of the *Ernhaus*. More significantly, they embellished those same private interiors and the furnishings they contained with an astonishingly rich, gaudy, flamboyant decoration quite beyond anything recollected from the old country and quite unlike other Americans' artistic expressions in the early nineteenth century.[27]

Some have interpreted these dichotomous, outside-inside, public-private aesthetics as evidence of a cultural split personality inflicted on minorities by the overweening hegemony of a master race of English descendants. The incandescent flowering of German American decorative arts does indeed suggest some little resistance and proud-hearted opposition to outside pressures to conform. Chances are that, when historians investigate acculturation among other large, stable ethnic groups as carefully as they have studied the Germans, they will discover similar crosscurrents in the mainstream of taste.

Be that as it may, now that we understand that gentility accommodated itself separately, differently, and piecemeal to each traditional culture it encountered, it seems highly likely that the process of Americanizing non-English peoples was also part of the idiosyncratic transformation of folkways into formalities that accounts for regional differences in middle-class culture everywhere after 1800. The dilemma facing

FIGURE 29

George Hehn Jr., the builder of this exceptionally large limestone and tile-roofed farmhouse, probably built in 1755 (inscription), was a third-generation descendant of Palatine immigrants to New York who later followed Conrad Weiser to Pennsylvania. A prosperous farmer, he ranked in the top 10 percent of tax-paying landowners in the township. The next owner to acquire the property in 1772, militia captain Conrad Kershner, was also well-off and another immigrant's grandson. Despite their American origins, both men's families practiced conservative German house habits, however grandly. They entered the house directly into a busy *Küche*. They ate and socialized in an elegant *Stube* heated by a five-plate iron stove stoked from the kitchen. They retired at night to an equally handsome and heated sleeping *Kammer* upstairs. They cooled milk and drew water from a spring in the basement, and they baked bread in a bakehouse located in a separate outbuilding. Kershner sold the house in 1803, and soon afterward the new owner made changes that modernized and gentrified the dwelling. He removed the ornamental ceiling in the parlor and pulled out the old stove to make room for a ground-floor bedchamber. The room above the kitchen was partitioned into two rooms and seemingly incorporated into a two-story range of rooms built against the east hillside. Large doors at ground level suggest an agricultural use for this addition, but a second staircase communicating with rooms upstairs and the relocation of the attic stairs look like segregated accommodations for farm workers. The kitchen stair, also rebuilt, now led to an open landing and into what had apparently declined into a second-best bedchamber.

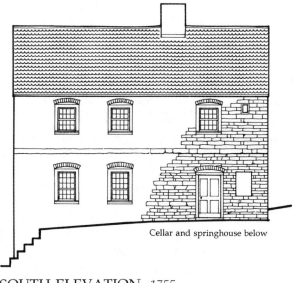

Cellar and springhouse below

SOUTH ELEVATION *1755*

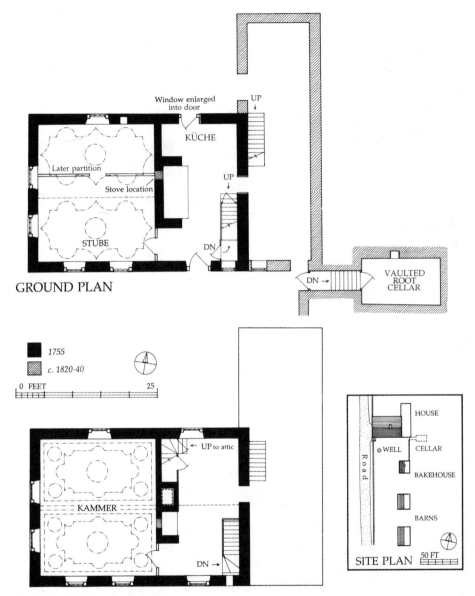

GROUND PLAN

Window enlarged into door

KÜCHE

UP

UP

DN

Later partition

Stove location

STUBE

DN →

VAULTED
ROOT
CELLAR

1755

c. 1820-40

0 FEET 25

SECOND FLOOR PLAN

← UP to attic

KAMMER

DN →

SITE PLAN

Road

HOUSE

○ WELL

CELLAR

BAKEHOUSE

BARNS

50 FT

Elevation, plans, and site plan, Hehn-Kershner House, Wernersville vicinity, Berks
County, Pennsylvania. The structure fell into ruin after interiors were removed to
the Winterthur Museum in 1957.

FIGURE 29 (*continued*)

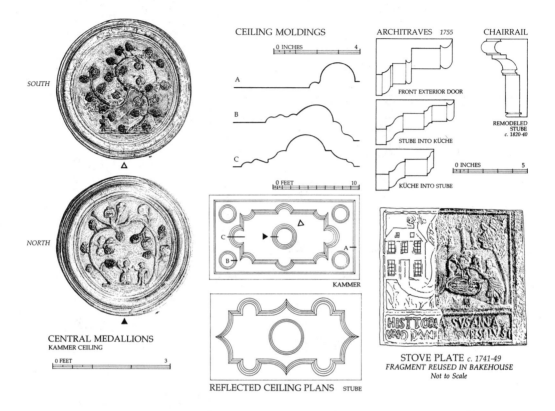

SOUTH

NORTH

CENTRAL MEDALLIONS
KAMMER CEILING

0 FEET · · · · · · · · · · 3

CEILING MOLDINGS

0 INCHES · · · · · · · · 4

A

B

C

0 FEET · · · · · · · · · · 10

REFLECTED CEILING PLANS STUBE

C

B

△

▶

A

KAMMER

ARCHITRAVES *1755*

FRONT EXTERIOR DOOR

STUBE INTO KÜCHE

KÜCHE INTO STUBE

CHAIRRAIL

REMODELED
STUBE
c. 1820-40

0 INCHES · · · · · · · · 5

STOVE PLATE *c. 1741-49*
FRAGMENT REUSED IN BAKEHOUSE
Not to Scale

HISTTORA VNO DANI · SVSANNA TVRES IN ST

Decorative elements of Hehn-Kershner House. The exuberantly molded ceilings in the *Stube* and *Kammer* took inspiration in equal part from German vernacular plasterwork and the German baroque. That said, Hehn's house made concessions to non-ethnic taste. The uniform size of the windows and their regular placement gave the front and the roadside gable a more formal appearance than most other German houses in the neighborhood. Inside, the use of stock hardware and conventionally trimmed door and window frames deliberately avoided the flamboyant ironwork and robust moldings still dear to many German builders. Englishisms were hard to keep out. They infiltrated into rural Pennsylvania in the guise of manufactured goods. The Englishman's architectural ideal was ever-present to Hehns and Kershners who gathered around the iron stove in their *Stube* or *Kammer*. One of its cast-iron plates (later reused and thus preserved in the nearby bakehouse) depicted the biblical story of Susanna and the Elders in a scene that included the virtuous woman's pattern-book town house (cf. fig. 22).

ROOF TILE
FRAGMENT EMBEDDED IN
FOUNDATION WALL

0 INCHES · · · · · · · · 3

FIGURE 30.

House with Six-Bed Garden, one of a pair of similar ink and watercolor drawings attributed to David Heubner, 1818, Upper Montgomery County, Pennsylvania. Poorly paid schoolmasters in German settlements earned pocket money by making baptismal certificates and other illuminated documents. They also rewarded diligent pupils with small Fraktur drawings or gave them to proud parents in hopes they would renew the teacher's annual contract. Such personal and personalized documents became treasured keepsakes. Fraktur was primarily a country art. Known prize winners and certificate holders seldom lived in towns or even villages. Cosmopolitan town dwellers were less enamored of folk artists' enthusiasm for colorful, playful, stylized flowers, birds, animals, and geometric pinwheels. This drawing of an Anglicized house in a Fraktur firmament is therefore an unusual expression of both id and ego in the half-acculturated German American personality.

Americans of Continental European descent seems therefore to have been less a choice between ethnic or English than one between folk or formal.[28] By the end of the eighteenth century isolated German, Swiss, Dutch, and Scotch Irish communities were opening up to the same outside influences that promoted gentility and use of consumer goods among country people everywhere. Under the circumstances even Dunkers, Dutchers, Jocks, and Paddywhacks may have conformed their house habits more or less willingly.

Others had no choice whatsoever. For every ethnic traditionalist forced against his or her will to accept the majority's tastes, there were probably a hundred whom the system snubbed and excluded. Snobbishness about possessions was never exclusively American, but it blossomed with special virulence here where the color of money outshone the quality of birth and where so many middling sorts jockeyed for position in society's compacted ranks. "True republicanism" was said to ensure "that every man shall have an equal chance—that every man shall be free to become as unequal as he can."[29] In competition where advantage was gained so decidedly by possessing material things, the possessors learned to manipulate and control the unpossessed in ways that again were not unknown elsewhere but reached new heights—or really new depths—of perfection in republican America.

The idea of status competition has weaved in and out of my account without ever becoming the main thread of the argument. Many other writers on consumption, from the moralists of the eighteenth century to latter-day Veblenites, would have emulation explain virtually everything about the rise of fashion. Others insist that it explains nothing.[30] I lean toward the latter view when it comes to first causes, for what impresses me most about early consumers' behavior is not so much their passion for exclusivity as their love for the rules, conventions, and symbols that identified kindred spirits and gave worthy claimants access to privileged social circles. But how then can historians account for consumers' puzzling addiction to novelty ever since the seventeenth century? Why the never-ending march of fashions if already fashionable people were happy to welcome successful emulators into their ranks? One well-publicized answer—that consumption actually has little to do with emulation and is better understood as a deep desire to experience the anticipated enjoyment of products and services not yet acquired—takes the subject down an interesting byway.[31] But no matter how widespread the pleasures of window-shopping had become by the end of the eighteenth century, this hedonism argument leaves unexplained the undeniable fact that fashionable elites had attracted imitators of their domestic lifestyles before 1700 and imitators of their sartorial styles more than a hundred years before that. The "epidemical madness" to consume was rampant for decades before the cerebral pleasures of contemplating future purchases became addictive.

Historians who will not dismiss status competition as a driving force behind fashion are obliged to give a better explanation for it than human nature. The goods themselves are one important clue to understanding how emulation worked to the advantage of some and the disadvantage of others. Inherent in the household furnishings and personal possessions that became status symbols for an international gentry were two qualities that impeached the lasting value of those symbols: they could be cheapened, and they could be mass produced. The old-fashioned marks of distinction could not. Pasture and ploughland were not easily expandable commodities in England, lineage was not usually for sale except by marriage, and labor was something would-be employers could either afford or not. Among the traditional status-bearing artifacts, painted canvas and base metals were shams that fooled no one. Only articles of clothing could be made cheaply, plentifully, and deceptively like the finery they imitated. No wonder sumptuary excesses caused such alarm, and no wonder annual fashions appeared first in the garment trades well before 1600.

When household furniture, tablewares, vehicles, and even buildings were subsequently pressed into service to communicate people's social identities, they opened to manufacturers a multitude of new product lines that could, like clothing, be made in a range of qualities and offered at prices to satisfy a wide marketplace demand. That demand came from two sources. At the low end were those who wanted in, the emulators and "mechanics struggling to be genteel."[32] These lesser social climbers were not the ultimate tastemakers, of course. They only wanted the "latest fashions" already displayed by those they aspired to copy. The demand for new things came from those whose privileged society the imitators desired to join. Because emulators became so numerous by the middle of the eighteenth century and because it was often so difficult on first acquaintance to tell a genuinely cultivated gentleperson from the many fraudulent look-alikes, the in-crowd that paid close attention to such things looked to high fashion as the elusive sine qua non that separated them from the clamorous herd of pretenders who flaunted last year's fads. The desire to bring on board those social equals who were entitled to respect was always counterbalanced by the impulse to pull up the ladder before mock ladies and gentlemen climbed higher than they deserved.

The history of consumer culture since the seventeenth century has to be understood as this tug-of-war between two great contending social needs: on the one hand, the desire for a new, universally accessible, portable system of status definition and, on the other, an effective means to differentiate and mark off one group from another. Affordable consumer goods used to engage in imitative genteel activities satisfied the first requirement; changing fashions and arcane gate-keeping rules of etiquette served the other.

The synergy between them was unusually strong in North America. Where so many strangers in a nation of nations set such great store by a person's possessions, fashionable consumption became an exaggerated symbol of personal worthiness and a dreadful instrument of social control. The new United States had no shortage of true gentlefolk who understood that "the best finished furniture or finest marble will lose half its luster" without the polish of good manners. But the future increasingly belonged to a baser crowd that saw nothing but their own advantage in "Rules for Ladies" that included the advice "Always keep callers waiting, till they have had time to notice the outlay of money in your parlors." Scolding writers of popular etiquette books could say a thousand times a thousand ways that wealth "ought not to be the passport into the higher orders of society," that instead "education should be the test of gentility." But lamentably in wide-open republican America "knaves and fools [were] often more successful than the wise and the good."[33]

Some knaves were nobody's fool. As store-bought products became ever more available to African Americans, many blacks, enslaved and free alike, used fashion to turn the tables on their masters and tormentors. As a proxy for status, fashion could mock as well as dazzle. Blacks knew whites were not fooled by their Sunday-go-to-meeting clothes, which someone derisively termed the Negroes' "Sabbath toilet." No amount of finery could camouflage a black man's or woman's race or render them socially acceptable. Nor was that false hope even entertained by the "exquisite dandies" and "howling swells" who flaunted "beauish" fashions and hairdos coiffed up wig-like in "the macaroni taste" or "such gorgeously dressed women" as one visitor to Charleston "never saw before." Blacks had their own good reasons for dressing sharp, reasons to which whites were mostly oblivious. But African Americans also perceived that swanning around in fancy clothes was guaranteed to rankle white folks' sensibilities, especially in towns where many blacks thronged together more or less unsupervised. There they overheard passersby censure their getups as foppish and "too good" for their sort. They learned that they could irk them still more by throwing in "a pot pourri" of jarring African color combinations and bizarre accessories. Their like drove scornful onlookers into blithering tirades against "the most ludicrous combination of incongruities that you can conceive" where "every color in the rainbow, and the deepest possible shades are blended in fierce companionship." Dressing fly was sweet revenge. It brandished a kind of group insolence that was impossible to punish. A traveler through South Carolina in 1772 observed "a great Difference in Appearance as well as Behavior between the Negroes of the Country, and those in Charles-Town." Plantation slaves were "generally clad suitable to their Condition"; those he met in town were "the very Reverse—abandonedly rude, unmannerly, insolent and shameless." With nothing to lose, this "dark gentry" turned politeness inside out.[34]

Gentility was no match for bigotry. Blacks expected nothing less. Some Native Americans were led to believe by the likes of Indian agent William Johnson that true converts to European-style respectability could expect a favorable reception from their white neighbors. Sometimes they were when little was at stake. Not so when land-hungry New Englanders coveted the ancestral homelands that belonged to Johnson's métis community of tea-drinking, waistcoat-wearing proselytes. "This Execrable Race" of bogus ladies and gentlemen was heartily despised because the trappings of gentility threatened to mask racial distinctions that were the ultimate justification for appropriating Indian territory.[35] The rules of etiquette never applied to everyone or everywhere.

Even when racial hatred was not an issue, social conflict between well-bred and ill-bred competitors was modern class warfare waged along new lines and fought with new weapons.[36] Usually the rich and powerful were able to turn the system of manners back in their own defense to gain psychological advantage over their "unworthy" rivals when those rivals (unlike blacks and Indians) could entertain some hope of eventual acceptance, however remote. Tastemakers cynically employed fashion and ceremony as instruments of intimidation. Dr. Alexander Hamilton of Annapolis was one of the first to describe how it worked. He even illustrated his *History of the [Ancient and Honorable] Tuesday Club* with sketches showing club members parading their pomp before the hoi polloi of the town (fig. 31). He explained that "this luxurious and effeminate age" required it. Where nature no longer distinguished the upper classes "from the common Rascallion herd," the newly risen "degenerate, puny, pigmy race" of rulers had only "these magnificent trappings and Embelishments . . . [to] keep the great Leviathan of Civil Society under proper discipline and order." Sure enough, when Hamilton and his cronies sallied forth into the town once a year resplendent in their full Tuesday Club regalia, they were "stared at, as they passed, by persons of all Ranks and degrees, who seemed to be as much astonished, as the mob is at a coronation procession, or any such Idle pageantry."[37] Just as kings and queens and ancient nobles once held the rabble in awe by their lavish feasts and stately ceremonies, now a lesser race of merchants, planters, physicians, and lawyers thought well to tranquilize the masses by showing off good manners.

Such display often achieved the desired effect. Men and women whose status was uncertain even to themselves and who therefore sought a firm footing in the lower ranks of genteel society were often rebuffed and cowed by the sheer arrogance of those who considered themselves their betters. Little people suffered most sorely the afflictions of a social system governed by annual fashions and mysterious initiations, little people like the artisan who wrote in despair to a Boston newspaper in 1792 that "from my situation in life, I am *virtually* debarred from any of the *common amusements* of this town." He explained that there were no actual regulations that excluded mechanics from concerts, assemblies, and public card parties. There did not have to be. "The *distance* that is always observed by those who move in the higher sphere, and the *mortification* which I and my family must inevitably undergo if we were with them, exclude us as much as if there was a solemn *act* of exclusion."[38]

Because fashionable consumption was no formulaic ritual, because every occasion for its display was a live performance that tested anew an individual consumer's social skills, there were always real winners and real losers. They could be found as well in Britain, northern Europe, and indeed wherever consumer culture followed the footsteps of people who traveled farther and farther from home and moved in wider and wider social circles. But the contest that produced winners and losers in polite society was played by a simplified set of singularly materialistic rules in America where otherwise virtually anybody was free to purchase property from a land office and lineage from a sign painter.[39] Showy material possessions and a passing acquaintance with their use increasingly became the most important measures of social standing in America as the country expanded beyond the older East Coast settlements and as manners were appropriated by people not to manners born.

So here at last my account of fashionable consumption is brought to the final corollary. However much Americans' enthusiasm for store-bought things created opportunities for social advancement and cultural assimilation, *the excessively materialistic values that attached to social status in the new United States had the effect of sharpening class differences—and sometimes racial differences for blacks who flaunted these rules—by making them visible, tangible, and inescapable. To emphasize differences is always the purpose of fashion. It often had sinister applications. In this country more than others it gave an upper class of purveyors and possessors a new kind of social control over an underclass of the less-possessed.*

With this acknowledgment that consumer culture cut both ways in the capitalistic society that the United States was fast becoming after 1800, I rest my case. This account is now brought forward to a point

FIGURE 31

Drawings depicting the "Grand Anniversary Processions" from Dr. Alexander Hamilton's *History of the [Ancient and Honorable] Tuesday Club* (1745–56). One after another the club's annual parades through the streets of Annapolis, Maryland, acquired the semblance of quasi-official ceremonies. Hamilton's satirical account records the process by which the pomp and grandeur of private citizens received attention, respect, and finally sanction from the town fathers. Thus, by degrees, public displays of civility came to reinforce the rule of well-bred gentlemen over the rest of society and the authority they exercised by dint of their superior manners. Participation in this annual event required not only the right clothes and correct comportment, but fashionable houses with formal reception rooms. Each procession convened at the town house of one pseudonymous "Sir John Oldcastle." He solemnly received the club

Drawing of the first of three "Grand Anniversary Processions," 1747. The inaugural parade attracted no more than curious stares from all who happened to be out on the street at the time, most notably from a coxcomb Hamilton dubbed "the Great Collonel Bumbasto" who showed them the courtesy of a "very Low bow."

Three years later in 1750 the outing was preceded by all the advance publicity of a circus parade. As Hamilton observed, "It was honored with a great number of Spectators of all Ranks [who gawked] from windows, walls, [and] Balconies, and even the Sides of the Streets were lined with Children and other Spectators, nay, the *Patres Conscripti,* or members of the Great provincial Senate, deigned to come forth of the doors of their house and look on this gallant Show."

brothers in his entry hall and then, "Introducing them into the Antichamber, Entertained them with Rich Lemonian punch and Generous wine." The company moved easily from such public architectural spaces to the outdoor parade route and, at its other end, to an outdoor courtyard facing the president's house. Here the procession halted again, the marchers pausing for refreshments. Eventually they "Translated themselves into his honor's great Saloon," another formal receiving room furnished with a "great Chair of State" for the club president. Thus the fusion of dress, deportment, and display with political authority was openly demonstrated and easily enforced in a culture that still made no hard and fast distinctions between public and private or indoors and out.

Third Grand anniversary Procession.

Grand Rehearsal of the anniversary ode.

The following year, 1751, the spectacle came even closer to receiving official recognition. The master of ceremonies, celebratory ode in hand, actually led the marchers past the club president's house, their ultimate destination, to the council's own chambers at the capitol.

There, in the dignified setting of the Maryland statehouse, the anniversary ode "was performed on many Instruments accompanied with voices with great applause, before a grand and Splendid assembly of the prime Gentlemen and Ladies" of the town. Following this public recital, members retraced their steps to the president's house to perform it all over again privately.

where it meets and engages an impressive body of recent scholarship that explores how nineteenth- and early twentieth-century inventions, events, and institutions made mass consumption synonymous with the American way of life. The themes running through this literature pull back and forth between the same contending interpretations of the good and evil consequences of materialism that have animated the luxury debate since the eighteenth century, particularly the American version. One scholar's "people of plenty" are another's hapless victims of consumer choices imposed on them by corporate captains and confidence men.[40] The judgment of history mirrors both the dreams and the nightmares of American consumers' own experience.

These writers on consumption in recent times appear to have read little history before the 1880s. Their statements about fundamental shifts from local to national market systems, from an economy of production to one of consumption, and from a clientele of elite customers to a mass market of ordinary buyers—*all supposedly taking place in the latter half of the nineteenth century*—reveal a lack of familiarity with a much longer chronology of historical events.[41] The value of starting the story at its real beginning three or even four hundred years ago is not merely to set the record straight or give early modern historians first say. Only a longer perspective can provide the focal length needed to perceive differences crucial to understanding the essential nature and complicated development of modern consumer culture. Those instructive differences include important distinctions between improved living standards and changing lifestyles, between gentility and fashion, between the market forces of supply and demand, and, most important of all, between prime causes and the many other factors that contributed to the growth, spread, and acceptance of consumer values. Once again, Americans' eagerness to believe the myth of our own uniqueness obscures the reality of our much older and more tangled ancestry.

7

TOWARD A HISTORY
OF MATERIAL LIFE

Adam Smith was a careful student and compulsive explainer of people's economic behavior. He pondered the same question about the origins of demand that historians have puzzled over productively as well. "To what purpose is all the toil and bustle of this world?" he asked with regard to the rising tempo of production in England's workshops. A sweeping answer would come as no surprise from the author of *The Wealth of Nations*. But on this occasion in 1759 he sought a deeper explanation in the psychology of individual consumers. "It is our vanity which urges us on," he concluded. "It is not wealth that men desire, but the consideration and good opinion that wait upon riches."[1] Men were earning those riches by toiling and bustling harder than ever before by the middle decades of the eighteenth century. They were earning the esteem they desired in new ways too. Landed property remained the most secure form of wealth in Britain, just as it paid the richest dividends in inflationary North America. But increasingly reputation was accorded to property owners and other wealth holders only when they used those resources to acquire the necessary leisure and learning to participate in genteel society. Vanity was no longer satisfied merely by the good opinion of neighbors. By Smith's day riches spent on fashionable good manners were investments in reputations recognized and honored worldwide.

The decade of the 1750s stands more or less at the center point of events that take on new significance when placed in a chronological narrative that spans the two centuries between 1650 and 1850. For the first hundred years or so, larger and larger numbers of quite ordinary men and women—who we know now were already enjoying a rising standard of living—increasingly found themselves in social circumstances where individuals were rewarded for learning to use a variety of domestic goods in ways that resembled the status-defining qualities of fashionable clothing. Between roughly 1650 and 1750 the desire to purchase amenities that distinguished polite society—the genteel orders—from the rough-scuff masses gradually exceeded the capacity of workbench craftsmen to meet the demand. Emerging capitalist entrepreneurs throughout northern Europe quickly spotted the opportunities that these earliest consumer developments offered. They saw profits to reap from the new inventions, technologies, power sources, labor supplies, distribution links, and sales strategies that already anticipated Adam Smith's busy world of the 1750s.

These and other innovations continued to gather momentum over the next hundred years—the hundred years following 1750—precipitating the second great revolution, industrialization. Somewhere along the way consumption and production became so reciprocally interactive that historians lose track of cause and effect. Mass abundance became a universal way of life in nineteenth-century England, America, and much of northern Europe. Or, more accurately, it became the universally accepted standard by which the good life was measured. By then, explanations for it are as complex as modern society itself.

I have tried in these pages to treat the earlier stages of the consumer revolution (when causes can still be distinguished from consequences) with some of the same precision that economic historians bring to their work on the origins of factory production. Unfortunately, cultural events seldom leave behind quantitative evidence of the sort that scholars need to answer definitively the most interesting questions they ask. The sources that best address the questions raised—why demand, why 1650 to 1750, why household goods and personal possessions rather than intrinsically valuable property—must be pieced together from a grab bag of museum and archaeological collections, vernacular buildings, probate inventories, travel journals, town histories, immigration studies, and folklorists' hindsights. Hodgepodge though it is, the evidence can be used fairly systematically to clarify some of the major unresolved theoretical problems in consumer revolution studies. By supplying answers to questions about new products and their uses, students of material culture can give the revolution definition and identify its leading indicators. By paying attention to the social status of tastemakers and trendsetters and observing where, when, and by whom their example was followed, they can isolate the leading sectors in the emerging consumption economy and date a "takeoff point" when demand for affordable luxuries began to reshape the means of production and supply.

Scholars have had trouble distinguishing the central event from its antecedents in sixteenth-century sumptuary practices and also from its remarkable aftermath in the nineteenth century when England and America became vast emporiums. Close attention to artifacts and manuscripts alike reveals recognizable stages in the development of consumer behavior from its ancient practice in courtly circles to its seminal fusion with seventeenth-century notions of gentility, its explosive elaboration into fashion-consciousness by the middle of the eighteenth century, its rambunctious accommodation to popular taste soon after 1800, and finally its wholesale commercialization from the 1880s onward. Economic historians are used to analyzing events in just such stages of growth and development; cultural historians less so. That difference leads to an asymmetry in colonial American scholarship. Production and trade are almost always discussed in the context of the British mercantile system. Consumption seldom is.[2] Consequently, American historians have been slow to acknowledge that the rise of a consumer society transformed the British Isles and British Empire as one. Indeed its effects were felt throughout northern Europe generally. It is therefore certainly a mistake to interpret American consumers' new lifestyles as evidence of nothing more than the colonies' success at finally catching up to English and European standards after the hardships of settlement. Taking the evidence of artifacts into account brings a fuller, more complicated story into view. Identifying recognizable stages in the growth and development of consumption practices makes connections with the whole sweep of early American history up to and including the struggle for American independence.

The creation and spread of an international gentry culture has figured off and on in the long-running historical debate about the influence of European antecedents on the formation of colonial American society. This culture-or-environment controversy warmed up again following publication of two major reinterpretations by David Hackett Fischer and Jack Greene in the 1980s. One school examined the English roots of seventeenth-century colonial society and found the cultural continuities decidedly stronger than the differences.[3] The other stressed the departures from English custom induced by the unusual conditions that colonists encountered in the New World.[4] On one thing they more or less agreed, that during the eighteenth century the colonies drew closer to the mother country again, culturally and intellectually as well as administratively. The traditionalists saw that as the unexceptional outcome of the colonists' tenacious hold on their old English heritage. Those who stressed the homesteaders' formative experience explained it as a gradual return to traditional ideals once colonial societies became larger, hardier, wealthier, and more socially elaborated. The term *anglicization* (or *reanglicization*) appears frequently in the literature to describe how American culture on the eve of the Revolution became more English than it had been since shortly after the initial migrations.[5]

Is that assertion true? The answer is a complicated yes and no. James Deetz's colorful analogy of a rocket that travels fastest as it blasts off the launch pad and again when gravity pulls it back to earth is often cited to illustrate the separation and later reunification of Anglo-American culture. But his further observation is usually omitted, that the rocket reentered an atmosphere in which British culture had changed significantly from its seventeenth-century form.[6] Archaeologists call that change *Georgianization,* a term as clumsy as it is inaccurate. The consumer revolution preceded the rule of the Hanover kings, drew inspiration from sources outside their realm, and spread its influence far beyond their writ. Its ideology and energy were overtly internationalist.

To overlook that fact, or to make a mishmash of old-fashioned folkways and new-fangled formalities as the traditionalists are prone to do, is tantamount to writing today about earth science in willful ignorance of plate tectonics. What insight can come from describing the influence of age-old English traditions when those traditions were undergoing profound transformation in England itself? *Of course* a gentleman in eighteenth-century Philadelphia resembled a contemporary Londoner! Who would expect anything else from someone who also shared a common culture with ladies and gentlemen in Stockholm, Dublin, Leiden, Paramaribo, and Williamsburg! It was not their British ancestry that was disputed when American writers anxiously explained to readers back home that "they live in the same manner, dress after the same fashion, and behave themselves exactly as the gentry in London." The point at issue was their broader claim to be inheritors of British *civilization*. That was their real patrimony. The British part was taken for granted. Being a *civilized* Briton was something else. It raised gentlepersons above the endemic barbarism of the real American wilderness and above the vulgarities of those "whose language and manners [were] strange to them" in the cultural wildernesses that could be encountered almost anywhere the world around.[7]

The environmentalists who stress the influence of local conditions on the formation of colonial culture sometimes fall into the same trap. Anglicization can be equated too simplistically with the process of becoming more English. Careful scholarship over the last generation has braided together diverse demographic, social, economic, and environmental variables into a developmental history of the American colonies that is sensitive to differences in timing and variations from place to place. Yet often that work has arrived at the overarching conclusion that all the mainland colonies became increasingly alike in the generations immediately preceding the Revolution. At first the argument appears unassailable partly because it builds on bedrock monographic research. The problem lies in its implication that these overseas societies resembled British society, especially its metropolitan culture, *as a consequence* of becoming more populous, more affluent, more settled, and more complex—in a word (the contemporary word for it) more "improved."

We have encountered this confusion once before. It recalls the view discussed earlier that the desire to acquire consumer goods awaited only the fulfillment of certain social and economic preconditions to achieve satisfaction. The stock character in that scenario was a closet consumer who was doggedly marking time until powerful restraints on his or her ambitions were finally relaxed. The stock character in the anglicization story is a hereditary gentleperson who allegedly always "displayed a strong desire to replicate British society" and, when conditions in the colonies finally allowed after 1690, "took pride in the extent to which those societies were coming increasingly to resemble that of the metropolis."[8]

All that is perfectly true as far as it goes. The trouble is that historians who argue that Americans "rejoined the Western world" in the eighteenth century have usually thought they were describing only one process of historical change.[9] In fact there were two. There is nothing wrong with a three-stage model in which transplanted British customs and institutions first were simplified, then elaborated by acculturation to local social and economic conditions, and finally replicated as a measure of cultural achievement by provincial societies far removed from the center of empire. Generally speaking, the histories of most immigrant groups cohesive enough to sustain their remembered traditions follow a roughly similar course regardless of time or place.

All that notwithstanding, the replication stage in the American colonies coincided with and was fundamentally shaped by the second formative process: international gentrification. The convergence was no historical accident. I have already explained how gentility and the physical things its demonstration required served the special needs of hundreds of thousands of long-distance migrants to North America. At the same time, I have also shown that the usefulness of a highly elaborated visual communications system was not confined to people or places involved in founding overseas societies. Civilized manners and their fashionable accessories were acquired by at least as many stay-at-home consumers whose enthusiasm for the gentle arts was much more than homage-paying to Mother England. Not one, but two transforming events came together in the hundred years between 1650 and 1750, first to reshape British and European cultural norms and then to impress their indelible hallmark on malleable America.

Generally historians have come around to the same conclusion that a traveler in America reached just before the Revolution, that "very little difference is, in reality, observable in the manners of the wealthy colonist and the wealthy Briton."[10] Is it therefore splitting hairs to argue over how that happened? Arguably not. First of all, appreciating the true internationalist character of these changes can save wasted effort. It renders null a troubling paradox for those who believe that "the Anglicization thesis obviously makes it hard to explain the American Revolution."[11] The colonists' increasing participation in a transatlantic consumer culture did indeed intrude on the developing quarrel with Great Britain in several ways. T. H. Breen has made that case convincingly.[12] But to go still further in search of reasons that explain away Americans' affinity for British culture at the same moment when they were throwing off British rule is an unnecessary exercise. Independence involved no serious repudiation of the values and tastes that both Britons and Americans shared. Moralists damned the excesses of fashionable consumption, patriots temporarily embargoed its products, and republicans later decried its snobbery. But gentility remained secure because its usefulness transcended national boundaries and outlasted international conflicts. Americans who developed a taste for French fashions during and after the war were simply switching brand-names and suppliers, and then not for long. The American Revolution made less difference to the consumer revolution than the other way around.

Something else worth knowing about early modern England and the colonies can be learned by observing that genteel Americans had become citizens of a wider world by the middle of the eighteenth century. Paying attention to consumer behavior has opened another rich field of inquiry to social historians, a field some call material history or, more accurately, the history of material life. These historians recognize that there is a social story to be told about the development of our own highly materialistic culture. Because the evidence for its study is so remarkably varied and so much of it unfamiliar to historians accustomed only to written records, students of material life have developed analytical skills and learned to play by rules that would benefit the field as a whole if they were better understood and practiced more widely.

Much historical writing on the seventeenth and eighteenth centuries deals one way or another with the events and forces that modernized Western societies. Political and economic historians bring an enviable precision to their accounts of this transformation largely because the official records and statistical evidence they use were written or compiled while performing the activities they seek to explain, such as buying services, selling goods, paying taxes, collecting customs, making laws, and casting votes. Social historians have accumulated impressive databases as well, but their evidence is different in kind. They cull much of their information from tax records, censuses, muster rolls, wills and inventories, and court books that were created in the course of keeping records for purposes very different from those that now interest the scholars who consult them to study social change. Lacking direct evidence, they must infer general explanations from patterns of recorded behavior largely unrelated to the subjects they inquire into. Over the years they have learned to make a functional distinction between the usefulness of much pattern-forming quantitative evidence for the purpose of asking questions and the efficacy of narrative evidence for testing their hypotheses. Genuine advances in historical understanding have followed when new ideas about social change were carefully framed in terms that genuinely explanatory evidence could answer, notably in the lively social history subfields of women's history, African American history, and the histories of childhood and the family. All those turned out to be subjects that are richly documented in a wide variety of sources.

So also is the social history of material life. It too is well recorded by abundant evidence that historians can use to penetrate social scientific abstractions and explain conclusively how and why we moderns begin to recognize ourselves when we hold up a mirror to the seventeenth and eighteenth centuries. Making a case for the history of material life and making a place for telling it in the broader narrative of American and Atlantic history have been the hidden agenda in this interpretive account of consumer demand.

Material history is not to be confused with the histories of material things themselves—we call that art history—or with social history merely illustrated with objects and images. The history of material life tells its own important story, an account of people's growing dependence on inanimate objects to communicate their relationships with one another and mediate their daily progress through the social worlds they inhabited. It has common characteristics with other testable social histories. It can be told as a narrative that is grounded in real places; follows a datable chronology; identifies specific causes, contributing factors, and measurable consequences; and records critical transitions from one stage of development to another. The evidence for past material life includes bodies of quantitative data that *indirectly* suggest their meaning by revealing patterns of acquisition, ownership, testation, and disposal of goods. From these, historians can make educated guesses about the uses those objects served. At the same time, there is also much other evidence that speaks *directly* to the question of use: surviving artifacts whose design discloses their function, shard collections from use-related archaeological contexts, travelers' descriptions of unfamiliar customs, advertisements and prescriptive handbooks, and genre paintings, prints, and other images including eventually photographs.[13] The primary sources that historians of material history can use to test and refine the bigger pictures suggested by the pattern-making evidence go on and on.[14]

An abundant historical record never guarantees that scholars will use it. Fashion in history-writing waits on events. The civil rights movement and the push for gender equality gave grounds and urgency to race and women's studies beginning in the 1960s. Nor is it an accident now that social historians have joined forces with other researchers to study the origins of our modern consumer society. The 1980s launched Americans on a spending spree that only faltered when the buy-now-pay-later bubble burst twenty-five years later, and even then not for long. Over the same period, other astonishing consumer spectacles unfolded beyond our borders. All across Eastern Europe, the former Soviet Union, China, and more recently the Middle East, people who were long denied amenities that we in the West took for granted toppled the governments, dissolved the nations, and repudiated the philosophies they blamed for their deprivation. "My countrymen interpret the term 'standard of living' to mean consumer goods," marveled an uncomprehending East German Communist Party official in 1989. "They are going West where they can find better and more plentiful goods."[15] Fast-forward twenty-five years again: today 91 percent of adult Americans have access to a cell phone; worldwide 6 billion do, out of an estimated global population of 7 billion. Meanwhile only 4.4 billion have working toilets, recalling another time two and a half centuries ago when tewares outnumbered chamber pots among poor-to-middling social climbers in Britain's American colonies.[16]

At first glance, such phenomenal sales figures suggest that the wealth of consumer goods today is widely shared. On closer inspection, those numbers prove to be misleading. In reality, tens of millions of ordinary people have been left out or left behind, not just in developing nations, but in this country as well. Here the consumption boom coincides with a record high percentage of people whose incomes fall below the poverty line. Even before the recent debt-driven recession, full-time employment no longer guaranteed access to the good life for many people. Workers' wages stagnated while managers' salaries soared. Corporate chief executives' earnings rose fifty to a hundred times higher than the average wage-earner's take-home pay.[17] The mood has soured at home and abroad. Parents report they are pessimistic about their children's chances to improve or even equal the living standards they themselves achieved. A younger generation feels cheated out of its birthright to a brighter future. People of all ages are dismayed that so many of us value immediate material gratification above everything else. What does it mean? Where is it heading? What do gross inequalities between rich and poor, or more significantly, between rich and middle—what do they portend? Where will it end? While historians are not seers or oracles, it is our special calling to temper the newness of now with frames of reference from the past. Obligingly social historians have chosen this moment to come forward with a history of material life.

The time for jeremiads against materialism is long passed. The consumer habit is too ingrained in modern culture to renounce and unlearn. Indeed, its utility as a worldwide communications system spreads ever farther, ever faster as venal and repressive regimes are denounced by disillusioned citizens. Their rage feeds on many complicated frustrations, not least of all the conviction that life is too short to spend queueing up for everyday amenities and too long to stay cooped up in countries with broken-down economies. They compare their own poverty and lack of opportunity with the affluence and mobility they see elsewhere in an increasingly globalized world, and from that they learn a history lesson that we in the West are prone to overlook. Easy access to consumer goods has been, on balance historically, a liberating force in modern society—up to a point. Plentiful, affordable goods, far more than political philosophies, have oiled the wheels of democracy—up to a point. They have also been a potent solvent to dissolve people's murderous loyalties to clans, races, religions, and nation-states—up to a point. Consumer goods, the things they do, and the harmless human pleasures they can provide have become for millions the fullest expression of their liberal Jeffersonian right to the pursuit of happiness—up to a point.

That point being, of course, that materialism is often carried to excess. No one knows better than historians that the rise of consumer culture has been attended at every step by greed, discrimination, exploitation, environmental degradation, and moral emptiness. Nonetheless, few know as well as historians that answers to the question that opened this book, *why demand,* need not cause thoughtful people to despair. The answers should instead concentrate our minds on choices still to be made, choices that will determine whether the world's resources in the future can be shared more widely and equitably at the same time that they are more wisely used and responsibly conserved.

The conviction that a knowledge of a people's material condition comes with an obligation to better that condition is a venerable tradition in American history-writing. No less a chronicler than Thomas Jefferson went out of his way to observe strangers' living standards wherever he traveled, and he traveled exhaustively. "I am constantly roving about, to see what I have never seen before," he told his friend the Marquis de Lafayette in 1787. "I am never satiated with rambling through the fields and farms, examining the culture and cultivators, with a degree of curiosity which makes some take me to be a fool, and others to be much wiser than I am." He had long since developed a keen eye for appearances. He urged his friend to follow his example and explore the French countryside "incognito" in order to observe the rustic inhabitants close at hand: "You must ferret the people out of their hovels as I have done, look into their kettles, eat their bread, loll on their beds under pretence [*sic*] of resting yourself, but in fact to find if they are soft." He promised that Lafayette would "feel a sublime pleasure in the course of this investigation." A still "sublimer one" awaited the nobleman when a man of his generous sensibilities weighed the implications of his findings and acknowledged his duty as a man of influence. The purpose of such inquisitiveness would ultimately be fulfilled "when you shall be able to apply your knowledge to the softening of their beds, or the throwing a morsel of meat into their kettle of vegetables."[18]

The history of material life is an account of the past—our past—whose time has come again.

Notes

Preface

1. United States Capitol Historical Society conference, "Of Consuming Interests: The Style of Life in the Eighteenth Century," Russell Senate Office Building, Washington, D.C., March 21–22, 1986. The proceedings, bearing the conference title, were edited by Cary Carson, Ronald Hoffman, and Peter J. Albert and published for the United States Capitol Historical Society by the University Press of Virginia (Charlottesville), in 1994. See pp. 483–697 for Cary Carson, "The Consumer Revolution in Colonial British America: Why Demand?"

2. Jan de Vries, *The Industrious Revolution: Consumer Behavior and the Household Economy, 1650 to the Present* (Cambridge: Cambridge University Press, 2008); T. H. Breen, *The Marketplace of Revolution: How Consumer Politics Shaped American Independence* (Oxford: Oxford University Press, 2004).

3. See chapter 1, note 6.

4. Woodruff D. Smith, *Consumption and the Making of Respectability, 1600–1800* (New York and London: Routledge, 2002); Linda Levy Peck, *Consuming Splendor: Society and Culture in Seventeenth-Century England* (Cambridge: Cambridge University Press, 2005); Maxine Berg, *Luxury and Pleasure in Eighteenth-Century Britain* (Oxford: Oxford University Press, 2005); Kate Haulman, *The Politics of Fashion in Eighteenth-Century* America (Chapel Hill: University of North Carolina Press, 2011); Phyllis Whitman Hunter, *Purchasing Identity in the Atlantic World: Massachusetts Merchants, 1670–1780* (Ithaca, N.Y.: Cornell University Press, 2001); David Jaffee, *A New Nation of Goods: The Material Culture of Early America* (Philadelphia: University of Pennsylvania Press, 2010), and with it a companion-piece from decorative arts literature, Sumpter Priddy, *American Fancy: Exuberance in the Arts, 1790–1840* (Milwaukee, Wisc.: Chipstone Foundation, 2004).

5. For a fuller explanation of my thinking about illustrations see the "Method" section in Cary Carson, "Banqueting Houses and the 'Need of Society' among Slave-Owning Planters in the Chesapeake Colonies," *William and Mary Quarterly*, 3rd series, 70 (2013): 757–59, and Cary Carson, "Architecture as Social History," in Cary Carson and Carl R. Lounsbury, eds., *The Chesapeake House: Architectural Investigation by Colonial Williamsburg* (Chapel Hill: University of North Carolina Press, 2013), 17–25.

1. Why Demand

1. R. K. Webb, *Modern England: From the Eighteenth Century to the Present* (New York: Dodd, Mead, 1968), 102, is typical of many older surveys that could be cited. Textbook writers frequently acknowledge that historians have greatly extended the period of the Industrial Revolution backwards and forwards from 1760, but even now few seriously question the basic sequence of events in which major technological and organizational innovations vastly increased the productive capacity of industry, thus flooding a mass market with popular goods and services in every price range. Harold J. Perkin, *The Origins of Modern English Society, 1780–1880* (London and Toronto: Routledge & Kegan Paul, 1969), was one of the first survey texts to argue strongly that "the most important economic factor in the genesis of industrialism [was] consumer demand" (91).

2. Daniel J. Boorstin and Brooks Mather Kelley, *A History of the United States* (Lexington, Mass.: Ginn & Co., 1971), 214–15.

3. Henry Fielding, *An Enquiry into the Causes of the Late Increase in Robbers* (London, 1751), xi.

4. Lawrence Mishel, Jared Bernstein, and John Schmitt, *The State of Working America, 2000–2001* (Ithaca, N.Y.: IRL Press for the Economic Policy Institute, 2001); Don Peck, *Pinched: How the Great Recession Has Narrowed Our Futures and What We Can Do About It* (New York: Crown Publishers, 2011). Inequality and the concentration of wealth are not American problems exclusively, nor are they strictly modern phenomena, we learn from Thomas Piketty, *Capital in the Twenty-First Century*, trans. Arthur Goldhammer (Cambridge. Mass.: Belknap Press of Harvard University Press, 2014).

5. A central theme from George Santayana to Daniel J. Boorstin. Theirs is a view of American history that is dismissed too easily by historians today whose well-meant efforts to recapture the ethnic, regional, and social diversities of American life nevertheless neglect the fact that our history is also a true story of nation-making. Boorstin's permanent exhibition at the Smithsonian Institution, "A Nation of Nations" (National Museum of American History, Washington, D.C., 1976–1991), and the third volume in *The Americans* trilogy, *The Democratic Experience* (New York: Random House, 1973) make an eloquent case in words and images for the unifying influence of a consumer revolution in the *nineteenth-century*. Boorstin, like other writers on the subject, deals more with con-

sequences than causes, partly because he accepts the myth that "in the older world"—that is, America before 1800—"almost everything a man owned was one-of-a-kind" (90) and partly too because he chooses not to see that consumer goods have always been used to separate and exclude as well as to join and unify.

6. Lorna Weatherill, *Consumer Behaviour and Material Culture in Britain, 1660–1760* (New York and London: Routledge, 1988); Carole Shammas, *The Pre-Industrial Consumer in England and America* (Oxford: Clarendon Press, 1990); Richard L. Bushman, *The Refinement of America: Persons, Houses, Cities* (New York: Alfred A. Knopf, 1992); John Brewer and Roy Porter, eds., *Consumption and the World of Goods* (London and New York: Routledge, 1993): Jean-Christophe Agnew, "Coming Up For Air: Consumer Culture in Historical Perspective," in Brewer and Porter, *Consumption and the World of Goods*, 19–39; Ann Bermingham and John Brewer, eds., *The Consumption of Culture, 1600–1800: Image, Object, Text* (London and New York: Routledge, 1995); Jon Butler, *Becoming America: The Revolution before 1776* (Cambridge. Mass.: Harvard University Press, 2000), ch. 4, "Things Material," 131–84; Phyllis Whitman Hunter, *Purchasing Identity in the Atlantic World: Massachusetts Merchants, 1670–1780* (Ithaca, N.Y.: Cornell University Press, 2001); Woodruff D. Smith, *Consumption and the Making of Respectability, 1600–1800* (New York and London: Routledge, 2002); Cary Carson, "Consumption," in Daniel Vickers, ed., *Blackwell Companion to Early American History* (Oxford: Blackwell Publishing, 2003), 334–65; Mark Overton, Jane Whittle, Darron Dean, and Andrew Hann, *Production and Consumption in English Households, 1600–1750* (London and New York: Routledge, 2004); T. H. Breen, *The Marketplace of Revolution: How Consumer Politics Shaped American Independence* (Oxford: Oxford University Press, 2004); David Jaffee, *A New Nation of Goods: The Material Culture of Early America* (Philadelphia: University of Pennsylvania Press, 2010). For complementary studies of consumer behavior in northern Europe see note 27, below.

7. Compared with supply-side studies of the Industrial Revolution, the literature on home demand and the consumer revolution remained thin until recently. The rare exceptions were early canonical works by Elizabeth Waterman Gilboy, "Demand as a Factor in the Industrial Revolution," in R. M. Hartwell, ed., *The Causes of the Industrial Revolution* (London: Methuen, 1967), 121–38; Joel Mokyr reformulated the "Gilboy thesis" in testable form in "Demand vs. Supply in the Industrial Revolution," *Journal of Economic History* 37 (1977): 981-l008; D. E. C. Eversley, "The Home Market and Economic Growth in England, 1750–1780," in Eric L. Jones and G. E. Mingay, eds., *Land, Labour, and Population in the Industrial Revolution: Essays Presented to J. D. Chambers* (London: Edward Arnold, 1967), 206–59; Eric L. Jones, "The Fashion Manipulators: Consumer Tastes and British Industries, 1660–1800," in Louis P. Cain and Paul J. Uselding, eds., *Business Enterprise and Economic Change: Essays in Honor of Harold F Williamson* (Kent, Ohio: Kent State University Press, 1973), 198–226; and Joan Thirsk, *Economic Policy*

and Projects: The Development of a Consumer Society in Early Modern England (Oxford: Clarendon Press, 1978). Coinciding with the turn of the new century, several leading economic historians weighed in with major reassessments of the Industrial Revolution and its consequences on Britain, northern Europe, and by implication their overseas colonies, notably Keith Wrightson, *Earthly Necessities. Economic Lives in Early Modern Britain* (New Haven: Yale University Press, 2000); Jan de Vries, *The Industrious Revolution: Consumer Behavior and the Household Economy, 1650 to the Present* (Cambridge: Cambridge University Press, 2008); Robert C. Allen, *The British Industrial Revolution in Global Perspective* (Cambridge: Cambridge University Press, 2009); and Joel Mokyr, *The Enlightened Economy: An Economic History of Britain, 1700–1850* (New Haven: Yale University Press, 2009). Noteworthy books and articles that take account of consumer demand in colonial American economies include Alice Hanson Jones, *Wealth of a Nation to Be: The American Colonies on the Eve of the Revolution* (New York: Columbia University Press, 1980); Gloria L. Main, *Tobacco Colony: Life in Early Maryland, 1650–1720* (Princeton: Princeton University Press, 1982), 140–236; John J. McCusker and Russell R. Menard, *The Economy of British America, 1607–1789* (Chapel Hill: University of North Carolina Press, 1985), chap. 13; Lorena S. Walsh, Gloria L. Main, and Lois Green Carr, "Toward a History of the Standard of Living in British North America," *William and Mary Quarterly,* 3rd ser., 45 (1988): 116–66; Lois Green Carr and Lorena S. Walsh, "Changing Lifestyles and Consumer Behavior in the Colonial Chesapeake," in Cary Carson, Ronald Hoffman, and Peter J. Albert, eds., *Of Consuming Interests. The Style of Life in the Eighteenth Century* (Charlottesville: University Press of Virginia, 1994), 59–166.

8. Joyce Oldham Appleby, "Ideology and Theory: The Tension between Political and Economic Liberalism in Seventeenth-Century England," *American Historical Review* 81 (1976): 499–515; Joyce Oldham Appleby, *Economic Thought and Ideology in Seventeenth-Century England* (Princeton: Princeton University Press, 1978), 163–98. Drew R. McCoy explores the subject in late eighteenth-century American thought in *The Elusive Republic: Political Economy in Jeffersonian America* (Chapel Hill: University of North Carolina Press, 1980).

9. John Sekora, *Luxury: The Concept in Western Thought, Eden to Smollett* (Baltimore: Johns Hopkins University Press, 1977), 23–131; Maxine Berg, *Luxury and Pleasure in Eighteenth-Century Britain* (Oxford: Oxford University Press, 2005); Linda Levy Peck, *Consuming Splendor: Society and Culture in Seventeenth-Century England* (Cambridge: Cambridge University Press, 2005). For the American literature on the subject see Robert Micklus, "'The History of the Tuesday Club': A Mock-Jeremiad of the Colonial South," *William and Mary Quarterly,* 3rd ser., 40 (1983): 42–61.

10. J. H. Plumb, *The Pursuit of Happiness: A View of Life in Georgian England* (New Haven: Yale Center for British Art, 1977); Ellen G. D'Oench, *The Conversation Piece: Arthur Devis and His Contemporaries* (New Haven: Yale Center for British Art, 1980); Ste-

phen Deuchar, *Sporting Art in Eighteenth-Century England: A Social and Political History* (New Haven: Yale University Press, 1988); Karin Calvert, "Children in American Family Portraiture, 1670 to 1810," *William and Mary Quarterly,* 3rd ser., 39 (1982): 87–113; T. H. Breen, "The Meaning of 'Likeness': American Portrait-Painting in an Eighteenth-Century Consumer Society," in Ellen G. Miles, ed., *The Portrait in Eighteenth-Century America* (Newark: University of Delaware Press, 1993): 37–60; Margaretta M. Lovell, *Art in a Season of Revolution. Painters, Artisans, and Patrons in Early America* (Philadelphia: University of Pennsylvania Press, 2005), esp. 8–25.

11. Norbert Elias, *The Civilizing Process: The Development of Manners,* vol. 1, trans. Edmund Jephcott (New York: Pantheon, 1978), 51–217; J. H. Plumb, *Georgian Delights* (Boston: Little Brown, 1980), pt. 1 and introductions to portfolios; Richard L. Bushman, "American High-Style and Vernacular Cultures," in Jack P. Greene and J. R. Pole, eds., *Colonial British America: Essays in the New History of the Early Modern Era* (Baltimore: Johns Hopkins University Press, 1984), 345–83; Michal Rozbicki, *The Complete Colonial Gentleman: Cultural Legitimacy in Plantation America* (Charlottesville: University Press of Virginia, 1998); C. Dallett Hemphill, *Bowing to Necessities. A History of Manners in America, 1620–1860* (New York: Oxford University Press, 1999).

12. The most authoritative recent work is John Archer, *The Literature of British Domestic Architecture, 1715–1842* (Cambridge: Massachusetts Institute of Technology Press, 1985), which is mainly a study of the book trade. Nevertheless, his sections on audiences, the format and content of building manuals, and treatises on the classical orders (pp. 20–28) show how "good taste" in architecture was sold to a mass market. The extent to which the American colonies figured in that market is documented from library catalogues and booksellers' lists first compiled by Helen Park in *A List of Architectural Books Available in America before the Revolution* (Los Angeles: Hennessey and Ingalis, rev. ed. 1973), now thoroughly updated in Janice G. Schimmelman, *Architectural Books in Early America: Architectural Treatises and Building Handbooks Available in American Libraries and Bookstores through 1800* (New Castle, Del.: Oak Knoll Press, 1999). American scholars have only begun to explain the inroads that pattern books made on vernacular building traditions in the eighteenth century, most having preferred to demonstrate the influence of specific publications on specific large houses, as in Mario di Valmarana, ed., *Building by the Book*, 3 vols. (Charlottesville: University Press of Virginia, 1984–86). See Carl Lounsbury, "The Design Process," in Cary Carson and Carl R. Lounsbury, eds., *The Chesapeake House: Architectural Investigation by Colonial Williamsburg* (Chapel Hill: University of North Carolina Press), 64–85, and for a somewhat later period Dell Upton, "Pattern Books and Professionalism: Aspects of the Transformation of Domestic Architecture in America, 1800–1860," *Winterthur Portfolio* 19 (1984): 107–50. The fullest treatment of the subject for seventeenth- and early eighteenth-century England is still M. W. Barley, *The English Farmhouse and Cottage* (London: Routledge & Kegan Paul, 1961), pt. 5.

13. Maxine Berg, *The Age of Manufactures: Industry, Innovation, and Work in Britain, 1700–1820* (London: Fontana, 1985); Christine MacLeod, *Inventing the Industrial Revolution: The English Patent System, 1660–1800* (Cambridge: Cambridge University Press, 1988); Beverly Lemire, *Fashion's Favourite: The Cotton Trade and the Consumer in Britain, 1660–1800* (Oxford: Oxford University Press, 1991); Beverly Lemire, *Dress, Culture, and Commerce: The English Clothing Trade before the Factory, 1660–1800* (New York: St. Martin's Press, 1997); John Styles, *The Dress of the People: Everyday Fashion in Eighteenth-Century England* (New Haven: Yale University Press, 2007).

14. Besides Neil McKendrick's chapters on Josiah Wedgwood and George Packwood in Neil McKendrick, John Brewer, and J.H. Plumb, eds., *The Birth of a Consumer Society: The Commercialization of Eighteenth-Century England* (Bloomington: Indiana University Press, 1982), 100–194, see his articles "Josiah Wedgwood: An Eighteenth-Century Entrepreneur in Salesmanship and Marketing Techniques," *Economic History Review*, 2nd ser., 12 (1960): 408–33, and "Josiah Wedgwood and Thomas Bentley: An Inventor-Entrepreneur Partnership in the Industrial Revolution," *Transactions of the Royal Historical Society*, 5th ser., 14 (1964): 1–33. Also Lorna Weatherill, *The Pottery Trade and North Staffordshire, 1660–1760* (Manchester, England: Manchester University Press, 1971), and Lorna Weatherill, "The Business of Middleman in the English Pottery Trade before 1780," *Business History* 28 (1986): 51–76.

15. John Brewer, "Commercialization and Politics," in McKendrick, Brewer, and Plumb, *Birth of a Consumer Society,* 197–262; John Brewer, *Party Ideology and Popular Politics at the Accession of George III* (New York: Cambridge University Press, 1976), 159–60, and 173–174 for John Wilkes's sophisticated marketing of propaganda. For the American colonies, see T. H. Breen, *The Marketplace of Revolution: How Consumer Politics Shaped American Independence* (Oxford: Oxford University Press, 2004); and Kate Haulman, *The Politics of Fashion in Eighteenth-Century America* (Chapel Hill: University of North Carolina Press, 2011).

16. William Cobbett, *Rural Rides* (London: Letchworth, 1932), 190–94. The consumption mania had spread widely throughout lowland England by the time Cobbett wrote this passage in 1825.

17. W. G. Hoskins, "The Rebuilding of Rural England, 1570–1640," *Past and Present* 4 (1953): 44–59, reprinted in Hoskins, *Provincial England: Essays in Social and Economic History* (London: Macmillan and Co., 1964), 13148.

18. R. Machin, "The Great Rebuilding: A Reassessment," *Past and Present* 77 (1977): 33–56; Matthew H. Johnson, "Rethinking the Great Rebuilding," *Oxford Journal of Archaeology* 12 (1993): 117–25; Edward Roberts, "W. G. Hoskins's 'Great Rebuilding' and Dendrochronology in Hampshire," *Vernacular Architecture* 38 (2007): 15–18; J. T. Smith, "The Evolution of the English Peasant House to the Late Seventeenth Century: The Evidence of Buildings," *Journal of the British Archaeological Association,* 3rd ser., 33 (1970):

122–47; Eric Mercer, *English Vernacular Houses: A Study of Traditional Farmhouses and Cottages* (London: H.M.S.O., 1975), 1–7, 23; Matthew Johnson, *English Houses, 1300–1800: Vernacular Architecture, Social Life* (London: Longman, 2010), 87–112; Nat Alcock and Dan Miles, *The Medieval Peasant House in Midland England* (Oxford: Oxbow Books, 2012), 41–49.

19. Abbott Lowell Cummings, "Massachusetts and Its First Period Houses: A Statistical Survey," in *Architecture in Colonial Massachusetts* (Boston: Colonial Society of Massachusetts, 1979), 113–221, with building dates revised in light of later dendrochronological research in Abbott Lowell Cummings, "Recent Tree-Ring Studies of Early New England Buildings: An Evaluation," *Vernacular Architecture* 35 (2004): 66–71, and Anne Grady, "First Period Buildings in Eastern Massachusetts: Research in Progress," paper presented at a meeting of the Vernacular Architecture Forum, New England Chapter, April 10, 2010, Sturbridge, Massachusetts. Also Kevin M. Sweeney, "Mansion People: Kinship, Class, and Architecture in Western Massachusetts in the Mid-Eighteenth Century," *Winterthur Portfolio* 19 (1984): 231–55; William N. Hosley Jr., "Architecture," in Gerald W. R. Ward and William N. Hosley Jr., eds., *The Great River: Art and Society of the Connecticut River Valley, 1635–1820* (Hartford, Conn.: The Atheneum, 1985), 63–72; Michael Steinitz, "Rethinking Geographical Approaches to the Common House: The Evidence from Eighteenth-Century Massachusetts," in Thomas Carter and Bernard L. Herman, eds., *Perspectives in Vernacular Architecture* 3 (Columbia, Mo.: Vernacular Architecture Form, 1989), 16–26; Cary Carson, Norman F. Barka, William M. Kelso, Garry Wheeler Stone, and Dell Upton, "Impermanent Architecture in the Southern American Colonies," *Winterthur Portfolio* 16 (1981): 135–96; Edward A. Chappell, "Housing a Nation: The Transformation of Living Standards in Early America," in Carson, Hoffman, and Albert, *Of Consuming Interests,* 167–232.

20. Johnson, *English Houses,* 87–102, 145–50, 179–81; Cary Carson, "Segregation in Vernacular Buildings," *Vernacular Architecture* 7 (1976): 24–29; Hoskins, *Provincial England,* 138–39; N. W. Alcock, "Physical Space and Social Space: The Interpretation of Vernacular Architecture," in Martin Locock, ed., *Meaningful Architecture: Social Interpretations of Buildings* (Avebury, England: Ashgate Publishing Ltd., 1994), 207–30. See also David H. Flaherty, *Privacy in Colonial New England* (Charlottesville: University Press of Virginia, 1972), 33–84.

21. William Harrison, *The Description of England,* ed. Georges Edelen (1577; Ithaca, N.Y.: Cornell University Press, 1968), 201.

22. The earliest studies were confined to southern Maryland, but they established the fact of remarkably primitive living conditions, which later research substantiated and extended to other regions of the Chesapeake. See Barbara G. Carson and Cary Carson, "Styles and Standards of Living in Southern Maryland, 1670–1752," paper presented at the Forty-second Annual Meeting of the Southern Historical Association, Atlanta, No-

vember 1976, and a companion piece by Lois G. Carr and Lorena S. Walsh, "Inventories and the Analysis of Wealth and Consumption Patterns in St. Mary's County, Maryland, 1658–1777," *Historical Methods* 13 (1980): 81–104. The larger picture that emerged from subsequent research is summarized in Lorena S. Walsh, Gloria L. Main, and Lois G. Carr, "Towards a History of the Standard of Living in British North America," *William and Mary Quarterly* 3rd. ser., 45 (1988): 116–66; James P. P. Horn, "'The Bare Necessities': Standards of Living in England and the Chesapeake, 1650–1700," *Historical Archaeology* 22 (1988): 74–91; Carr and Walsh, "Changing Lifestyles and Consumer Behavior in the Colonial Chesapeake," in Carson, Hoffman, and Albert, *Of Consuming Interests*, 59–166; and Main, *Tobacco Colony*, chaps. 4–7. Systematic study of archaeological assemblages from early domestic sites in Maryland and Virginia has produced data that correct for under-representation of ceramics, tools, and table utensils in probate inventories. See Dennis J. Pogue, "The Transformation of America: Georgian Sensibility, Capitalist Conspiracy, or Consumer Revolution?," *Historical Archaeology* 35 (2001): 41–57. Living standards are interpreted against a broader economic and social background in Main, *Tobacco Colony*, chaps. 4–7.

23. John Fontaine, "Memoirs of a Huguenot Family," quoted in *Virginia Magazine of History and Biography* 3 (1895): 171. The gentleman in question, Robert Beverley of Beverley Park, may have been more eccentric in his tastes than Fontaine implied in this often-cited passage. A probate inventory of the estate of Beverley's father came to light in a private collection in 1992. When Maj. Robert Beverley died in 1686, he left a hall-and-parlor house full of expensive fashionable furniture, including calico bed curtains and twenty-three leather chairs. His son's back-to-basics lifestyle in 1715, whatever the explanation, was not for lack of parental example.

24. Abbott Lowell Cummings, ed., *Rural Household Inventories [Suffolk, Massachusetts]: Establishing the Names, Uses, and Furnishings of Rooms in the Colonial New England House, 1625–1775* (Boston: Society for the Preservation of New England Antiquities, 1964); John Demos, *A Little Commonwealth: Family Life in Plymouth Colony* (New York: Oxford University Press, 1970), chap. 2; Carole Shammas, "The Domestic Environment in Early Modern England and America," *Journal of Social History* 14 (1980): 3–24; Jackson Turner Main, *Society and Economy in Colonial Connecticut* (Princeton: Princeton University Press, 1985), 89–114, 142–73; Peter Benes, "Sleeping Arrangements in Early Massachusetts: The Newbury Household of Henry Lunt, Hatter," and Gloria L. Main, "The Distribution of Consumer Goods in Colonial New England: A Subregional Approach," in Peter Benes, ed., *Early American Probate Inventories* (Boston: Boston University, 1989), 140–68; Gloria L. Main, "The Standard of Living in Southern New England, 1640–1773," *William and Mary Quarterly*, 3rd ser., 45 (1988): 124–34; Jack Michel, "'In a Manner and Fashion Suitable to Their Degree': A Preliminary Investigation of Material Culture of Early Rural Pennsylvania," *Working Papers from the Regional Economic History*

Research Center 5 (1981): 1–83; Paul G. E. Clemens, "The Consumer Culture of the Middle Atlantic, 1760–1820," *William and Mary Quarterly*, 3rd ser., 62 (2005): 577–624; R. C. Nash, "Domestic Material Culture and Consumer Demand in the British Atlantic World: Colonial South Carolina, 1670–1770," in David S. Shields, ed., *Material Culture in Anglo-America: Regional Identity and Urbanity in the Tidewater, Lowcountry, and Caribbean* (Columbia: University of South Carolina Press, 2009), 221–66, esp. 223–34.

25. Cary Carson et al., "Impermanent Architecture," 135–48, 160–78; Gloria L. Main and Jackson T. Main, "Economic Growth and the Standard of Living in Southern New England, 1640–1774," *Journal of Economic History* 48 (1988): 37–39. In Pennsylvania this homesteading process was remarked on as early as the eighteenth century by Benjamin Rush in "An Account of the Manners of the German Inhabitants of Pennsylvania" (1789) and Jacques-Pierre Brissot de Warville in "Progress of Cultivation in Pennsylvania" (1792), both reprinted and discussed in Cynthia G. Falk, *Architecture and Artifacts of the Pennsylvania Germans. Constructing Identity in Early America* (University Park: Pennsylvania State University Press, 2008), appendices A and B.

26. Similarly, Patricia Trautman finds that quality and quantity, not the cut of people's clothing, distinguished rich from poor in seventeenth-century Massachusetts. See her "Dress in Seventeenth-Century Cambridge, Massachusetts: An Inventory-Based Reconstruction," in Benes, *Early American Probate Inventories,* 51–73. The colony's sumptuary laws notwithstanding, "differences between upper- and lower-class men's suits lay in fabric quality and number of coordinated pieces" (57–58). Likewise, women's accessories "were owned and worn by all classes of Cambridge residents." Those of higher standing simply had more of them (61–62).

27. The most recent and ambitious use of English probate inventories to study standards of living are Weatherill, *Consumer Behaviour and Material Culture;* Shammas, *Pre-Industrial Consumer*; and Mark Overton, et al., *Production and Consumption*. James P. P. Horn applies American research strategies to Anglo-American comparative studies in *Adapting to a New World: English Society in the Seventeenth-century Chesapeake* (Chapel Hill: University of North Carolina Press, 1994), 293–333. Craig Muldrew, *Food, Energy, and the Creation of Industriousness: Work and Material Culture in Agrarian England, 1550–1780* (Cambridge: Cambridge University Press, 2011) analyzes English laborers' inventories. Valuable Irish, Dutch, French, and German studies give a wider view of living conditions across northern Europe. See Toby Barnard, *Making the Grand Figure: Lives and Possessions in Ireland, 1641–1770* (New Haven: Yale University Press, 2004); Jan de Vries, "Peasant Demand Patterns and Economic Development: Friesland, 1550–1750," in William N. Parker and Eric L. Jones, eds., *European Peasants and Their Markets: Essays in Agrarian Economic History* (Princeton: Princeton University Press, 1975), 205–66; Micheline Baulant, "Niveaux de Vie Paysans Autour de Meaux en 1700 et 1750," *Annales: economies, sociétés, civilisations* 30 (1975): 505–18; Ad van der Woude and Anton

Schuurman, eds., *Probate Inventories: A New Source for the Historical Study of Wealth, Material Culture and Agricultural Development: Papers Presented at the Leeuwenborch Conference, Wageningen, May 5–7, 1980* (Utrecht, Netherlands: HES, 1980); Daniel Roche, *The People of Paris: An Essay in Popular Culture in the 18th Century,* trans. Marie Evans (Berkeley: University of California Press, 1987), esp. pts. 1 and 2; Daniel Roche, *A History of Everyday Things: The Birth of Consumption in France, 1600–1800,* trans. Brian Pearce (Cambridge: Cambridge University Press, 2000); Simon Schama, *The Embarrassment of Riches: An Interpretation of Dutch Culture in the Golden Age* (New York: Knopf, 1987); Peter Burke, *"Res et Verba*: Conspicuous Consumption in the Early Modern World," in Brewer and Porter, *Consumption and the World of Goods,* 148–61; and Wouter Ryckbosch, "A Consumer Revolution under Strain: Consumption, Wealth, and Status in Eighteenth-Century Aalst (Southern Netherlands)," PhD diss., University of Antwerp, 2012.

28. J. C. Drummond and Anne Wilbraham, *The Englishman's Food: A History of Five Centuries of English Diet* (London: J. Cape, 1939); Christopher Dyer, "English Diet in the Later Middle Ages," in T. H. Aston, P. R. Cross, Christopher Dyer, and Joan Thirsk, eds., *Social Relations and Ideas: Essays in Honour of J. H. Hilton* (Cambridge: Cambridge University Press, 1983), 191–216; Jay Allan Anderson, "'A Solid Sufficiency': An Ethnography of Yeoman Foodways in Stuart England," PhD diss., University of Pennsylvania, 1971; Stephen Mennell, *All Manners of Food: Eating and Taste in England and France from the Middle Ages to the Present* (Oxford: B. Blackwell, 1985); Carole Shammas, "The Eighteenth-Century English Diet and Economic Change," *Explorations in Economic History* 21 (1984): 254–69. For early America, see James T. Lemon, "Household Consumption in Eighteenth-Century America and Its Relationship to Production and Trade: The Situation among Farmers in Southeastern Pennsylvania [1740–1790]," *Agricultural History* 41 (1967): 59–70; Audrey Noël Hume, *Food* (Williamsburg, Va.: Colonial Williamsburg Foundation, 1978); Peter Benes, ed., *Foodways in the Northeast* (Boston: Boston University, 1984); Sarah F. McMahon, "Provisions Laid Up for the Family: Towards a History of Diet in New England, 1600–1850," *Historical Methods* 14 (1981): 4–21; Sarah F. McMahon, "A Comfortable Subsistence: The Changing Composition of Diet in Rural New England, 1620–1840," *William and Mary Quarterly,* 3rd ser., 42 (1985): 26–65; Henry M. Miller, "An Archaeological Perspective on the Evolution of Diet in the Colonial Chesapeake" in Lois Green Carr, Philip D. Morgan, and Jean B. Russo, eds., *Colonial Chesapeake Society* (Chapel Hill: University of North Carolina Press, 1988), 176–99; Cary Carson, Joanne Bowen, William Graham, Martha McCartney, and Lorena Walsh, "New World, Real World: Improvising English Culture in Seventeenth-Century Virginia," *Journal of Southern History* 74 (2008): 36–49; Joanne Bowen, "Foodways in the 18th-Century Chesapeake," in Theodore R. Reinhart, ed., *The Archaeology of 18th-Century Virginia* (Richmond: Archaeological Society of Virginia, 1996), 87–130; Shammas, *Pre-Industrial Consumer,* 121–57.

29. Margaret Spufford, *The Great Reclothing of Rural England: Petty Chapmen and Their Wares in the Seventeenth Century* (London: Hambledon Press, 1984) and Lemire, *Fashion's Favourite* are the classic economic histories of ordinary people's clothing. Both are still useful. Newer work includes David Kuchta, *The Three-Piece Suit and Modern Masculinity: England, 1550–1850* (Berkeley: University of California Press, 2002); Styles, *Dress of the People*; and Diana DiPaolo Loren, *The Archaeology of Clothing and Bodily Adornment in Colonial America* (Gainsville: University Press of Florida, 2010). See also Beverly Lemire, "Consumerism in Preindustrial and Early Industrial England: The Trade in Secondhand Clothes," *Journal of British Studies* 27 (1988): 1–24.

30. Allen, *The British Industrial Revolution in Global Perspective,* 36–41; Stephen Broadberry, Bruce Campbell, Alexander Klein, Mark Overton, and Bas van Leeuwen, "British Economic Growth, 1270–1870," July 14, 2010, project paper for "Reconstructing the National Income of Britain and Holland, c. 1270/1500 to 1850," Leverhulme Trust, London, ref. no. F/00215AR, and for collaborative project HI-POD, European Commission, 7th Framework Programme for Research, contract no. SSH7-CT-2008–225342; David Herlihy, *The Black Death and the Transformation of the West* (Cambridge, Mass.: Harvard University Press, 1997); de Vries, *Industrious Revolution*, 6–9.

31. For example, Fernand Braudel (in *Civilization and Capitalism, 15th–18th Century,* vol. 1, *The Structures of Everyday Life: The Limits of the Possible,* trans. Siãn Reynolds [New York: Harper & Row, 1982]) writes broadly on these subjects and with great originality, but large external events—climates, new crops, international markets—are the agents of change in his history. He never questions the assumption that all peoples in all times and places always desire to raise their standards of living. Yet anthropologists argue that material standards are subject to the same cultural influences that shape a people's other values, and therefore that differences and changes in those standards require cultural explanations as well.

32. This important difference between folk and popular culture, so familiar to geographers, is the organizing concept in Henry Glassie, *Pattern in the Material Folk Culture of the Eastern United States* (Philadelphia: University of Pennsylvania Press, 1969), 33–36.

33. I owe my appreciation for these distinctions to Dell Upton and Fraser Neiman, who called my attention to Meyer Schapiro, "Style," in A. L. Kroeber, ed., *Anthropology Today: An Encyclopedic Inventory* (Chicago: University of Chicago Press, 1953), 287, and James R. Sackett, "The Meaning of Style in Archaeology: A General Model," *American Antiquity* 42 (1977): 370–79. Upton describes how style and mode worked in eighteenth-century Virginia churches in *Holy Things and Profane: Anglican Parish Churches in Colonial Virginia* (Cambridge: Massachusetts Institute of Technology Press, 1986), 101–96.

34. Robert Beverley to [John Bland], December 27, 1762; Beverley to Samuel Athawes, April 15 and July 16, 1771; Robert Beverley Letterbook, 1761–93, Library of Congress, Washington, D.C.

35. George Washington to Robert Cary and Co., September 28, 1760, in John C. Fitzpatrick, ed., *The Writings of George Washington,* 39 vols. (Washington, D.C.: U.S. Government Printing Office, 1931), 2:350.

36. William Eddis, *Letters from America,* ed. Aubrey C. Land (Cambridge, Mass.: Belknap Press of Harvard University Press, 1969), 19, 57–58.

37. James J. F. Deetz, "Ceramics from Plymouth, 1635–1835: The Archaeological Evidence," Marley R. Brown III, "Ceramics from Plymouth, 1621–1800: The Documentary Evidence," and Garry Wheeler Stone, J. Glenn Little III, and Stephen Israel, "Ceramics from the John Hicks Site, 1723–1743: The Material Culture," in Ian M. G. Quimby, ed., *Ceramics in America* (Charlottesville: University Press of Virginia, 1973), 15–74, 103–40. See also James J. F. Deetz, *In Small Things Forgotten: The Archaeology of Early American Life* (Garden City, N.Y.: Anchor Press/Doubleday, 1977), chap. 3; William M. Kelso, *Kingsmill Plantations, 1619–1800: Archaeology of Country Life in Colonial Virginia* (Orlando, Fla.: Academic Press, Inc., 1984), 176–79, 204–6.

38. Beverley to [Bland], December 27, 1762, Beverley Letterbook.

39. Plumb, *Georgian Delights,* pt. 1 and introductions to portfolios; Peter Clark, *The English Alehouse: A Social History, 1200–1830* (New York and London: Longman, 1983), 222–332; Peter Borsay, *The English Urban Renaissance: Culture and Society in the Provincial Town, 1660–1770* (Oxford: Oxford University Press, 1989).

40. The earliest documented social club in Maryland or Virginia was the Tuesday Club of Annapolis, made famous by Dr. Alexander Hamilton in *The History of the Ancient and Honorable Tuesday Club* (1745–56), 3 vols., ed. Robert Micklus (Chapel Hill: University of North Carolina Press, 1990). Freemasons and college fraternities clubbed together in taverns and coffeehouses in Williamsburg and Fredericksburg in the 1750s and 1760s, according to Jane Carson, *James Innes and His Brothers of the F.H.C.* (Williamsburg, Va.: Colonial Williamsburg, 1965), 1–2, and Patricia A. Gibbs, "Taverns in Tidewater Virginia, 1700–1774," master's thesis, College of William and Mary, 1968. See also Kym S. Rice, *Early American Taverns: For the Entertainment of Friends and Strangers* (Chicago: Regnery Gateway, 1983); Sharon V. Salinger, *Taverns and Drinking in Early America* (Baltimore: Johns Hopkins University Press, 2002); Peter Thompson, *Rum Punch and Revolution: Taverngoing and Public Life in Eighteenth-Century Philadelphia* (Philadelphia: University of Pennsylvania Press, 1999); David W. Conroy, *In Public Houses: Drink and the Revolution of Authority in Colonial Massachusetts* (Chapel Hill: North Carolina University Press, 1995); and Jane Carson, *Colonial Virginians at Play* (Williamsburg, Va.: Colonial Williamsburg, 1965), 102–270.

41. Barbara G. Carson, "Early American Tourists and the Commercialization of Leisure," in Carson, Hoffman, and Albert, *Of Consuming Interests,* 373–405.

42. In addition to David D. Hall, "Books and Reading in Eighteenth-Century America," in Carson, Hoffman, and Albert, *Of Consuming Interests,* 354–72, see Cynthia Z. Stiverson and Gregory A. Stiverson, "The Colonial Retail Book Trade: Availability and

Affordability of Reading Material in Mid-Eighteenth-Century Virginia," in William L. Joyce et al., eds., *Printing and Society in Early America* (Worcester, Mass.: American Antiquarian Society, 1983), 132–73; William J. Gilmore, *Reading Becomes of Necessity of Life: Material and Cultural Life in Rural New England, 1780–1835* (Knoxville: University of Tennessee Press, 1989); Cathy N. Davidson, *Revolution and the Word: The Rise of the Novel in America* (New York: Oxford University Press, 1986); Cynthia Adams Hoover, "Music and Theater in the Lives of Eighteenth-Century Americans," in Carson, Hoffman, and Albert, *Of Consuming Interests*, 307–53.

43. Richard L. Bushman, "Shopping and Advertising in Colonial America," in Carson, Hoffman, and Albert, *Of Consuming Interests,* 233–51. Ann Smart Martin, *Buying into the World of Goods: Early Consumers in Backcountry Virginia* (Baltimore: Johns Hopkins University Press, 2008).

44. Bushman, "American High-Style and Vernacular Cultures," 373–76. The complicated process by which localities did or did not modernize is worked out with remarkable subtlety in Gilmore, *Reading Becomes a Necessity of Life.*

45. *Journal and Letters of Philip Vickers Fithian, 1773–1774: A Plantation Tutor of the Old Dominion,* Hunter Dickinson Farish, ed. (Williamsburg, Va.: Colonial Williamsburg, 1957), 33, 168; *Lower Norfolk County, Virginia, Antiquary* 5 (1906): 33–35n.

46. Nancy L. Struna, *People of Prowess: Sport, Leisure, and Labor in Early Anglo-America* (Urbana and Chicago: University of Illinois Press, 1996).

47. A. W. Coates, "Changing Attitudes to Labour in the Mid-Eighteenth Century," *Economic History Review,* 2nd ser., 11 (1958): 35–51; de Vries, *Industrious Revolution,* 40–185.

48. Harold J. Perkin, "The Social Causes of the British Industrial Revolution," *Transactions of the Royal Historical Society,* 5th ser., 18 (1968): 123–43; Jones, "The Fashion Manipulators," 210–16; Harold J. Perkin, *The Origins of Modern English Society, 1780–1880* (New York: Routledge & Kegan Paul, 1985), 73–98.

49. Joseph Harris, *An Essay upon Money and Coins* (n.p., 1757), pt. 1: 70. Until recently few questioned that Britain led the consumer world in the eighteenth century and that aristocratic France, by contrast, remained mired in tradition. Not so, argues Cissie Fairchilds in "A Comparison of the Consumer Revolutions in Britain and France" (paper presented to the Meeting of the Economic History Association, Boston, September 1992). Her research shows high levels of consumption of domestic amenities, clothing, and foodstuffs among town dwellers in France from 1680 to 1720. French peasants lagged behind prosperous English tenant farmers at first, but began catching up after 1730 or so.

50. Neil McKendrick, "The Commercialization of Fashion," in McKendrick, Brewer, and Plumb, *Birth of a Consumer Society,* 34–99.

51. McKendrick, "Commercialization of Fashion," 13–33; Neil McKendrick, "Home Demand and Economic Growth: A New View of the Role of Women and Children in the

Industrial Revolution," in Neil McKendrick, ed., *Historical Perspectives: Studies in English Thought and Society in Honour of J. H. Plumb* (London: Europa Publications, 1974), 152–210; Eversley, "Home Market and Economic Growth"; de Vries, *Industrious Revolution*, 12–18; Allen, *British Industrial Revolution in Global Perspective*, 14–16; Philip T. Hoffman, David Jacks, Patricia A. Levin, and Peter H. Lindert, "Real Inequality in Europe since 1500," *Journal of Economic History* 62 (2002): 322–55.

52. De Vries, *Industrious Revolution,* 73–121, 186–257; see also Gary S. Becker, "A Theory of the Allocation of Time," *Economic Journal* 75 (1965): 493–517, and Gary S. Becker and Robert T. Michael, "On the New Theory of Consumer Behavior," in Gary S. Becker, ed., *The Economic Approach to Human Behavior* (Chicago: University of Chicago Press, 1976), 131–49. For complicating evidence, see Mark Overton, et al., *Production and Consumption*, 33–121, 173–74.

53. Sir James Steuart, *An Inquiry into the Principles of Political Economy* (London, 1767), eds. Andrew F. Skinner, Noboru Kobayashi, and Hiroshi Mizuta (London: Pickering & Chatto, 1998), 53–54.

54. De Vries, *Industrious Revolution;* Jan de Vries, "Between Purchasing Power and the World of Goods: Understanding the Household Economy in Early Modern Europe," in Brewer and Porter, *Consumption and the World of Goods*, 114 (quote); McKendrick, "Home Demand and Economic Growth," 152–210.

55. Plumb, *Georgian Delights,* 10.

56. The causal relationships described here are clearly laid out in Carr and Walsh, "Changing Lifestyles and Consumer Behavior," in Carson, Hoffman, and Albert, *Of Consuming Interests,* 59–166. For regional studies, see S. Max Edelson, *Plantation Enterprise in Colonial South Carolina* (Cambridge, Mass.: Harvard University Press, 2006), 92–199; Lorena S. Walsh, *Motives of Honor, Pleasure, and Profit: Plantation Management in the Colonial Chesapeake, 1607–1763* (Chapel Hill: University of North Carolina Press, 2010), 201–50; and Lorena Walsh, "The Differential Cultural Impact of Free and Coerced Migration to Colonial America," in David Eltis, ed., *Coerced and Free Migration: Global Perspectives* (Stanford, Calif.: Stanford University Press, 2002), 117–51.

57. British Public Record Office [National Archives], C.O. 5/1330, Francis Fauquier, "Answers to the Queries Sent to Me by the Right Honourable the Lords Commissioners for Trade and Plantation Affairs," January 30, 1763.

58. Cary Carson, "Banqueting Houses and the 'Need of Society' among Slave-Owning Planters in the Chesapeake Colonies," *William and Mary Quarterly,* 3rd ser., 70 (2013): 725–80. The ownership of slaves itself became another trademark of gentility after 1700; see Eric Otremba, "Conspicuous Production: Slaves, Consumables, and Material Culture in the Chesapeake, 1710–1780," paper presented at Omohundro Institute of Early American History and Culture conference, "The Early Chesapeake: Reflections and Projections," Solomons Island and St. Mary's City, Maryland, November 19–21, 2009.

59. James A. Henretta, *The Evolution of American Society, 1700–1815: An Interdisciplinary Analysis* (Lexington, Mass.: Heath, 1973), chap. 2; John J. McCusker and Russell R. Menard, *The Economy of British America, 1607–1789* (Chapel Hill: University of North Carolina Press, 1991), chaps. 5, 9, 13; Carole Shammas, "Consumer Behavior in Colonial America," *Social Science History* 6, no. 1 (Winter 1982): 67–86; T. H. Breen, "An Empire of Goods: The Anglicization of Colonial America, 1690–1776," *Journal of British Studies* 25 (1986): 478–85; Winifred Barr Rothenberg, *From Market-Places to a Market Economy. The Transformation of Rural Massachusetts, 1750–1850* (Chicago: University of Chicago Press, 1992). Main and Main, "Economic Growth," 36–39, note that, while the economic experience of New Englanders varied widely by locality and their stock of assets fluctuated with ups and downs in the economy, the value of land and its improvements rose fairly steadily in the region as a whole. By comparison the value of consumer goods declined early in the eighteenth century and remained relatively constant thereafter. Notwithstanding, the Mains firmly believe that the volume of consumer goods increased and the makeup of these eighteenth-century household goods and personal possessions drove New Englanders' standards of living steadily higher.

60. McKendrick, "Home Demand and Economic Growth," 198; Lois Green Carr and Lorena S. Walsh second his statement in "The Standard of Living in the Colonial Chesapeake," *William and Mary Quarterly,* 3rd ser., 45 (1988): 142.

61. De Vries, "Between Purchasing Power and the World of Goods," 114.

62. Plumb, *Georgian Delights,* 10.

63. This part of my account draws on Neil McKendrick, "The Cultural Response to a Consumer Society: Coming to Terms with the Idea of Luxury in Eighteenth-Century England" (paper presented at a conference on comparative English and American social history sponsored by the Institute of Early American History and Culture, Williamsburg, September 1985).

64. This and the following quotation, cited by McKendrick in "Cultural Response to a Consumer Society" are from Fielding, *Enquiry into the Causes of the Late Increase in Robbers,* 3–4.

65. "The Prevalence of Luxury: With a Burgo-Master's Excellent Admonition against It," *Maryland Gazette,* March 9, 1748, cited in Micklus, "'The History of the Tuesday Club,'" 46.

66. Ferdinand Marie Bayard, *Travels of a Frenchman in Maryland and Virginia with a Description of Philadelphia and Baltimore in 1791,* trans. and ed. Ben C. McCary (Ann Arbor, Mich.: Edwards Brothers, 1950), 130.

67. *Boston Gazette,* January 18, 1773.

68. *Maryland Gazette,* December 23, 1746; *Gentleman's Progress: The Itinerarium of Dr. Alexander Hamilton, 1744,* ed. Carl Bridenbaugh (Chapel Hill: University of North Carolina Press, 1948), 54–55.

69. Harry Alonzo Cushing, ed., *The Writings of Samuel Adams,* 4 vols. (New York: G. Putnam, 1904–8), 4:31516. The letter to John Adams, written from Boston on July 2, 1785, lashed out against the "unmeaning & fantastick Extravagance" flaunted by the uppity poor. "You would be surprizd," the writer wagered, "to see the Equipage, the Furniture & expensive Living of too many, the Pride & Vanity of Dress which pervades thro every class."

70. Richard D. Brown, *Modernization: The Transformation of American Life, 1600–1865* (New York: Hill and Wang, 1976). Among writers on American material life, a thinly disguised modernization model has found favor with Deetz, *In Small Things Forgotten,* 36–43; Henry Glassie, *Folk Housing in Middle Virginia: A Structural Analysis of Historic Artifacts* (Knoxville: University of Tennessee Press, 1975), 88–113, 188–93; and some of their protégés. For a critical discussion of historians' uses and abuses of the modernization concept, see Christopher Lasch, "The Family and History," serialized in the *New York Review of Books,* November 13 and 27 and December 11, 1975.

2. Folk Consumers

1. J. Ambrose Raftis, *Tenure and Mobility: Studies in the Social History of the Medieval English Village* (Toronto: Pontifical Institute of Mediaeval Studies, 1964), 173–75; Edwin B. DeWindt, *Land and People in Holywell-cum-Needingworth [Huntingdonshire]: Structures of Tenure and Patterns of Social Organization in an East Midlands Village, 1252–1457* (Toronto: Pontifical Institute of Mediaeval Studies, 1972), 166–205; Rodney H. Hilton, *The English Peasantry in the Later Middle Ages* (Oxford: Clarendon Press, 1975), 15, 76–94; Keith Wrightson and David Levine, *Poverty and Piety in an English Village, Terling [Essex], 1525–1700* (New York: Academic Press, 1979), 73–91, 102–9; Peter McClure, "Patterns of Migration in the Late Middle Ages: The Evidence of English Place-Name Surnames," *Economic History Review,* 2nd ser., 32 (1979): 167–82; Ian D. Whyte, *Migration and Society in Britain, 1550–1830* (New York: St. Martin's Press, 2000), 22–48, 63–137.

2. Wrightson and Levine, *Poverty and Piety,* 74–82; Ann Kussmaul, *Servants in Husbandry in Early Modern England* (Cambridge: Cambridge University Press, 1981), 97–119.

3. Wrightson and Levine, *Poverty and Piety,* 82–109; Hilton, *English Peasantry,* 20–36; Keith Wrightson, *English Society, 15801680* (New Brunswick, N.J.: Rutgers University Press, 1982), 17–65.

4. Information about ordinary farmers' domestic furnishings is extraordinarily scarce before the mid-sixteenth century. The most revealing evidence is presented by R. K. Field, "Worcestershire Peasant Buildings, Household Goods, and Farming Equipment in the Later Middle Ages," *Medieval Archaeology* 9 (1965): 105–45, and discussed in Penelope

Eames, "Inventories as Sources of Evidence for Domestic Furnishings in the Fourteenth and Fifteenth Centuries," *Furniture History* 9 (1973): 33–40. On the absence of bedsteads, Eames concluded that either they were built-in or not inventoried, but the American evidence (see chapter 1, note 22 above) reopens the strong possibility that many ordinary men and women in England may have slept directly on the floor as colonists still were doing three hundred years after the Worcestershire survey was made. Christopher Dyer treats peasants' possessions in the context of *Standards of Living in the Later Middle Ages: Social Change in England, c. 1200–1500* (New York: Cambridge University Press, 1989), 160–77. See also Richard Bebb, *Welsh Furniture, 1250–1950: A Cultural History of Craftsmanship and Design*, 2 vols. (Kidwelly, Carmarthenshire, Wales: Saer Books, 2007), 1:118–21, 135–60; Nat Alcock, "A Medieval Kitchen," *Vernacular Architecture Group Newsletter* (1987): 6–7; Carole A. Morris, "Anglo-Saxon and Medieval Woodworking Crafts: The Manufacture and Use of Domestic and Utilitarian Wooden Artifacts in the British Isles, 400–1500 AD," DPhil diss., Cambridge University, 1984; Rosemary Weinstein, "Kitchen Chattels: The Evolution of Familiar Objects, 1200–1700," *Oxford Symposium on Food and Cookery, 1988 Proceedings: The Cooking Pot* (London, 1989), 168–82. Weinstein offers the useful reminder that medieval cookery and cookwares have a changing history too and that "by the 16th century the variety of wares had increased beyond useful classification, so much so that students consider the period ca. 1480–1500 a ceramic revolution" (171).

5. Linda Levy Peck demonstrates that this view is less true of royalty and the high aristocracy in Jacobean England in *Consuming Splendor: Society and Culture in Seventeenth-Century England* (Cambridge: Cambridge University Press, 2005).

6. Kathryn Davies, *Artisan Art: Vernacular Wall Paintings in the Welsh Marches, 1550–1650* (Little Logaston, Woonton, Almeley, Herefordshire, England: Logaston Press, 2008), 32–52, 114–22.

7. Randle Holme, *The Academy of Armory; or A Storehouse of Armory and Blazon*, 2 vols., ed. I. H. Jeayes (Chester, England, 1688; London: Roxburgh Club, 1905), 2: bk. 3, chap. 14, p. 14. The entire Ms. is reproduced on a CD-ROM in N. W. Alcock and Nancy Cox, *Living and Working in Seventeenth Century England: An Encyclopedia of Drawings and Descriptions from Randle Holme's Original Manuscripts for "The Academy of Armory"* (London: British Library, 2001). Holme compiled his manuscript before 1649.

8. This and the preceding discussion are the very original contributions of Penelope Eames, *Medieval Furniture: Furniture in England, France, and the Netherlands from the Twelfth to the Fifteenth Century* (London: Furniture History Society, 1977), and Penelope Eames, "Documentary Evidence Concerning the Character and Use of Domestic Furnishings in England in the Fourteenth and Fifteenth Centuries," *Furniture History* 7 (1971): 41–57. Eames's study of late medieval furniture and her interpretation of its meaning are important advances on the older but still useful Eric Mercer, *Furniture, 700–1700* (New York: Meredith Press, 1969).

9. Animism is poorly studied in English sources. What little is known has been said by Keith Thomas, *Religion and the Decline of Magic* (New York: Charles Scribner's Sons, 1971), 222–31, and Charles Pythian-Adams, *Local History and Folklore: A New Framework* (London: National Council of Social Service, 1975), 12–17. See also Peter Burke, *Popular Culture in Early Modern Europe* (New York: New York University Press, 1978). Jon Butler discusses the use of magical charms in American occult practices in *Awash in a Sea of Faith: Christianizing the American People* (Cambridge, Mass.: Harvard University Press, 1990), 72–74, and Mechal Sobel writes about the African American spirit world in *The World They Made Together: Black and White Values in Eighteenth-Century Virginia* (Princeton: Princeton University Press, 1987), 9698. On spiritualism in American folk pottery specifically, see John M. Vlach's chapter on African influences in face vessels from Edgefield, South Carolina, in Catherine Wilson Home, ed., *Crossroads of Clay: The Southern Alkaline-Glazed Tradition* (Columbia: McKissick Museum, University of South Carolina Press, 1990), 16–39.

10. Albeit reported by a European slaver who may or may not have understood what he saw; see Hugh Crow, *The Memoirs of Captain Hugh Crow: The Life and Times of a Slave Trade Captain,* intro. John Pinfold (Oxford: Bodleian Library, 2007), 155.

11. Robert Blair St. George discusses "architectural pathology" in old and New England in *Conversing by Signs: Politics of Implication in Colonial New England Culture* (Chapel Hill: University of North Carolina Press, 1998), 135–41. A curious assortment of horse bones excavated on a late seventeenth-century site in Virginia is interpreted as a possible talisman by William M. Kelso, *Kingsmill Plantations, 1619–1800: Archaeology of Country Life in Colonial Virginia* (Orlando, Fla.: Academic Press, Inc., 1984), 182–83. Amulets to "keep de witches away" are described in Theresa A. Singleton, "The Archaeology of Slave Life," in Edward D. C. Campbell Jr., ed., with Kym S. Rice, *Before Freedom Came: African-American Life in the Antebellum South* (Richmond and Charlottesville: Museum of the Confederacy and University Press of Virginia, 1991), 155–75, and Patricia Samford, "The Archaeology of African-American Slavery and Material Culture," *William and Mary Quarterly*, 3rd ser., 53 (1996): 107–10.

12. Proving the point, a genre painting by Dutch artist Pieter Aertsen pictures a large stoneware face jug prominently seated at table on a three-legged stool and enjoying the boisterous company of *Feestende boeren* [feasting peasants] in 1550 (coll. Kunsthistorisches Museum, Vienna, Austria; illustrated and discussed in Peter van der Coelen and Friso Lammertse, *De Ontdekking van het Dagelijks Leven van Bosch tot Bruegel* [Rotterdam, The Netherlands: Museum Boijmans van Beuningen, 2015], 178, 198).

13. Slipware harvest jug (1764), Barnstable, Devon, England (Colonial Williamsburg Foundation, Williamsburg, Virginia, acc. no. 1963-658). Vessels that use the personal pronoun should not be confused with a larger number that bear political slogans or repeat popular doggerel of the day. Ceramic collections surveyed for this chapter include

those at the Colonial Williamsburg Foundation, the Henry Francis du Pont Winterthur Museum, Winterthur, Delaware, and the Burnap Collection at the William Rockhill Nelson Gallery, Kansas City, Missouri. For specimens in tin-glazed earthenware see also Louis L. Lipski and Michael Archer, *Dated English Delftware: Tin-Glazed Earthenware, 1600–1800* (London: Sotheby Publications, 1984), esp. 228–34. Inscribed ceramics are preceded by a long line of English face jugs and figure vessels going back to the fourteenth century at least. See Ross E. Taggart, ed., *The Frank P. and Harriet C. Burnap Collection of English Pottery in the William Rockhill Nelson Gallery* (Kansas City, Mo.: Nelson-Atkins Gallery of Art, 1967), 17, nos. 1–2; John G. Hurst, David S. Neal, and H. J. E. van Beuningen, *Pottery Produced and Traded in North-West Europe, 1350–1650* (Rotterdam: Stichting Het Nederlandse Gebruiksvoorwerp, 1986), 93–94, 142–46, 210–21, 255; and Bernard Rackham, *Medieval English Pottery* (London: Faber and Faber, 1948). Puzzle jugs, fuddling cups, pitchers in the shape of cats, and other inscribed drinking vessels used in merrymaking were given a new lease on life by the tin-glazed potters who supplied both folk and up-scale markets in England and the colonies after 1600, according to Lipski and Archer, *Dated English Delftware,* 156–235.

14. Harvest jug (1764), Colonial Williamsburg Foundation; slip decorated puzzle jug (c. 1800), possibly Sussex, England (Nelson Gallery, acc. no. B-756 [BI. 33]).

15. Sgraffito harvest jug (1698), North Devon, England, possibly imported to and used in Sussex County, Delaware (Winterthur Museum, acc. no. 64.25) is illustrated (but the verse incorrectly transcribed) in C. Malcolm Watkins, *North Devon Pottery and Its Export to America in the 17th Century* (Washington, D.C.: Smithsonian Institution, 1960), 39.

16. J. D. Chambers, *Population, Economy, and Society in Pre-Industrial England* (Oxford: Oxford University Press, 1972); R. B. Outhwaite, *Inflation in Tudor and Stuart England* (London: Macmillan & Co., Ltd., 1969); Margaret Spufford, *Contrasting Communities: English Villages in the Sixteenth and Seventeenth Centuries* (Cambridge: Cambridge University Press, 1974); Kussmaul, *Servants in Husbandry*, 97–119; Nuala Zahedieh, "London and the Colonial Consumer in the Late Seventeenth Century," *Economic History Review* 47 (1994): 239–61.

17. Immanuel Wallerstein, *The Modern World System: Capitalist Agriculture and the Origins of the European World-Economy in the Sixteenth Century,* 2 vols. (New York: Academic Press, 1974–80), 1: esp. chaps. 5–6.

18. Alan Everitt, "Social Mobility in Early Modern England," *Past and Present* 33 (1966): 56–73, deals with geographical mobility as well; Julian Cornwall, "Evidence of Population Mobility in the Seventeenth Century," *Bulletin of the Institute of Historical Research* 40 (1967): 143–52; John H. C. Patten, *Rural-Urban Migration in Pre-Industrial England* (Oxford: Oxford University Press, 1973); Peter Laslett, "Clayworth and Cogenhoe," in Peter Laslett, ed., *Family Life and Illicit Love in Earlier Generations* (Cambridge:

Cambridge University Press, 1977), 50101; E. A. Wrigley and R. S. Schofield, *The Population History of England, 1541–1871: A Reconstruction* (Cambridge, Mass.: Harvard University Press, 1981), 219–28; David Souden, "Migrants and the Population Structure of Later Seventeenth-Century Provincial Cities and Market Towns," in Peter Clark, ed., *The Transformation of English Provincial Towns, 1600–1800* (London: Hutchinson, 1984), 133–68; Peter Clark and David Souden, eds., *Migration and Society in Early Modern England* (Totowa, N.J.: Barnes & Noble Books, 1987).

19. Introduction to Clark and Souden, *Migration and Society,* 28–38, and Clark's essay in that volume, "Migration in England during the Late Seventeenth and Early Eighteenth Centuries," 213–52.

20. Bernard Bailyn, *The Peopling of British North America: An Introduction* (New York: Alfred A. Knopf, 1986), 24, is my source of information for estimates of London's population and the other figures cited in the following discussion, although even more recently calculated population estimates for sixteenth-century London are presented in Steven Rappaport, *Worlds within Worlds: Structures of Life in Sixteenth-Century London* (Cambridge: Cambridge University Press, 1989), 61–86. Also see Lawrence Stone, "Social Mobility in England, 1500–1700," *Past and Present* 33 (1966): 16–55, esp. 29–33, for population movement to towns, and 51–55 for the rise of a "pseudo-gentry" who prefixed their names with "Mr."

21. Bailyn, *Peopling of British North America,* chap. 1; David W. Galenson, *White Servitude in Colonial America: An Economic Analysis* (Cambridge: Cambridge University Press, 1981); David Souden, "'Rogues, Whores, and Vagabonds'? Indentured Servant Emigration to North America and the Case of Mid-Seventeenth-Century Bristol," in Clark and Souden, *Migration and Society,* 150–71; Bernard Bailyn, *Voyagers to the West: A Passage in the Peopling of America on the Eve of the Revolution* (New York: Alfred A. Knopf, 1986); Bernard Bailyn, "From Protestant Peasants to Jewish Intellectuals: The Germans in the Peopling of America," *German Historical Institute Annual Lecture Series* 1 (Oxford, Hamburg, and New York: Berg Publishers, 1988), 1–12; Henry A. Gemery, "Emigration from the British Isles to the New World, 1630–1700: Inference from Colonial Populations," *Research in Economic History* 5 (1980): 179–213; and Henry A. Gemery, "European Emigration to North America, 1700–1820: Numbers and Quasi-Numbers," *Perspectives in American History,* new ser., 1 (1984): 283–342.

22. [Janet Schaw], *Journal of a Lady of Quality,* eds. Evangeline Walker Andrews and Charles M. Andrews (New Haven: Yale University Press, 1921), 185. The year was 1775.

23. Gemery, "European Emigration," table 3, pp. 303, 317–20; Galenson, *White Servitude,* table H.3, pp. 216–17; John J. McCusker and Russell R. Menard, *The Economy of British America, 1607–1789* (Chapel Hill: University of North Carolina Press, 1991), fig. 10.2, p. 220. The consumption indicators are discussed below.

24. Neil McKendrick, "Commercialization of Fashion," in Neil McKendrick, John Brewer, and J. H. Plumb, eds., *The Birth of a Consumer Society: The Commercialization of Eighteenth-Century England* (Bloomington: Indiana University Press, 1982), 34–42. Neil McKendrick, "Home Demand and Economic Growth: A New View of the Role of Women and Children in the Industrial Revolution," in Neil McKendrick, ed., *Historical Perspectives: Studies in English Thought and Society in Honour of J. H. Plumb* (London: Europa Publications, 1974), 197–98, borrows its argument from Joan Thirsk, "The Fantastical Folly of Fashion: The English Stocking Knitting Industry, 1500–1700," in N. B. Harte and K. G. Ponting, eds., *Textile History and Economic History* (Manchester: Manchester University Press, 1973), 50–73. Fashion in clothing is Grant McCracken's starting point in *Culture and Consumption: New Approaches to the Symbolic Character of Consumer Goods and Activities* (Bloomington and Indianapolis: Indiana University Press, 1990), 11–16. See also F. J. Fisher, "The Development of London as a Center of Conspicuous Consumption in the Sixteenth and Seventeenth Centuries," *Transactions of the Royal Historical Society*, 4th ser., 30 (1948): 37–50, and Alan Hunt, *Governance of the Consuming Passions: A History of Sumptuary Law* (New York: St. Martin's Press, 1996). American sumptuary legislation is discussed in Patricia Trautman, "When Gentlemen Wore Lace: Sumptuary Legislation and Dress in Seventeenth-Century New England," *Journal of Regional Cultures* 2 (1983): 9–21.

25. Phillip Stubbes, *The Anatomie of Abuses*, 4th ed. (London, 1595), 9–10.

26. Susan M. Kingsbury, ed., *The Records of the Virginia Company of London*, 4 vols. (Washington, D.C.: Government Printing Office, 1906–35), 3:221; Lyon Gardiner Tyler, ed., *Narratives of Early Virginia* (New York: Barnes & Noble, Inc., 1907), 285. John Pory was equally scandalized to report that "our cowekeeper here of James citty on Sundays goes accowtered all in freshe flaming silke" (ibid.).

27. Ivor Noël Hume and Audrey Noël Hume, *The Archaeology of Martin's Hundred*, Part I: Interpretive Studies (Philadelphia: University of Pennsylvania Museum of Archaeology and Anthropology, and Williamsburg, Va.: Colonial Williamsburg Foundation, 2001), 178–79.

28. Quoted in Alice Morse Earle, *Two Centuries of Costume in America, 1620–1820*, 2 vols. (New York and London: Macmillan & Co., Inc., 1903), 1:61.

29. William Vaughan, *The Golden Grove* (London, 1600), n.p.

30. Discussed in Thirsk, "Folly of Fashion," 55–60, and Joan Thirsk, *Economic Policy and Projects: The Development of a Consumer Society in Early Modern England* (Oxford: Clarendon Press, 1978), 106–32.

31. Neil McKendrick, "Josiah Wedgwood and the Commercialization of the Potteries," and "George Packwood and the Commercialization of Sharing: The Art of Eighteenth-Century Advertising; or, 'The Way to Get Money and Be Happy,'" in McKendrick, Brewer,

and Plumb, *Birth of a Consumer Society,* 99–194; Robin Reilly, *Josiah Wedgwood, 1730–1795* (London: Macmillan, 1992), 202–25.

32. Alan Macfarlane, *The Origins of English Individualism: The Family, Property, and Social Transition* (Oxford: Blackwell, 1978). A review by Lawrence Stone in the *New York Review of Books,* April 19, 1979, drew the battle lines for the fracas that followed.

33. C. B. Macpherson, *The Political Theory of Possessive Individualism: Hobbes to Locke* (Oxford: Oxford University Press, 1962), 46–70. Joyce Oldham Appleby discusses the clash of interests and philosophies between old-fashioned mercantilists who saw England as a giant workhouse and a new breed who viewed the economy as an aggregation of self-interested individual producer-consumers in "Ideology and Theory: The Tension between Political and Economic Liberalism in Seventeenth-Century England," *American Historical Review* 81 (1976): 499–515, and *Economic Thought and Ideology in Seventeenth-Century England* (Princeton: Princeton University Press, 1978).

34. The practice descended the social scale in the eighteenth and nineteenth centuries as consumer habits invaded traditional communities and as ethnic subgroups accommodated their material culture to mainstream English taste. For examples in many media, see Scott T. Swank et al., *Arts of the Pennsylvania Germans* (New York: Norton, 1983).

35. My confidence in these unsupported statements comes from many years of fieldwork recording English and American vernacular buildings and from observations drawn from the study of museum collections. It remains for someone to do a systematic frequency distribution study of dated and personalized buildings and domestic artifacts in Britain and America. For vernacular buildings their model should be Linda J. Hall, *The Rural Houses of North Avon and South Gloucestershire, 1400–1720,* (Bristol, England: City Museum and Art Gallery, 1983), 87–93. For initialed and dated American furniture, see Laurel Ulrich, "Hannah Barnard's Cupboard," in *The Age of Homespun: Objects and Stories in the Creation of an American Myth* (New York: Alfred A. Knopf, 2001), 108–41; Patricia E. Kane, "The Seventeenth-Century Furniture of the Connecticut Valley: The Hadley Chest Reappraised," in Ian M. G. Quimby, ed., *Arts of the Anglo-American Community in the Seventeenth Century* (Charlottesville: University Press of Virginia, 1975), 79–122; and Patricia E. Kane, "The Joiners of Seventeenth-Century Hartford County," *Connecticut Historical Society Bulletin* 35 (1970): 82–85. The practice of personalizing furniture is discussed briefly in [Barbara McLean Ward et al.], *A Place for Everything: Chests and Boxes in Early Colonial America* (Winterthur, Del.: H. F. du Pont Winterthur Museum, 1986), 5–7.

36. Locked chests became an obsession for Virginia planters who shared their dwellings with an ever-changing population of indentured servants and slaves. Inventory takers in York County, Virginia, for instance, meticulously recorded trunks and chests with locks and keys. See York County Deeds, Orders, Wills, 1–6 (1637–84), Virginia State Library, Richmond.

37. Henrico County Deeds, Orders, Wills, 2 (1678–93), Virginia State Library inventory (1677/8) of Col. William Farrar, f. 51.

38. Slipware bottle (1752), Staffordshire (Colonial Williamsburg Foundation, acc. no. 1952–408); posset bowl (1720), England (Nelson Gallery, acc. no. B675 [BI. 1231); slipware harvest jug (1764), Devon (Colonial Williamsburg Foundation).

39. Francis Markham, *The Booke of Honour* (London, 1625), 8.

3. New Consumers

1. Robert Blair St. George, "'Set Thine House in Order': The Domestication of the Yeomanry in Seventeenth-Century New England," in Jonathan L. Fairbanks and Robert F. Trent, eds., *New England Begins: The Seventeenth Century,* 3 vols. (Boston: Museum of Fine Arts, 1982), 2:162–63. The practice lasted into the nineteenth century in many parts of New England; see Thomas C. Hubka, *Big House, Little House, Back House, Barn: The Connected Farm Buildings of New England* (Hanover, N.H.: University Press of New England, 1984) and J. Ritchie Garrison, *Two Carpenters: Architecture and Building in Early New England, 1799–1859* (Knoxville: University of Tennessee Press, 2006).

2. Cary Carson and Carl R. Lounsbury, eds., *The Chesapeake House: Architectural Investigation by Colonial Williamsburg* (Chapel Hill, University of North Carolina Press, 2013), 86–114, 179–203.

3. Durand de Dauphiné, *A Huguenot Exile in Virginia,* ed. Gilbert Chinard (New York: The Press of the Pioneers, Inc., 1934), 119–20.

4. Quoted in Cary Carson, Norman F. Barka, William M. Kelso, Garry Wheeler Stone, and Dell Upton, "Impermanent Architecture in the Southern American Colonies," *Winterthur Portfolio* 16 (1981): 146, 153.

5. When T. H. Breen writes that historians "can only speculate about the motivation of the colonial buyer," he is dealing with consumer psychology on a personal level, that is, "each person entered the market for slightly different reasons." He reaches for a deeper explanation when he goes on to say, "In addition, consumer goods provided socially mobile Americans with boundary markers, an increasingly recognized way to distinguish betters from their inferiors, for . . . in whatever group one traveled . . . one knew that consumer goods mediated social status" ("An Empire of Goods: The Anglicization of Colonial America, 1690–1776," *Journal of British Studies* 25 [1986]: 495–96).

6. The first fashionable buildings in North America (as I am using that term here) appeared in Boston and Virginia in the 1660s and 1670s and made no inroads on vernacular building tradition for another generation. See Abbott Lowell Cummings, "The Beginnings of Provincial Renaissance Architecture in Boston, 1690–1725," *Journal of the Society of Architectural Historians* 42 (1983): 43–53, and Cary Carson, "Banqueting

Houses and the 'Need of Society' among Slave-Owning Planters in the Chesapeake Colonies," *William and Mary Quarterly*, 3rd ser., 70 (2013): 725–80.

7. Dramatically demonstrated by Robert Blair St. George in ratios showing furniture value per square foot of floor space in Fairbanks and Trent, *New England Begins*, 2:171–72. Parlor furniture was worth almost two and a half times as much as the next best furnished rooms in the Dedham and Saugus houses he studied.

8. Abbott Lowell Cummings, ed., *Rural Household Inventories [Suffolk, Massachusetts]: Establishing the Names, Uses, and Furnishings of Rooms in the Colonial New England House, 1625–1775* (Boston: Society for the Preservation of New England Antiquities, 1964), 62–64.

9. Actually John Weld kept another, even more valuable, featherbed and a chest of drawers filled with sheets and napkins in his kitchen chamber, an atypical arrangement that might be explained if we could identify all the inmates of the house.

10. This statement and the following general account of household furniture draw on a remarkable body of scholarship by Benno M. Forman and several exceptional students he trained at the Winterthur Museum. Their work, in which connoisseurship is informed by historical research and which I borrow from here, usually without further citation, includes Benno M. Forman, *American Seating Furniture, 1630–1730* (New York: W. W. Norton, 1988); Benno Forman, "The Chest of Drawers in America, 1635–1730: The Origins of the Joined Chest of Drawers," *Winterthur Portfolio* 20 (1985): 1–30; Robert F. Trent, "The Chest of Drawers in America, 1635–1730: A Postscript," *Winterthur Portfolio* 20 (1985): 31–48; Benno M. Forman, "Furniture for Dressing in Early America, 1650–1730: Forms, Nomenclature, and Use," *Winterthur Portfolio* 22 (1987): 149–64; Robert F. Trent, "New England Joinery and Turning before 1700," in Fairbanks and Trent, *New England Begins*, 3:501–50. The approach they follow and many of their ideas about contemporary uses of furniture were borrowed from the work of English and European curators and architectural historians, superbly brought together in Peter Thornton, *Seventeenth-Century Interior Decoration in England, France, and Holland* (New Haven: Yale University Press, 1978). Recent works no less rigorous in their scholarship include Adam Bowett, *English Furniture 1660–1714: From Charles II to Queen Anne* (Woodbridge, England: Antiques Collectors' Club, 2002), and *American Furniture in the Metropolitan Museum of Art*, 2 vols., Vol. I: *Early Colonial Period: The Seventeenth-Century and William and Mary Styles* by Frances Gruber Safford (New York: Metropolitan Museum of Art, 2007). See also Reinier Baarsen, Gervase Jackson-Stops, Philip M. Johnson, and Elaine Evans Dee, *Courts and Colonies: The William and Mary Style in Holland, England, and America* (New York: Cooper-Hewitt Museum, 1988), 12–61.

11. Robert F. Trent, "The Concept of Mannerism," in Fairbanks and Trent, *New England Begins*, 3:368–79; Trent, "New England Joinery," 504–6; Martha H. Willoughby,

"Patronage in Early Salem: The Symonds Shops and Their Customers," *American Furniture* (2000): 169–84; Robert F. Trent, Peter Follansbee, and Alan Miller, "First Flowers of the Wilderness: Mannerist Furniture from a Northern Essex County, Massachusetts, Shop," *American Furniture* (2001): 1–64. Joseph Manca, a specialist in Italian Renaissance painting and interiors, challenged the conventional wisdom that north European and American seventeenth-century furniture should be considered mannerist at all in "A Matter of Style: The Question of Mannerism in Seventeenth-Century American Furniture," *Winterthur Portfolio* 15 (2003): 1–36. For a closely reasoned and persuasive rebuttal, see Glenn Adamson, "Mannerism in Early American Furniture: Connoisseurship, Intention, and Theatricality," *American Furniture* (2005): 22–62.

12. Robert Blair St. George, "Style and Structure in the Joinery of Dedham and Medfield, Massachusetts, 1635–1685," *Winterthur Portfolio* 13 (1979): 1–46, esp. 20–24; Robert Blair St. George, *The Wrought Covenant: Source Material for the Study of Craftsmen and Community in Southeastern New England, 1620–1700* (Brockton, Mass.: Brockton Art Center-Fuller Memorial, 1979), fig. 41a; Robert Tarule, *The Artisan of Ipswich: Craftsmanship and Community in Colonial New England* (Baltimore: Johns Hopkins University Press, 2004), 114–24.

13. David Pye, *The Nature and Art of Workmanship* (Cambridge: Cambridge University Press, 1968), 13–24; Trent, "New England Joinery," 504–5. Not all early furniture made in the colonies was designed pro forma. Robert Trent et al. illustrate a number of unique pieces in the mannerist style made for members of the Puritan gentry in Massachusetts in "First Flowers of the Wilderness," 1–2, passim.

14. Benno Forman describes how ideas about style traveled from one country to another in "The Chest of Drawers," 13. For the no less complex process by which design ideas developed locally, see the insightful work of Richard Bebb, *Welsh Furniture, 1250–1950: A Cultural History of Craftsmanship and Design,* 2 vols. (Kidwelly, Carmarthenshire, Wales: Saer Books, 2007), 2:379–419, especially the section on "The Craftsman-Customer Relationship in the Pre-Industrial Period," 402–6.

15. Adamson, "Mannerism in Early American Furniture," especially the part subtitled "The Theatricality of Anglo-American Furniture," 38–58.

16. This is as much "social learning theory" as I will burden readers with here. For more, see Peter J. Richerson and Robert Boyd, *Not By Genes Alone: How Culture Transformed Human Evolution* (Chicago: University of Chicago Press, 2004); Stephen J. Shennan, *Genes, Memes and Human History: Darwinian Archaeology and Cultural Evolution* (London: Thames and Hudson, 2002); Stephen J. Shennan, "Culture Transmission and Culture Change," in Sander E. van der Leeuw and Robin Torrence, eds., *What's New? A Closer Look at the Process of Innovation* (New York: Unwin Hyman, 1989), 330–46. See also Tibor Scitovsky, *The Joyless Economy* (Oxford: Oxford University Press, 1976, rev. ed. 1992), 74, 225.

17. John L. Cotter, *Archaeological Excavations at Jamestown, Virginia* (Washington, D.C.: National Park Service, U.S. Department of the Interior, 1959), 188; John L. Cotter and J. Paul Hudson, *New Discoveries at Jamestown* (Washington, D.C.: National Park Service, U.S. Department of the Interior, 1957), 44–45; Anne Dowling Grulich, *Façon de Venise Drinking Vessels on the Chresapeake Frontier: Examples from St. Mary's City, Maryland* (St. Mary's City, Md.: Historic St. Mary's City, 2004).

18. Illustrated in Cotter, *Archaeological Excavations at Jamestown,* 183, but correctly identified and knowledgeably discussed in Ivor Noël Hume, *Here Lies Virginia: An Archaeologist's View of Colonial Life and History* (New York: Knopf, 1963), 289 and figs. 20, 121, and Ivor Noël Hume, "Rhenish Grey Stonewares in Colonial America," *Antiques* 92 (1967): 349–53 and fig. 2. The jugs were half a century old when they were finally broken and the pieces thrown away in an archaeological context of c. 1650–60. For more recent information, including an additional fragment excavated inside Jamestown Fort, see Beverly Straube, "European Ceramics in the New World: The Jamestown Example," in *Ceramics in America* (2001): 64–68. See also Janine E. Skerry and Suzanne Findlan Hood, *Salt-Glazed Stoneware in Early America* (Williamsburg, Va.: Colonial Williamsburg Foundation, 2009), 7–64.

19. Trent, "Concept of Mannerism," 377, and Joy Kenseth, "A World of Wonders in One Closet Shut," in Joy Kenseth, ed., *The Age of the Marvelous* (Hanover, N.H.: Hood Museum of Art, Dartmouth College, 1991), 81–101 and entries 29–39. Such objects were owned in the neighborhood of Jamestown—for example, William Hughes's "small black jack [a leather tankard] tipp'd with Silver" (York County Deeds, Orders, Wills, 3 [1657–62], ff.154, inventory dated 1661, Virginia State Library, Richmond). Hughes was a planter and a merchant.

20. York County Deeds, Orders, Wills, 3, ff.77, inventory (1659) of Francis Wheeler, a merchant, Virginia State Library, Richmond. The can was valued at £3 l0s. A remarkable Höhrware presentation piece, a large jug bearing a portrait of William III, was excavated on the site of Westwood Manor, Charles County, Maryland, occupied in the 1680s and 1690s by John Baynes, a "merchant of London"; see "The Westwood Manor Archaeological Collection, Preliminary Interpretations," report prepared by Archaeology Practicum Class, St. Mary's College of Maryland (2010), 86, fig. 45. Excavations on Richard John's late seventeenth-century plantation in Calvert County, the Angelica Knoll site (18CV60), produced shards from a similar vessel; see Robert A. Elder Jr.'s report in *Maryland Archeology* 27 (1991): 1–47.

21. William M. Kelso, *Kingsmill Plantations, 1619–1800: Archaeology of Country Life in Colonial Virginia* (Orlando, Fla.: Academic Press, Inc., 1984), 183 and fig. 129; Julia B. Curtis, "Chinese Ceramics and the Dutch Connection in Early Seventeenth-Century Virginia," *Vereniging van Vrienden der Asiatische Kunst* 15 (1985): 6–13; Cotter, *Archaeological Excavations at Jamestown,* 182–85; Cotter and Hudson, *New Discoveries at Jamestown,* 34–45; Henry M. Miller, *Discovering Maryland's First City: A Summary Report on*

the 1981–1984 Archaeological Excavations in St. Mary's City, Maryland (St. Mary's City, Md.: Historic St. Mary's City, 1986), 16–18, 61, 83–92, and 111–13; Ivor Noël Hume, *A Guide to Artifacts of Colonial America* (New York: Knopf, 1970), is full of accurately dated specimens, but it does not always name the American sites where similar shards have been found; C. Malcolm Watkins, "Ceramics in the Seventeenth-Century English Colonies," in Ian M. G. Quimby, ed., *Arts of the Anglo-American Community in the Seventeenth Century* (Charlottesville: University Press of Virginia, 1975), 275–99; Alaric Faulkner and Gretchen Fearon Faulkner, *The French at Pentagoet, 1635–1674: An Archaeological Portrait of the Acadian Frontier* (Augusta: Maine Historic Preservation Commission, 1987), 196–97, 208–16, 237–42; James A. Tuck and Barry Gaulton illustrate one of two tall, goblet-like, Portuguese-made presentation pieces (1638–c. 1650) excavated on the site of Sir David Kirke's Ferryland colony in "*Terra Sigillata* from a Seventeenth-Century Settlement in Newfoundland," *Ceramics in America* (2002): 202–4, fig. 3.

22. York County Deeds, Orders, and Wills, 3, ff. 23, inventory (1657) of Gyles Mode, a planter and physician, Virginia State Library, Richmond.

23. The following discussion takes its facts from Forman, "Furniture for Dressing," 149–60. Closely parallel developments in English upper-class circles are summarized in Edward T. Joy, *Getting Dressed* (London: H.M.S.O., 1981), 8–27. The earliest English publication devoted exclusively to cosmetics was *Beauties Treasury; or, The Ladies Vade Mecum* (London, 1705). Recipes for facial preparations had been included in numerous cookbooks since the 1660s.

24. The earliest dated delftware barber bowl is 1681; see Louis L. Lipski and Michael Archer, *Dated English Delftware: Tin-Glazed Earthenware, 1600–1800* (London: Sotheby Publications, 1984), 295.

25. To earlier generations grooming meant shaving and beard trimming for men and haircuts for both sexes, but seldom the application of facial cosmetics. Early inventories are likely to list looking glasses in association with razors, scissors, combs, and wash bowls, the whole kit occasionally described as a "barbers case with some instruments and a small looking glasse to it." See York County [Virginia] Deeds, Orders, Wills, 3, ff. 23–24, 69, 135, inventories of Hugh Stanford (1657), John Goslings (1658), Thomas Bucke (1659), and John Heyward (1661), Virginia State Library, Richmond.

26. Ethan W. Lasser argues in "Reading Japanned Furniture," *American Furniture* (2007): 168–90, that merchants and sea captains were often the intended audience for high-fashion japanned and varnished chests of drawers and looking glasses sometimes found en suite in townhouse parlors in the decades after 1700.

27. Cummings, *Rural Household Inventories*, 54–57, inventory of John Bowles (1691).

28. Quoted in Forman, "Furniture for Dressing," 158.

29. For most of what follows, see Forman, "The Chest of Drawers," 1–17. In the Netherlands clothing formerly kept in chests began being stored more conveniently on shelves

inside *kasten* about 1600; see Reinier Baarsen *Furniture in Holland's Golden Age* (Amsterdam: Rijksmuseum and Nieuw Amsterdam, 2007), 21–23.

30. No chests are listed in rural Suffolk County, Massachusetts, garrets or cellars until after 1700, then with increasing frequency throughout the eighteenth century; see [Barbara McLean Ward et al.], *A Place for Everything: Chests and Boxes in Early Colonial America* (Winterthur, Del.: H. F. du Pont Winterthur Museum, 1986), 6.

31. Lorna Weatherill, "Consumer Behavior, Textiles, and Dress in the Late Seventeenth Century and Early Eighteenth Centuries," in N. B. Harte, ed., *Fabrics and Fashion: Studies in the Economic and Social History of Dress* (London: Pasold Research Fund, 1991), 297–310; Beverley Lemire, "Transforming Consumer Custom: Linens, Cottons and the English Market, 1660–1800," in Brenda Collins and Philip Ollerenshaw, eds., *The European Linen Industry in Historical Perspective* (Oxford: Oxford University Press, 2003), 187–207; and Beverley Lemire, "Fashioning Cottons; Asian trade, Domestic Industry and Consumer Demand, 1660–1780," in David T. Jenkins, ed., *The Cambridge History of Western Textiles*, vol. 1 (Cambridge: Cambridge University Press, 2003), 493–512.

32. Testamentary Proceedings, 3:127–59, Maryland State Archives, Annapolis, inventory of Capt. William Smith (1668). Smith, though a wealthy innkeeper, leased a residence formerly owned by the governor of the colony. York County Deeds, Orders, Wills, 4 (1665–68), ff. 212–13, 230, inventories of Adam Miles (1668) and John Hubberd (1667), Virginia State Library, Richmond. Hubberd was a merchant and Miles may have dabbled in trade. Both chests of drawers were valued at £1 10s.

33. Wash basins developed wide rims to prevent water damage to the wooden stands they stood on or nested into. The earliest dated example of an improved wash basin in delftware is 1680 (Lipski and Archer, *Dated English Delftware*, 297).

34. *The Journeys of Celia Fiennes,* ed. Christopher Morris (London and New York: Cresset Press, 1949), 154. Fiennes was visiting Chippenham Park, Cambridgeshire, in 1698.

35. Jonathan L. Fairbanks, "Portrait Painting in Seventeenth-Century Boston: Its History, Methods, and Materials," in Fairbanks and Trent, *New England Begins,* 3:413–79; Margaretta M. Lovell, *Art in a Season of Revolution: Painters, Artisans, and Patrons in Early America* (Philadelphia: University of Pennsylvania Press, 2005), 8–25; Carolyn J. Weekley, *Painters and Paintings in the Early American South* (New Haven: Yale University Press and Colonial Williamsburg Foundation, 2013), 63–124.

36. John Elsum, *The Art of Painting After the Italian Manner* (London, 1704), 9.

37. Quoted in Fairbanks, "Portrait Painting in Boston," 413, 421.

38. York County Deeds, Orders, Wills, 3, ff.108, inventory of Lt. Col. Thomas Ludlowe (1660), Virginia State Library, Richmond. Among the earliest surviving paintings are those of John Winthrop (English portrait and miniature imported 1630), Puritan

divine Dr. William Ames (Dutch portrait imported by his widow 1637), Gov. Pieter Stuyvesant (several family portraits painted in Breda and imported to New Amsterdam 1647), Gov. Edward Winslow (portrait painted on a return visit to London in 1651), and the Rev. Increase Mather (portrait by a Dutch painter working in London for whom Mather sat on a trip to England in 1688). See Fairbanks and Trent, *New England Begins,* 1:10–13, 2:157–58, 304–6, 3:413–15, 455; Edgar Preston Richardson, *Painting in America: The Story of 450 Years* (New York: Crowell, 1956), 25. Wayne Craven dates the earliest locally painted portraits in Virginia to the 1690s in *Colonial American Portraiture: The Economic, Religious, Social, Cultural, Philosophical, Scientific, and Aesthetic Foundations* (Cambridge, Mass.: Harvard University Press, 1986), 178–95. See also Richard H. Saunders, "The Portrait in America, 1700–1750," in Richard H. Saunders and Ellen G. Miles, *American Colonial Portraits, 1700–1776* (Washington: Smithsonian Institution Press, 1987), 1–27.

39. Valerie Steele, "Appearance and Identity," in Claudia Brush Kidwell and Valerie Steel, eds., *Men and Women: Dressing the Part* (Washington, D.C.: Smithsonian Institution Press, 1989), 6–22.

40. Fairbanks and Trent, *New England Begins,* 3:420–21; Richardson, *Painting in America,* 30–48; Graham Hood, *Charles Bridges and William Dering: Two Virginia Painters, 1735–1750* (Williamsburg, Va.: Colonial Williamsburg Foundation, 1978); Lovell, *Art in a Season of Revolution.*

41. T. H. Breen, "The Meaning of 'Likeness': American Portrait-Painting in an Eighteenth-Century Consumer Society," in Ellen G. Miles, ed., *The Portrait in Eighteenth-Century America* (Newark: University of Delaware Press, 1993), 37–60. For an insightful case study of a portraitist and his sitters in republican America, see Richard L. Bushman, "Portraiture and Society in Late Eighteenth-Century Connecticut," in Elizabeth Mankin Kornhauser et al., *Ralph Earl: The Face of the Young Republic* (New Haven: Yale University Press for the Wadsworth Atheneum, 1991), 69–83.

42. Kathleen M. Brown, *Foul Bodies: Cleanliness in Early America* (New Haven: Yale University Press, 2009), 98–158. Richard L. Bushman and Claudia L. Bushman, "The Early History of Cleanliness in America," *Journal of American History* 74 (1988): 1213–38; Richard L. Bushman, *The Refinement of America: Persons, Houses, Cities* (New York: Alfred A. Knopf, 1992), 39–46, 61–78.

43. Forman, "Furniture for Dressing," 159–60.

44. Sir Henry Wotten, *The Elements of Architecture* (London, 1624; modern reprint of 1651 ed., Springfield, Mass.: F.A. Bassette Co., n.d.), 271. Philip Zea used the theater motif to good effect in organizing the inaugural exhibition of the Flynt Center of Early New England Life at Historic Deerfield, Massachusetts, and in the book it inspired, *Useful Improvements, Innumerable Temptations: Pursuing Refinement in Rural New England, 1750–1850* (Deerfield, Mass.: Historic Deerfield, Inc., 1998).

4. Fashion Performed

1. Identified in Jonathan L. Fairbanks and Robert F. Trent, eds., *New England Begins: The Seventeenth Century,* 3 vols. (Boston: Museum of Fine Arts, 1982), 2:279–80, and discussed p. 377.

2. Ivor Noël Hume, *A Guide to Artifacts of Colonial America* (New York: Knopf, 1970), 184–92.

3. Dwight P. Lanmon, *The Golden Age of English Glass, 1650–1775* (Woodbridge, Suffolk, England: Antique Collectors' Club, 2011). The origins of the lead-crystal industry in England are summarized in Christine MacLeod, "Accident or Design? George Ravencroft's Patent and the Invention of Lead-Crystal Glass," *Technology and Culture* 28 (1987): 776–803. For table glass used in Virginia, see Ivor Noël Hume, *Glass in Colonial Williamsburg's Archaeological Collections* (Williamsburg, Va.: Colonial Williamsburg, 1969), 9–28.

4. Both techniques are shown, for example, in Godfrey Kneller's portrait of the Duke of Newcastle (c. 1718), illustrated in G. Bernard Hughes, *English, Scottish and Irish Table Glass from the Sixteenth Century to 1820* (London: B. T. Batsford, 1956), fig. 32. An overmantel painting (c. 1750) from the Moses Marcy House, Southridge, Massachusetts, pictures a complacent New England merchant raising a celebratory glass in proper genteel fashion (Old Sturbridge Village, Sturbridge, Mass., acc. no. 20.19.1).

5. *Journal and Letters of Philip Vickers Fithian, 1773–1774: A Plantation Tutor of the Old Dominion,* Hunter Dickinson Farish, ed. (Williamsburg, Va.: Colonial Williamsburg, 1957), 138.

6. *William Fitzhugh and His Chesapeake World, 1676–1701: The Fitzhugh Letters and Other Documents,* ed. Richard Beale Davis (Chapel Hill: University of North Carolina Press, 1963), 244–46, 249–50, 258–59, 382.

7. Peter Thornton, *Seventeenth-Century Interior Decoration in England, France, and Holland* (New Haven: Yale University Press, 1978), 391n13. He describes the use of monteiths on p. 284.

8. Thomas Blount, *Glossographia; A Dictionary, Interpreting All ... Words .. Now Used in Our Refined English Tongue,* 2nd ed. (London, 1661), s.v. "Salver." A recipe for "Taking Spots and Stains Out of Garments, Linnen, etc." was important enough to include in *The Family Dictionary; or, Household Companion*, published in London in 1605.

9. Mark R. Wenger sets Fitzhugh's table in "The Dining Room in Early Virginia," in Thomas Carter and Bernard L. Herman, eds., *Perspectives in Vernacular Architecture* 3 (Columbia, Mo.: Vernacular Architecture Forum, 1989): 149–59, although he draws somewhat different conclusions from mine.

10. William Cobbett, *Rural Rides* (London: Letchworth, 1932), 192.

11. Despite much recent interest in culinary history, little has been written about common people's table customs before the eighteenth century. Until recently the best

one could do was to work backwards from such statements as Alice Smith's in the *Art of Cookery; or, The Compleat-Housewife* (London, 1758), that "in the old way, when there was but a tolerably large company, it was almost impossible the Mistress of the house should taste a bit of anything" because she was so busy waiting on others. If such were true for gentlewomen when they entertained guests, a hypothesis worth testing might hold that serving at table was a gender-specific chore expected of all classes of women. Newer works have begun to fill in the picture, notably, Hugh Willmott, "Tudor Dining: Object and Image at the Table," in Maureen Carroll, D. M. Haley, and Hugh Willmott, eds., *Consuming Passions: Dining from Antiquity to the Eighteenth Century* (Stroud, Gloucestershire, England: Tempus Publications, 2005), 126–29; and Gilly Lehmann, "Meals and Mealtimes, 1600–1800," in *The Meal: Proceedings of the Oxford Symposium on Food and Cookery, 2001* (Devon, England: Prospect Books, 2002), 139–54.

12. Gerald W. R. Ward, "Tables and Their Social Role," in David L. Barquist, *American Tables and Looking Glasses in the Mabel Brady Garvan and Other Collections at Yale University* (New Haven: Yale University Art Gallery, 1992), 14–26; Peter M. Kenny, "Flat Gates, Draw Bars, Twists, and Urns: New York's Distinctive, Early Baroque Oval Tables with Falling Leaves," *American Furniture* (1994): 106–35.

13. "The John Trot Fault: An English Dinner Table in the 1750s," *Petits Propos Culinaires* 15 (1983): 55–59; [John Trusler], *The Honours of the Table; or, Rules for Behaviour during Meals* (Dublin, 1791), 4–5.

14. Smith, *Art of Cookery*. The convenience of round tables is discussed in Thornton, *Seventeenth-Century Interior Decoration*, 226.

15. Thornton, *Seventeenth-Century Interior Decoration*, 378n10, 391n6; Adam Bowett, *English Furniture 1660–1714: From Charles II to Queen Anne* (Woodbridge, England: Antiques Collectors' Club, 2002), 106–11, 274–78.

16. British Public Record Office [National Archives], Court of Chancery: Thomas Cornwaleys vs. Richard Ingle, examination of Cuthbert Fenwick, Oct. 20, 1646, C24 690/14. The very fine table, standing in the parlor, was worth £3. York County Deeds, Orders, Wills, 4, ff.330–35, inventory (1667) of Mathew Hubberd, a planter, Virginia State Library, Richmond. His neighbor, Maj. Joseph Croshaw, another large planter, owned the other earliest oval table in 1668 and a round one as well (ibid., f.190). Robert F. Trent, *Historic Furnishings Report: Saugus Iron Works National Historic Site* (Harpers Ferry, W.Va.: National Park Service, 1982), 33, 46, 60–61.

17. As early as 1710 on the Eastern Shore of Maryland, for example (Somerset County Court Records, EB 14/365, Maryland State Archives, Annapolis, inventory of Col. Francis Jenkins), or as late as 1745 in conservative Suffolk County, Massachusetts; see Abbott Lowell Cummings, ed., *Rural Household Inventories [Suffolk, Massachusetts]: Establishing the Names, Uses, and Furnishings of Rooms in the Colonial New England House, 1625–1775* (Boston: Society for the Preservation of New England Antiquities, 1964), 130.

18. Benno M. Forman, *American Seating Furniture, 1630–1730* (New York: W. W. Norton, 1988), 84–88, 145–46.

19. Thornton, *Seventeenth-Century Interior Decoration,* 185–92; Peter Thornton, "Back-Stools and Chaises à Demoiselles," *Connoisseur* 185 (1974): 99–105; Bowett, *English Furniture,* 68–83.

20. Forman, *American Seating Furniture,* 195–213.

21. York County Deeds, Orders, Wills, 8 (1687–91), ff.37–38, inventory of Josias Moody (1676), Virginia State Library, Richmond; Somerset County Court Records, EB 14/365, Maryland State Archives, Annapolis, inventory of Col. Francis Jenkins (1710). Moody, a planter, was called a "Gentleman"; Jenkins was a very wealthy merchant and ship owner.

22. Quoted in Forman, *American Seating Furniture,* 197.

23. R. W. Symonds, "Turkey Work, Beech, and Japanned Chairs," *Connoisseur* 93 (1934): 221–27. Forman believed that the first immigrant upholsterer was at work in Boston by 1662 (see Forman, *American Seating Furniture,* 208).

24. R. W. Symonds, "Charles II: Couches, Chairs, and Stools," pt. 1 (1660–70) and pt. 2 (1670–80), *Connoisseur* 93 (1934): 15–23, 86–95; R. W. Symonds, "Cane Chairs of the Late 17th and Early 18th Centuries," *Connoisseur* 93 (1934): 173–81; R. W. Symonds, "English Cane Chairs," pts. 1 and 2, *Connoisseur* 127 (1951): 8–15, 83–91; Forman, *American Seating Furniture,* 229–80; Bowett, *English Furniture,* 84–93, 260–71.

25. Company of Joyners petition, quoted in Forman, *American Seating Furniture,* 238.

26. Quoted in Symonds, "English Cane Chairs," 13–14.

27. Forman, *American Seating Furniture,* 281–356, quote p. 283. Tall backed cane and leather-covered chairs made in England were also exported in great numbers to Holland and thence probably to New Netherlands as well; see Reinier Baarsen, *Furniture in Holland's Golden Age* (Amsterdam: Rijksmuseum and Nieuw Amsterdam, 2007), 211–12.

28. Jay Allan Anderson, "'A Solid Sufficiency': An Ethnography of Yeoman Foodways in Stuart England," PhD diss., University of Pennsylvania, 1971: 234–73.

29. William Harrison, *The Description of England,* ed. Georges Edelen (1577; Ithaca, N.Y.: Cornell University Press, 1968), 142, 144. Barbara Ketcham Wheaton, *Savoring the Past: The French Kitchen and Table from 1300 to 1789* (Philadelphia: University of Pennsylvania Press, 1983), chap. 6, dates the rise of French cuisine "governed by accepted rules" to the middle of the seventeenth century.

30. W. E. Esquire, *The Philosophers Banquet . . .* (London, 1614), title page. There is no known copy of the first edition.

31. Arnold Whitaker Oxford, *English Cookery Books to the Year 1850* (1913; reprinted, London: Holland Press, 1977), 9–10, 17.

32. John Murrell, *A Delightful Daily Exercise for Ladies and Gentlewomen* (London, 1621), preface.

33. W. J., Gent., *A True Gentlewomans Delight . . .* (London, 1653), title page.

34. Oxford, *English Cookery Books.* These should be regarded as minimums. Other titles have been located since 1913.

35. *The Genteel House-Keeper's Pastime* (London, 1693), title page.

36. Robert Beverley, *The History and Present State of Virginia* (1705), ed. Louis B. Wright (Chapel Hill: University of North Carolina Press, 1947), 291; Louise Conway Belden, *The Festive Tradition: Table Decoration and Desserts in America, 1650–1900* (New York: W. W. Norton, 1983), 97. The earliest American imprint of an English cookbook was Eliza Smith's *Compleat Housewife*, published in 1742; see Glynis Ridley, "The First American Cookbook," *Eighteenth-Century Life*, new ser., 23 (1999): 114–23.

37. The best account of ordinary table furnishings in Tudor and Stuart England is Anderson, "'Solid Sufficiency,'" 236–40; Gerard Brett, *Dinner Is Served: A Study in Manners* (London: Archon Books, 1969), presents a concise assessment of the alterations in tablewares brought about by changing table customs after 1600. For later American practice, see Jane Carson, *Colonial Virginia Cookery* (Williamsburg, Va.: Colonial Williamsburg, 1968), 6–13; Helen Sprackling, *Customs of Table Top: How New England Housewives Set Out Their Tables* (Sturbridge, Mass.: Old Sturbridge Village, 1958).

38. *Gentleman's Progress: The Itinerarium of Dr. Alexander Hamilton, 1744,* ed. Carl Bridenbaugh (Chapel Hill: University of North Carolina Press, 1948), 8.

39. James J. F. Deetz, "Ceramics from Plymouth, 1635–1835: The Archaeological Evidence," 28–29, and Marley R. Brown III, "Ceramics from Plymouth, 1621–1800: The Documentary Evidence," 56, in Ian M. G. Quimby, ed., *Ceramics in America* (Charlottesville: University Press of Virginia, 1973); William M. Kelso, *Kingsmill Plantations, 1619–1800: Archaeology of Country Life in Colonial Virginia* (Orlando, Fla.: Academic Press, Inc., 1984), 177–79; Fraser Neiman, *The "Manner House" Before Stratford: Discovering the Clifts Plantation* (Stratford, Va.: Robert E. Lee Memorial Association, 1980), 36–47; Anne Yentsch, "Minimum Vessel Lists as Evidence of Change in Folk and Courtly Traditions of Food Use," *Historical Archaeology* 24 (1990): 2453.

40. Alison Grant, *North Devon Pottery: The Seventeenth Century* (Exeter, England: University of Exeter, 1983), 114–30; Linda Blanchard, ed., *Archaeology in Barnstable, 1987–88,* (Barnstable, England: North Devon District Council, Rescue Archaeology Unit, n.d.); C. Malcolm Watkins, *North Devon Pottery and Its Export to America in the 17th Century* (Washington, D.C.: Smithsonian Institution, 1960) for the archaeological dating evidence, pp. 34–41; Beverly Straube, "European Ceramics in the New World: The Jamestown Example," in *Ceramics in America* (2001): 47–71; Merry Abbitt Outlaw, "Scratched in Clay: Seventeenth-Century North Devon Slipware at Jamestown, Virginia," *Ceramics in America* (2002): 17–38; Henry M. Miller, Alexander H. Morrison, and Garry Wheeler Stone, *A Search for the "Citty of Saint Maries": Report on the 1981 Excavations at St. Mary's City, Maryland* (St. Mary's City, Md.: St. Mary's City Commission, 1983),

87, 97–98; Ivor Noël Hume and Audrey Noël Hume, *The Archaeology of Martin's Hundred,* Part 1: Interpretive Studies (Philadelphia: University of Pennsylvania Museum of Archaeology and Anthropology, and Williamsburg, Va.: Colonial Williamsburg Foundation, 2001), 237–39, 300–303. Sgraffito slipware appears somewhat earlier on the site of Maryland's capital and earlier by fifty years—before 1622—at Wolstenholme Town along the James River, but the bulk of excavated shards in the Chesapeake region belong to the last quarter of the century. See also Leslie B. Grigsby, *English Slip-Decorated Earthenware at Williamsburg* (Williamsburg, Va.: Colonial Williamsburg Foundation, 1993), 28–37. New England archaeologists have excavated sgraffito-decorated slipware on a Plymouth Colony site occupied c. 1635–50 (see Deetz, "Ceramics from Plymouth," 24–25). Thomas Pettus's "valuable Chinese porcelain and matched dinnerware sets" are briefly mentioned in Kelso, *Kingsmill Plantations,* 178, and the marbleized tin-glazed earthenware is illustrated in Kelso, "1973 Interim Report on the Excavations at Kingsmill Plantation" (Richmond: Virginia Historic Landmarks Commission, 1974), plate 3.

41. York County Deeds, Orders, Wills, f.323, Virginia State Library, Richmond. A hundred years later pewter still set many fashionable tables despite the availability of fine china. See Ann Smart Martin, "The Role of Pewter as Missing Artifact: Consumer Attitudes toward Tablewares in Late 18th-Century Virginia," *Historical Archaeology* 23 (1989): 1–27.

42. Belden, *Festive Tradition,* 41–45; York County Deeds, Orders, Wills, 4, ff.190–1, inventory (1668) of Maj. Joseph Croshaw, Virginia State Library, Richmond. He had "weeker rings for dishes seaven," equipment to mount a splendid meal.

43. Giles Rose, *A Perfect School of Instructions for the Officers of the Mouth* (London, 1682), title page; Albert S. Roe and Robert F. Trent, "Robert Sanderson and the Founding of the Boston Silversmiths' Trade," in Fairbanks and Trent, *New England Begins,* 3:481–82; Edward J. Nygren, "Edward Winslow's Sugar Boxes: Colonial Echoes of Courtly Love," *Yale University Art Gallery Bulletin* 33 (1971): 39–52; York County Deeds, Orders, Wills, 4, ff.191–92, inventory (1667) of Edward Lockey whose occupation is uncertain, but was related by blood and marriage to London shopkeepers and merchants, Virginia State Library, Richmond; Louis L. Lipski and Michael Archer, *Dated English Delftware: Tin-Glazed Earthenware, 1600–1800* (London: Sotheby Publications, 1984), 235. If no. 1036 was not intended for sauce, it certainly appears to be a container for some other table delicacy.

44. Lipski and Archer, *Dated English Delftware,* 100; Michael Archer, *Delftware: The Tin-Glazed Earthenware of the British Isles: A Catalogue of the Collection in the Victoria and Albert Museum* (London: H.M.S.O., 1997), 261–62. For archaeological evidence, see Kieron Tyler, Ian Betts, and Roy Stephenson, *London's Delftware Industry: The Tin-Glazed Pottery Industries of Southwark and Lambeth* (London: Museum of London, 2008).

45. John C. Austin, *British Delft at Williamsburg* (Williamsburg, Va.: Colonial Williamsburg Foundation, 1994), no. 80; Aileen Dawson, *English and Irish Delftware, 1570–1840* (London: British Museum Press, 2010), 112; Lipski and Archer, *Dated English Delftware,* 156–218, 235–306; Watkins, *North Devon Pottery,* figs. 12, 14.

46. Austin, *British Delft at Williamsburg,* nos. 81 and 82; Dawson, *English and Irish Delftware,* 180–81

47. Archer, *Delftware,* 282–85.

48. More than one American archaeologist has observed an "increase in the absolute numbers of ceramic drinking vessels" on sites occupied during the first quarter through the first half of the eighteenth century (Deetz, "Ceramics from Plymouth," 29). Teacups account for many of them. Probably so does the trend toward individualized food service, although that correlation is harder to demonstrate. See Kelso, *Kingsmill Plantations,* 178–79n27 and fig. 124; Neiman, *The "Manner House,"* 36–40.

49. British Public Record Office [National Archives], Chancery, Cornwaleys vs. Ingle, C24 690/14. The earliest porcelain tablewares recovered on James River sites are wine cups dating from the first quarter of the seventeenth century. Enormous quantities of utilitarian tea bowls and dinnerwares were imported at the end of the century and in ever more standardized forms after 1712. See Julia B. Curtis, "Perceptions of an Artifact: Chinese Porcelain in Colonial Tidewater Virginia," in Mary C. Beaudry, ed., *Documentary Archaeology in the New World* (Cambridge: Cambridge University Press, 1993), 20–31.

50. Lipski and Archer, *Dated English Delftware,* 43.

51. York County Deeds, Orders, Wills 3, f.60, inventory (1659) of William White, a clerk, Virginia State Library, Richmond; Testamentary Proceedings, Maryland State Archives, Annapolis, 3:127–59, inventory of Capt. William Smith, a wealthy innkeeper.

52. Lipski and Archer, *Dated English Delftware,* 72.

53. In Fernand Braudel's often cited discourse on the use of forks (*Civilization and Capitalism, 15th–18th Century,* vol. 1, *The Structures of Everyday Life: The Limits of the Possible,* trans. Siān Reynolds [New York: Harper & Row, 1982], 1:203–9), he makes the unsubstantiated claim that "there is no mention of table forks in any [English] inventory before 1660." Reaching the same conclusion, but with more evidence to show for it are G. Bernard Hughes, "Evolution of the Silver Table Fork," *Country Life,* September 24, 1959: 364–65; Ivor Noël Hume, *A Guide to Artifacts of Colonial America* (New York: Knopf, 1970), 177–84; and Suzanne von Drachenfels, "The Design of Table Tools and the Effects of Form on Etiquette and Table Setting," in Sarah D. Coffin et al., *Feeding Desire: Design and the Tools of the Table, 1500–2005* (New York: Cooper-Hewitt, National Design Museum, 2006), 165–73. For evidence of American use see Lois Green Carr and Lorena S. Walsh, "Changing Lifestyles and Consumer Behavior in the Colonial Chesapeake," in Cary Carson, Ronald Hoffman, and Peter J. Albert, eds., *Of Consuming Interests: The Style of Life in the Eighteenth Century* (Charlottesville: University Press of

Virginia, 1994), tables 1–6; and Gloria L. Main and Jackson T. Main, "Economic Growth and the Standard of Living in Southern New England, 1640–1774," *Journal of Economic History* 48 (1988): table 5.

54. Lipski and Archer, *Dated English Delftware,* 52–126; Dawson, *English and Irish Delftware,* 242–43; Sarah Richards, *Eighteenth-Century Ceramics: Products for a Civilised Society* (Manchester, England: Manchester University Press, 1999), 107–8. Archaeological fragments have been found in Maryland at Horne Point plantation, Dorchester County (18DO58) and on the site of an ordinary (c. 1690–1700) at St. Mary's City; see Silas D. Hurry, "What Is 'What' in St. Mary's City," *Ceramics in America* (2005): 220–22.

55. Not unexpectedly, American towns and cities continued in the eighteenth century to collect immigrants in proportionally larger concentrations than did rural populations. See Gary B. Nash, *The Urban Crucible: Social Change, Political Consciousness, and the Origins of the American Revolution* (Cambridge, Mass.: Harvard University Press, 1979), 103–11. It is perhaps a little surprising that even in such small towns as Williamsburg, Virginia, foreign-born residents still accounted for almost half the population as late as 1770, by then four times the number of immigrants to be found in the countryside outside the town. See Lorena S. Walsh, "York County Urban and Rural Residents Compared," in "Urbanization in the Tidewater South, Part II: The Growth and Development of Williamsburg and Yorktown," final York County Project Report to the National Endowment for the Humanities, grant no. RO 20869-85 1989, 12–13.

56. F. J. Fisher, "The Development of London as a Center of Conspicuous Consumption in the Sixteenth and Seventeenth Centuries," *Transactions of the Royal Historical Society,* 4th ser., 30 (1948); E. A. Wrigley, "A Simple Model of London's Importance in Changing English Society and Economy, 1650- 1750," *Past and Present* 37 (1967): 44–70; Lorna Weatherill, *Consumer Behaviour and Material Culture in Britain, 1660–1760* (London and New York: Routledge, 1988), 70–90; Peter Borsay, "The English Urban Renaissance: The Development of Provincial Urban Culture, c. 1680–1760," *Social History* 5 (1977): 581–603; Peter Clark and Paul Slack, *English Towns in Transition, 1500–1700* (Oxford: Oxford University Press, 1976), 141–57; Penelope J. Corfield, *The Impact of English Towns, 1700–1800* (Oxford: Oxford University Press, 1982); Joyce M. Ellis, *The Georgian Town, 1680–1840* (Houndmills, Basingstoke, England, and New York: Palgrave, 2001), 65–86, 120–28. Phyllis Whitman Hunter, *Purchasing Identity in the Atlantic World: Massachusetts Merchants, 1670–1780* (Ithaca, N.Y.: Cornell University Press, 2001); Susan Mackiewicz, "Philadelphia Flourishing: The Material World of Philadelphians, 1682–1760," PhD diss., University of Delaware, 1988; Main and Main, "Economic Growth," 40–41; Lorena S. Walsh, "Urban Amenities and Rural Sufficiency: Living Standards and Consumer Behavior in the Colonial Chesapeake, 1643–1777," *Journal of Economic History* 43 (1983): 109–17; specifically for Williamsburg and York-

town, see Walsh, "York County Urban and Rural Residents," 1–20; and Carr and Walsh, "Changing Lifestyles and Consumer Behavior," tables 5–6; Kathleen Warden Manning, "Two Studies of North Carolina Material Culture in the Eighteenth Century," pt. 2, master's thesis, University of North Carolina at Greensboro, 1978. Ann Smart Martin, "'Fashionable Sugar Dishes, Latest Fashion Ware': The Creamware Revolution in the Eighteenth-Century Chesapeake," in Paul A. Shackle and Barbara J. Little, eds., *Historical Archaeology of the Chesapeake* (Washington, D.C.: Smithsonian Institution Press, 1994), 169–88, demonstrates in a study of storekeepers' records that urban consumers enjoyed a much larger selection of fashionable tea and tablewares than country buyers were offered. She found that the contrast between Williamsburg and most York County consumers still persisted in 1815; see Ann Morgan Smart, "The Urban/Rural Dichotomy of Status Consumption: Tidewater Virginia, 1815," master's thesis, College of William and Mary, 1986, and Ann Smart Martin, *Buying into the World of Goods: Early Consumers in Backcountry Virginia* (Baltimore: Johns Hopkins University Press, 2008), 67–144.

57. Carole Shammas observes fewer differences between wealthy town and country consumers in Britain than in England's colonies owing, she argues, to the special problem of acquiring consumer durables in rural America. See her essay "Changes in English and Anglo-American Consumption from 1550 to 1800," in John Brewer and Roy Porter, eds., *Consumption and the World of Goods* (London and New York: Routledge, 1993), 199. Other scholars challenge her conclusions even for Britain; for example, Janet Sleep, "Patterns of Consumption across an Urban Hierarchy, 1650–1725," PhD diss., University of East Anglia, 1996; Bowett, *English Furniture*, 24–26; and Archer, *Delftware*, 6–7.

58. Lorna Weatherill (*Consumer Behaviour and Material Culture*, 79–90) asks the right question—"Why should living in a town result in a greater likelihood of owning domestic goods?"—and she steers clear of the most commonly given wrong answer by correctly asserting that "there was more to individual consumption than social competition, fashion, and emulation." Yet her own explanation ultimately falls short of the mark too. It may be true that "material goods could compensate for some of the inconveniences of town life" and that overcrowding might cause urban dwellers "to look inwardly to the living space and make this as aesthetically pleasing and comforting as possible." But the proximity argument not only fails to explain consumption in places where crowding was not a problem, its emphasis on goods that provided greater privacy (window curtains) and prettiness (pictures) ignores the more important social uses of most new consumer goods and the activities in which they assisted. Weatherill comes closer to a real explanation when she writes that people in towns "were liable to meet others and to learn about consumption and to have the opportunity to present themselves in a variety of different situations" (79, 81, 83, 89). Consumer goods appeared first and most frequently in the possession of citizens with the farthest-flung connections because town house parlors and dining rooms were the venues where such people exchanged their social credentials.

59. The 1710 inventory of Col. Francis Jenkins of Somerset County, Maryland, provides one of the best examples. Jenkins owned sixteen maps, all presumably mounted and hung, including "3 maps of the quarters of the World," "1 Map of the Celestial and Terestrial Globe," a London map, and another of Virginia. His walls also displayed "Small Draughts of Pauls Monument Exchange," "2 large heads of K Wm and Q Mary in frames," and four more unidentified "Heads" (Somerset County Court Records, EB 14/365, Maryland State Archives, Annapolis).

60. For Virginia see statistical analysis presented in Cary Carson, "Banqueting Houses and the 'Need of Society' among Slave-Owning Planters in the Chesapeake Colonies," *William and Mary Quarterly,* 3rd ser., 70 (2013): 729–36.

61. Few historians of this period have asked how immigrants were received, by whom, and what strategies they adopted to assimilate themselves into new communities. It is the missing chapter in David Cressy, *Coming Over: Migration and Communication between England and New England in the Seventeenth Century* (Cambridge: Cambridge University Press, 1987). The most suggestive work is Peter Clark, "Migrants in the City: The Process of Social Adaptation in English Towns, 1500–1800," in Peter Clark and David Souden, eds., *Migration and Society in Early Modern England* (Totowa, N.J.: Barnes & Noble Books, 1987), 267–91. Bernard Bailyn has something to say about the sale and distribution of servants and convicts in *Voyagers to the West: A Passage in the Peopling of America on the Eve of the Revolution* (New York: Alfred A. Knopf, 1986), 324–52.

62. Lorena S. Walsh, "The African Slave Trade: Regional Patterns, African Origins, and Some Implications," *William and Mary Quarterly* 3rd ser., 58 (2001), 139–70; Philip D. Morgan, "The Cultural Implications of the Atlantic Slave Trade: African Regional Origins, American Destinations, and New World Developments," in David Eltis and David Richardson, eds., *Routes to Slavery: Direction, Ethnicity and Mortality in the Atlantic Slave Trade,* (London: Frank Cass, 1997), 122–45.

63. Martha B. Katz-Hyman and Kym S. Rice, eds., *World of a Slave: Encyclopedia of the Material Life of Slaves in the United States,* 2 vols. (Santa Barbara, Ca.: Greenwood, 2011), passim; Philip D. Morgan, *Slave Counterpoint: Black Culture in the Eighteenth-Century Chesapeake and Lowcounry* (Chapel Hill: University of North Carolina Press, 1998), 125–33.

64. "Virginia in 1732, The Travel Journal of William Hugh Grove," Gregory A. Stiverson and Patrick H. Bulter III, eds., *Virginia Magazine of History and Biography* 85 (January 1977): 31–32. For the traditional choice among some Africans to wear few clothes, especially when working, see Lorena S. Walsh, *From Calabar to Carter's Grove: The History of a Virginia Slave Community* (Charlottesville: University Press of Virginia, 1997), 97–100.

65. Barbara J. Heath, "Buttons, Beads, and Buckles: Contextualizing Adornment within the Bounds of Slavery," in Maria Franklin and Garrett Fesler, eds., *Historical Ar-*

chaeology, Identity Formation, and the Interpretation of Ethnicity (Williamsburg, Va.: Colonial Williamsburg Research Publications, 1999), 47–69. The presence of glass beads on archaeological sites in Jamaica and Virginia correlates with the importation of enslaved Africans, not with their American-born offspring; see Jillian E. Galle, "Assessing the Impacts of Time, Agricultural Cycles, and Demography on the Consumer Activities of Enslaved Men and Women in Eighteenth-Century Jamaica and Virginia," in James A. Delle, Mark W. Hauser, and Douglas V. Armstrong, eds., *Out of Many, One People: The Historical Archaeology of Colonial Jamaica* (Tuscaloosa: University of Alabama Press, 2011), 211–41.

66. Heath, "Buttons, Beads, and Buckles," 54; Shane White and Graham White, "Slave Hair and African-American Culture in the Eighteenth and Nineteenth Centuries," *Journal of Southern History* 61 (1995): 45–76.

67. Linda Baumgarten, "'Clothes for the People': Slave Clothing in Early Virginia," *Journal of Early Southern Decorative Arts* 14 (1988): 26–70; Jonathan Prude, "To Look Upon the 'Lower Sort': Runaway Ads and the Appearance of Unfree Laborers in America, 1750–1800," *Journal of American History* 78 (1991): 124–59; Shane White and Graham White, "Slave Clothing and African-American Culture in the Eighteenth and Nineteenth Centuries," *Past and Present* 148 (1995): 149–86; Linda Baumgarten, *What Clothes Reveal: The Language of Clothing in Colonial and Federal America* (Williamsburg, Va., and New Haven, Conn.: Colonial Williamsburg Foundation and Yale University Press, 2002), 106–39; Morgan, *Slave Counterpoint*, 133.

68. Jillian E. Galle, "Costly Signaling and Gendered Social Strategies among Slaves in the Eighteenth-Century Chesapeake: An Archaeological Perspective," *American Antiquity* 75 (2010): 19–43; also Jillian E. Galle, "Strategic Consumption: Archaeological Evidence for Costly Signaling among Enslaved Men and Women in the Eighteenth-Century Chesapeake," PhD diss., University of Virginia, 2006.

69. F. L. Parker, *Stealing a Little Freedom: Advertisements for Slave Runaways in North Carolina, 1791–1840* (New York: Garland Publishing, Inc., 1994), 686.

70. White and White, "Slave Clothing," 174, 161.

71. Martin, *Buying into the World of Goods,* 173–93; Ira Berlin and Philip D. Morgan, "Introduction," and John T. Schlotterbeck, "The Internal Economy of Slavery in Rural Piedmont Virginia," in Ira Berlin and Philip D. Morgan, eds., *The Slaves' Economy: Independent Production by Slaves in the Americas* (London: Frank Cass, 1991), 1–27, 170–81.

72. Barbara Heath, "Engendering Choice: Slavery and Consumerism in Central Virginia," in Jillian E. Galle and Amy L. Young, eds., *Engendering African American Archaeology* (Knoxville: University of Tennessee Press, 2004): 19–38; White and White, "Slave Clothing," 160–61.

73. Ongoing work by Fraser Neiman, Jillian Galle, and staff at the Digital Archaeological Archive of Comparative Slavery (DAACS), Thomas Jefferson Foundation, Char-

lottesville, Virginia, www.daacs.org; Patricia Samford, *Subfloor Pits and the Archaeology of Slavery in Colonial Virginia* (Tuscaloosa: University of Alabama Press, 2007), 85–107.

74. Galle, "Costly Signaling," 31–35. Barbara Heath recognized similar patterns at Jefferson's other Virginia plantation, Poplar Forest; see her "Buttons, Beads, and Buckles," 57–62.

75. Quoted in White and White, "Slave Clothing," 179. Figure 17 illustrates men wearing short jackets with buttons, which appear to be cloth-covered. See Susan P. Shames, *The Old Plantation: The Artist Revealed* (Williamsburg, Va.: Colonial Williamsburg Foundation, 2010).

76. Julian U. Niemcewicz, *Under Their Vine and the Fig Tree; Travels through America in 1797–1799, 1805, with Some Further Account of Life in New Jersey,* trans. and ed. Metchie J. E. Bedka (Elizabeth, N.J.: Grassmann Publishing Co., 1965), 100.

77. Timothy J. Shannon, "Dressing for Success on the Mohawk Frontier: Hendrick, William Johnson, and the Indian Fashion," *William and Mary Quarterly,* 3rd ser., 53 (1996): 13–42; Emily Ballew Neff, "At the Wood's Edge: Benjamin West's 'The Death of Wolfe' and the Middle Ground," 64–103, and Janet Catherine Berlo, "Men of the Middle Ground: The Visual Culture of Native-White Diplomacy in Eighteenth-Century North America," 104–15, both in Emily Ballew Neff and Kaylin H. Weber, eds., *American Adversaries: West and Copley in a Transatlantic World* (Houston, Texas: The Museum of Fine Arts, 2013).

78. Laura Elaine Johnson, "'Goods to Clothe Themselves': Native Consumers, Native Images on the Pennsylvania Trading Frontier, 1712–1730," master's thesis, University of Delaware (Winterthur Program), 2004, includes an appendix that catalogs, illustrates, and analyzes an important collection of artifacts excavated at Conestoga Town and now curated by the Pennsylvania Historical and Museum Commission.

79. Clark, "Migrants in the City," 269–76. Kin ties may again have smoothed the reception of urban newcomers in the eighteenth century as townspeople's living standards continued to rise. For internal migration in preindustrial England, see E. J. Buckatzch, "The Constancy of the Local Populations and Migration in England before 1800," *Population Studies* (1951–52): 62–69; Julian Cornwall, "Evidence of Population Mobility in the Seventeenth Century," *Bulletin of the Institute of Historical Research* 40 (1967): 143–52; and more recent works cited in Peter Clark, "Migration in England during the Late Seventeenth and Early Eighteenth Centuries," in Peter Clark and David Souden, eds., *Migration and Society in Early Modern England* (Totowa, N.J.: Barnes & Noble Books, 1987), 213–52. A useful comparative study is W. R. Prest, "Stability and Change in Old and New England: Clayworth and Dedham," *Journal of Interdisciplinary History* 6 (1976): 359–74. John Murray, earl of Dunmore, to the earl of Dartmouth, in Reuben G. Thwaites and Louise P. Kellogg, eds., *Documentary History of Dunmore's War, 1774* (Madison: Wisconsin Historical Society, 1905), 368–95.

80. Especially when the population of mainland North America began to grow faster by natural increase than by immigration from abroad. Compare table H.3 in David W. Galenson, *White Servitude in Colonial America: An Economic Analysis* (Cambridge: Cambridge University Press, 1981), 216–17, and table 3 in J. Potter, "The Growth of Population in America, 1700–1860," in D. V. Glass and D. E. C. Eversley, eds., *Population in History: Essays in Historical Demography* (Chicago: Aldine Publishing Co., 1965), 642. Between 1710 and 1740 free white immigrants accounted for upwards of 12 percent of the population, but much less after the middle of the century.

81. The complex subject and imperfect literature are summarized by James P. P. Horn in an essay that examines a wider area than the title suggests, "Moving On in the New World: Migration and Out-Migration in the Seventeenth-Century Chesapeake," in Clark and Souden, *Migration and Society,* 172–212. The key regional studies include Daniel Scott Smith, "The Demographic History of Colonial New England," *Journal of Economic History* 32 (1972): 165–83; T. H. Breen and Stephen Foster, "Moving to the New World: The Character of Early Massachusetts Immigration," *William and Mary Quarterly,* 3rd ser., 30 (1973): 189–222; Ralph J. Crandall, "New England's Second Great Migration: The First Three Generations of Settlement, 1630–1700," *New England Historical and Genealogical Register* 129 (1975): 347–60; Douglas Lamar Jones, *Village and Seaport: Migration and Society in Eighteenth-Century Massachusetts* (Hanover, N.H.: University Press of New England, 1981), 40–69, 103–13, and a useful bibliographic note, pp. 124–33; Lorena S. Walsh, "Staying Put or Getting Out: Findings for Charles County, Maryland, 1650–1720," *William and Mary Quarterly,* 3rd ser., 44 (1987): 89–103; and Allan Kulikoff, *Tobacco and Slaves: The Development of Southern Cultures in the Chesapeake, 1680–1800* (Chapel Hill: University of North Carolina Press, 1986), 76–77, 14557, for eighteenth-century migration. See also Allan Kulikoff, "Migration and Cultural Diffusion in Early America, 1600–1860: A Review Essay," *Historical Methods* 19 (1986): 153–69.

82. John J. McCusker and Russell R. Menard, *The Economy of British America, 1607–1789* (Chapel Hill: University of North Carolina Press, 1985), 172, 203. Other new colonies grew even faster.

83. *Calendar of Virginia State Papers,* 11 vols., ed. W. P. Palmer (Richmond, 1875–93), 1:52.

84. British Public Record Office [National Archives], C.O. 1/47, f. 261.

85. Cited in Patricia Trautman, "Dress in Seventeenth-Century Cambridge, Massachusetts: An Inventory-Based Reconstruction," in Peter Benes, ed., *Early American Probate Inventories* (Boston: Boston University, 1989), 52.

86. Main and Main, "Economic Growth," 37–39; Kevin M. Sweeney, "From Wilderness to Arcadian Vale: Material Life in the Connecticut River Valley, 1635–1760," in Gerald W. R. Ward and William N. Hosley Jr., eds., *The Great River: Art and Society of the Connecticut River Valley, 1635–1820* (Hartford, Conn.: The Atheneum, 1985), 17–27.

87. William Eddis, *Letters from America,* ed. Aubrey C. Land (Cambridge, Mass.: Belknap Press of Harvard University Press, 1969), 37–38.

88. *Allgemeine Zeitung* (Augsburg), December 9, 1816, trans. Marcus Lee Hansen, *The Atlantic Migration, 1607–1860* (1940; reprint ed., New York: Harper & Row, 1961), 3.

89. The figures exclude 1698. See R. W. Symonds, "The Export Trade of Furniture to Colonial America," *Burlington Magazine* (November 1940): 152–63.

90. For instance, John Brush, a Williamsburg gunsmith worth a modest £90 when he died in 1727; see Karl J. Reinhard, "Analysis of Latrine Soils from the Brush-Everard Site, Colonial Williamsburg, Virginia," unpublished report, 1989, Colonial Williamsburg Foundation. "Virginia in 1732: The Travel Journal of William Hugh Grove," Gregory A. Stiverson and Patrick H. Butler, eds., *Virginia Magazine of History and Biography* 85 (January 1977): 18–44. It was said that the broccoli-eating gentlemen "at Their Tables have commonly dishes or plates" (29).

91. Brown, "Ceramics from Plymouth," 45. Demonstrated in the context of a single, early eighteenth-century town in Ivor Noël Hume, *Pottery and Porcelain in Colonial Williamsburg's Archaeological Collections* (Williamsburg, Va.: Colonial Williamsburg, 1969); also Julia B. Curtis, "Chinese Export Porcelain in Eighteenth-Century Tidewater Virginia," *Studies in Eighteenth-Century Culture* 17 (1987): 119–44.

92. Carr and Walsh, "Changing Lifestyles and Consumer Behavior"; Carson, "Banqueting Houses," 729–36; and, for Britain, Weatherill, *Consumer Behaviour and Material Culture,* 201–7. Unfortunately, English and American scholars have not used the same market basket of goods or employed the same social and economic categories to define wealth groups, thus making direct comparisons impossible. Nevertheless, Weatherill's tables 8.2, 8.3, and 8.4 show that yeomen and husbandmen in the countryside and most urban-dwelling artisans not engaged in the luxury trades were still making almost no use of forks, saucepans, fine china, or teawares by 1725, the last year for which she presents quantitative data.

93. Mary Clavers, *A New Home—Who'll Follow! or, Glimpses of Western Life* (New York, 1850), 82, recalling what passed for gentility on the Michigan frontier twenty years earlier; "Notes of Judge St. George Tucker," *William and Mary Quarterly,* 1st ser., 22 (1914): 252; Graham Hood, *The Governor's Palace in Williamsburg. A Cultural Study* (Williamsburg, Va.: Colonial Williamsburg Foundation, 1991), 287–88.

94. Carr and Walsh, "Changing Lifestyles and Consumer Behavior," 65–68; Main and Main, "Economic Growth," 44.

95. Walsh, *From Calabar to Carter's Grove,* 182–83; Lorena S. Walsh, "Fettered Consumers: Slaves and the Anglo-American 'Consumer Revolution,'" paper presented to the annual meeting of the Economic History Association, 1992 (ms. copy, Rockefeller Library, Colonial Williamsburg Foundation, Williamsburg, Virginia); Martin, *Buying into the World of Goods,* 173–93; Patricia Samford, "The Archaeology of African-American

Slavery and Material Culture," *William and Mary Quarterly*, 3rd ser., 53 (1996): 87–114; Theresa A. Singleton, "The Archaeology of Slave Life," in Edward D. C. Campbell Jr., ed., with Kym S. Rice, *Before Freedom Came: African-American Life in the Antebellum South* (Richmond and Charlottesville: Museum of the Confederacy and University Press of Virginia, 1991), 155–75; Frederick W. Lange and Shawn Bonath Carlson, "Distributions of European Earthenwares on Plantations on Barbados, West Indies," in Theresa A. Singleton, ed., *The Archaeology of Slavery and Plantation Life: Studies in Historical Archaeology* (Orlando, Fl.: Academic Press, Inc., 1985), 97–120; Galle, "Assessing the Impacts of Time, Agricultural Cycles, and Demography," 211–41.

96. Jean E. Howson, "Social Relations and Material Culture: A Critique of the Archaeology of Plantation Slavery," *Historical Archaeology* 24 (1990): 78–91; Daniel Mouer, "Chesapeake Creoles: The Creation of Folk Culture in Colonial Virginia," in Theodore R. Reinhart and Dennis J. Pogue, eds., *The Archaeology of 17th-Century Virginia* (Richmond: Archaeological Society of Virginia, Special Publication No. 30, 1993), 105–66.

97. Martin, *Buying into the World of Goods*, 181.

98. Singleton, "The Archaeology of Slave Life," 160–61.

5. Living En Suite

1. Peter Thornton, *Seventeenth-Century Interior Decoration in England, France, and Holland* (New Haven: Yale University Press, 1978), 1–106. Eric Jones describes early Parisian influence on fashion in "The Fashion Manipulators: Consumer Tastes and British Industries, 1660–1800," in Louis P. Cain and Paul J. Uselding, eds., *Business Enterprise and Economic Change: Essays in Honor of Harold F. Williamson* (Kent, Ohio: Kent State University Press, 1973), 208–10.

2. Mark Girouard, *Life in the English Country House: A Social and Architectural History* (New Haven: Yale University Press, 1978), 119–62; Nicholas Cooper, *Houses of the Gentry, 1480–1680* (New Haven: Yale University Press, 1978), 1–18, 55–107; Nicholas Cooper, "Display, Status and the Vernacular Tradition," *Vernacular Architecture* 33 (2002): 28–33.

3. Overlooked in Abbott Lowell Cummings, *The Framed Houses of Massachusetts Bay, 1625–1725* (Cambridge, Mass.: Belknap Press of Harvard University Press, 1979), the French-via-London model for advanced house designs and furnishings in mid-seventeenth-century Boston was first recognized by Robert F. Trent and his *Historic Furnishings Report: Saugus Iron Works National Historic Site* (Harpers Ferry, W.Va.: National Park Service, 1982), 43–64.

4. The uses to which rare early galleries may have been put is a matter that invites speculation. One was recorded between an unusual lean-to parlor and a lean-to chamber in the inventory of the Rev. John Cotton (died 1652), who acquired his Boston house,

built about 1636, from Sir Henry Vane, the son of a nobleman and the governor of the Massachusetts Bay colony. Trent conjectures (*Historic Furnishings Report,* 46) that "Vane may have intended the suite of parlor, gallery, and chamber to function as a suite in the grand manner, and accordingly he may have used his gallery for pictures." By contrast, an immensely wealthy Virginia merchant, Col. Joseph Bridges, kept only odds and ends in a gallery in his three-story house, which also contained one of the earliest dining rooms in 1686 (Isle of Wight County Deeds, Orders, Wills, 2 [1661–1719], ff.255–63, Virginia State Library, Richmond).

5. Discussed in Abbott Lowell Cummings, "The Beginnings of Provincial Renaissance Architecture in Boston, 1690–1725," *Journal of the Society of Architectural Historians* 42 (1983): 43–53, and Cary Carson, "Peter Tufts House Investigation," unpublished field report, June/August, 2010, addenda June 2014 (Historic New England archives, Boston).

6. Mark R. Wenger, "The Central Passage in Virginia: Evolution of an Eighteenth-Century Living Space," in Camille Wells, ed., *Perspectives in Vernacular Architecture* 2, (Columbia: University of Missouri Press, 1986): 137, states that the earliest known inventory reference to a passage in Virginia and earliest house plan showing one date to 1719. But see both a "Passage" and an "Upper Passage" in a 1689 inventory in York County Deeds, Orders, Wills, 8, ff. 362–63, Virginia State Library, Richmond, cited in Mary Ann Weiglhofer, "Inventories as a Barometer of Room Function in Colonial York County, Virginia," unpublished report, 1981 (Colonial Williamsburg Foundation), 9. Cary Carson, "Plantation Housing: Seventeenth Century" and Mark R. Wenger, "Town House and Country House: Eighteenth and Early Nineteenth Centuries," in Cary Carson and Carl R. Lounsbury, eds., *The Chesapeake House: Architectural Investigation by Colonial Williamsburg* (Chapel Hill: University of North Carolina Press, 2013), 102–14, 125–34.

7. In this case, it was the upper-class vestrymen of Truro Parish (Fairfax County, Virginia) who could not decide what to call the new hall in a glebe house they were building in 1737 (*Minutes of the Vestry: Truro Parish, Virginia, 1732–1785* [Lorton, Va.: Pohick Church, 1974], 15).

8. Isaac Weld, *Travels through the States of North America,* 2 vols. (1800; reprint ed., New York: Johnson Reprint Corp., 1968), 1:207, and Thomas Anburey, *Travels through the Interior Parts of America,* 2 vols. (1789; reprint ed., New York: New York Times, 1969), 2:359, cited and discussed in Wenger, "The Central Passage in Virginia," 142–43. It is significant when travelers comment on such American departures from architectural canon. Their surprise betrays their expectation that they would find gentlemen's houses laid out in ways to which they were already accustomed.

9. Mark R. Wenger is the acknowledged American expert on the subject of gentry houses in early Virginia. Conversations with him have shaped what I have written here, as have Dell Upton, "Vernacular Domestic Architecture in Eighteenth-Century Virginia," *Winterthur Portfolio* 17 (1982): 95–119; Edward A. Chappell, "Looking at Buildings,"

Fresh Advices: A Research Supplement to the Colonial Williamsburg Interpreter 5 (1984): i–vi; and chapters by Wenger, Chappell, and Willie Graham in Carson and Lounsbury, *The Chesapeake House.*

10. Edward Chappell and the staff of architectural historians at Colonial Williamsburg have recorded this neglected social-architectural information in a number of large gentry houses in Virginia, Maryland, Charleston, and Philadelphia. For the former, see Edward A. Chappell, "Fieldwork" and Willie Graham, "Interior Finishes" in Carson and Lounsbury, *The Chesapeake House,* 29–47, 312–47. Even the choice of paint colors, the number of coats to be applied, and sometimes the decision to paint at all were matters in which builders and clients took careful account of the relative importance of the rooms or architectural elements to be painted; see Edward Chappell, Willie Graham, and Carl Lounsbury, "The Social Significance of Paint Color Schemes in Eighteenth-Century Public Buildings," memorandum, October 10, 1989 (Colonial Williamsburg Foundation). Orlando Ridout V, *Building the Octagon* (Washington, D.C.: American Institute of Architects Press, 1989), 107–24, discusses the same hierarchy of architectural ornament in the best American house history yet written.

11. For the fullest discussion of these developments among minor gentry builders in the southern and middle colonies, see Wenger, "Town House and Country House," 120–55; Carl R. Lounsbury, "The Development of Domestic Architecture in the Albemarle Region," in Doug Swaim, ed., *Carolina Dwelling* (Raleigh: North Carolina State University, 1978), 46–61; Catherine W. Bishir and Michael T. Southern, *A Guide of the Historic Architecture of Eastern North Carolina* (Chapel Hill: University of North Carolina Press, 1996), 17–33; Upton, "Vernacular Domestic Architecture"; Camille Wells, "The Eighteenth-Century Landscape of Virginia's Northern Neck," *Northern Neck of Virginia Historical Magazine* 37 (1987): 4217–55; Bernard L. Herman, *Architecture and Rural Life in Central Delaware, 1700–1900* (Knoxville: University of Tennessee Press, 1987), 14–41; Cynthia G. Falk, *Architecture and Artifacts of the Pennsylvania Germans: Constructing Identity in Early America* (University Park: Pennsylvania State University Press, 2008), 61–169. Oddly enough New England is still mostly virgin territory for fieldwork-based regional studies of eighteenth-century vernacular architecture. Scholars there know to expect buildings to be "expressions of a complex regional aesthetic" (William N. Hosley Jr., "Architecture," in Gerald W. R. Ward and William N. Hosley Jr., eds., *The Great River: Art and Society of the Connecticut River Valley, 1635–1820,* (Hartford, Conn.: The Atheneum, 1985), 63), but no one has carefully worked out how "architectural style was negotiated in a way that softened fashion's cutting edge."

12. Edward A. Chappell, "Housing a Nation: The Transformation of Living Standards in Early America," in Cary Carson, Ronald Hoffman, and Peter J. Albert, eds., *Of Consuming Interests: The Style of Life in the Eighteenth Century* (Charlottesville: University Press of Virginia, 1994), 167–232.

13. Cummings, *Framed Houses of Massachusetts Bay,* 192–201; Abbott Lowell Cummings, "Decorative Painting in Seventeenth-Century New England," in Ian M. G. Quimby, ed., *American Painting to 1776: A Reappraisal* (Charlottesville: University Press of Virginia, 1971), 71–125.

14. Cummings, *Framed Houses of Massachusetts Bay,* 192. The earliest Virginia inventory that lists chambers by color—red and green—was taken on the death of Col. Thomas Willoughby of Norfolk County in 1672 (Norfolk County Wills and Deeds E, [1666–75], ff.124–25, Virginia State Library, Richmond). Willoughby, son of a prominent Virginia merchant, was educated at Merchant Taylors School in London before returning to the colony.

15. The "Paper Room" belonged to John Welland of Boston (see Abbott Lowell Cummings, ed., *Rural Household Inventories [Suffolk, Massachusetts]: Establishing the Names, Uses, and Furnishings of Rooms in the Colonial New England House, 1625–1775* [Boston: Society for the Preservation of New England Antiquities, 1964], xxiv); the "Chintz Chamber" was one of a suite of rooms including a "Yellow Chamber," "Red Chamber," and "Dressing Chamber" at Belvoir, the home of George William Fairfax of Fairfax County, Virginia (Fairfax Family Papers, 1756–87, Virginia Historical Society, Richmond). See also Catherine Lynn, *Wallpaper in America from the Seventeenth Century to World War I* (New York: W. W. Norton, 1980), 17–24; Florence M. Montgomery, *Printed Textiles: English and American Cottons and Linens, 1700–1850* (London: Thames and Hudson, 1970), 36–82; Richard C. Nylander, *Wallpaper in New England: Selections from the Society for the Preservation of New England Antiquities* (Boston: S.P.N.E.A., 1986); and Margaret Beck Pritchard, "Wallpaper," in Carson and Lounsbury, *The Chesapeake House,* 376–92.

16. These and other advertisements collected in *The Arts and Crafts in Philadelphia, Maryland, and South Carolina, 1721- 1785: Gleanings from Newspapers,* 1st ser., comp. Alfred Coxe Prime (Topsfield, Mass.: The Walpole Society, 1929), 275, 279, 281, are cited in an intelligent discussion of the buyers of wallpaper and where they hung it in Lynn, *Wallpaper in America,* 154–61.

17. Thornton, *Seventeenth-Century Interior Decoration,* plates 85 and 131; H. J. Louw, "The Origin of the Sash-Window," *Architectural History* 26 (1983): 49–72.

18. Daniel Neal, *The History of New England,* 2 vols. (London, 1720), 2:590. New fashions leapt across the Atlantic in a matter of months: "There is no Fashion in London, but in three or four Months is to be seen in Boston" (614).

19. Garry Wheeler Stone, *Seventeenth-Century Wall Tile from the St. Mary's City Excavations, 1971–1985* (St. Mary's City, Md.: Historic St. Mary's City, 1987). Tin-glazed tiles decorated a fireplace opening in a dwelling of the same date in Providence, Maryland; see Al Luckenbach, *Providence 1649: The History and Archaeology of Anne Arundel County Maryland's First European Settlement* (Annapolis: Maryland State Archives, 1995), 12, plate 2.

20. Structure 138/53 leased as lodgings to Governor Effingham; see Cary Carson, et al., *Evaluation of Previous Archaeology, Jamestown Archaeological Assessment, 1992–1996* (Williamsburg, Va.: National Park Service, 2006), 138–43. The excavated house plan and selected plaster fragments are illustrated in Cary Carson, "Banqueting Houses and the 'Need of Society' among Slave-Owning Planters in the Chesapeake Colonies." *William and Mary Quarterly*, 3rd ser., 70 (2013): 740.

21. Charles F. Montgomery "Thomas Banister on the New Sash Windows, Boston, 1701," *Journal of the Society of Architectural Historians* 24 (1965): 169–70.

22. Abbott Lowell Cummings, "The Parson Barnard House," *Old Time New England* 47 (1956): 2940. The parlor chamber in this house, which Cummings dated circa 1715, is illustrated and discussed in broader context in his *Framed Houses of Massachusetts Bay,* 187–91.

23. Holly Hill (Anne Arundel County, Maryland) is further illustrated and discussed in Susan Buck and Willie Graham, "Paint," in Carson and Lounsbury, *The Chesapeake House,* 366, 371.

24. Culled from a typescript survey of "Virginia Room-by-Room Inventories," n.d., Architectural Research Department, Colonial Williamsburg Foundation.

25. *Moreau de St. Méry's American Journey, 1793–1798,* trans. and ed. Kenneth Roberts and Anna M. Roberts (Garden City, N.Y.: Doubleday & Company, Inc., 1947), 264; François Jean, Marquis de Chastellux, *Travels in North America in the Years 1780, 1781, and 1782,* ed. Howard C. Rice Jr., 2 vols. (Chapel Hill: University of North Carolina Press, 1963), 2:441.

26. Cummings, *Rural Household Inventories,* 190; Thornton, *Seventeenth-Century Interior Decoration,* 149–225; Abbott Lowell Cummings, *Bed Hangings: A Treatise on Fabrics and Styles in the Curtaining of Beds, 1650–1850* (Boston: S.P.N.E.A., 1961); "Bed Hangings," in Florence M. Montgomery, *Textiles in America: A Dictionary Based on Original Documents* (New York: Norton, 1984), 15–47, and "Bed Hangings," in Montgomery, *Printed Textiles*, 49–65.

27. Sometimes "couches" were lightweight beds and nothing more, as they seem to have been frequently in the southern colonies. Their otherwise complicated history is told, as far as it is now known, by Thornton, *Seventeenth-Century Interior Decoration,* 149–79, 210–17, and Benno M. Forman, *American Seating Furniture, 1630–1730* (New York: W. W. Norton, 1988), 208–12. The story continues in Edward S. Cooke Jr., et al., *Upholstery in America and Europe from the Seventeenth Century to World War I* (New York: W. W. Norton, 1987), passim.

28. Tea drinking is the one most often cited and best studied, starting with Rodris Roth, *Tea Drinking in Eighteenth-Century America: Its Etiquette and Equipage,* U.S. National Museum Bulletin 225 (Washington, D.C.: Smithsonian Institution, 1961), and Barbara G. Carson, "Determining the Growth and Distribution of Tea Drinking in Eighteenth-

Century America," in Beatrice Hohenegger, ed., *Steeped in History: The Art of Tea* (Los Angeles: Fowler Museum, University of California, 2009), 158–71. Julia B. Curtis, "Chinese Export Porcelain in Eighteenth-Century Tidewater Virginia," *Studies in Eighteenth-Century Culture* 17 (1987): 121–29, makes the important observation that, while porcelain vessel forms became more standardized after 1712, suggesting a growing consensus about their use, teawares continued to be sold in a wide variety of fashionable patterns. Mary C. Beaudry, "Ceramics in York County, Virginia, Inventories, 1730–1750: The Tea Service" (paper presented at the Eighth Annual Conference of the Society for Historical Archaeology, Charleston, S.C., January 1975), and Ann Smart Martin, "'Fashionable Sugar Dishes, Latest Fashion Ware': The Creamware Revolution in the Eighteenth-Century Chesapeake," in Paul A. Shackle and Barbara J. Little, eds., *Historical Archaeology of the Chesapeake* (Washington, D.C.: Smithsonian Institution Press, 1994), 169–88, present valuable new evidence about the status of tea drinkers, information corroborated from archaeological sources in Anne Yentsch, "Minimum Vessel Lists as Evidence of Change in Folk and Courtly Traditions of Food Use," *Historical Archaeology* 24 (1990): 2453. Barbara G. Carson, *Ambitious Appetites: Dining, Behavior, and Patterns of Consumption in Federal Washington* (Washington, D.C.: American Institute of Architects Press, 1990), describes how teawares and tea etiquette continued to respond to changing social customs after the Revolution. Chances are that other beverages inspired other protocols. The fantastical appearance of posset pots is surely owing to some extraordinary custom in their use, which still awaits discovery. See also Peter B. Brown and Marla H. Schwartz, *Come Drink the Bowl Dry: Alcoholic Liquors and Their Place in 18th Century Society* (York, England: York Civic Trust, 1996).

29. Inventories and newspaper advertisements started using adjectives that referred to the placing of pieces of furniture with some regularity after 1720 and most frequently in the 1760s and 1770s. I am grateful to Karin Goldstein for undertaking for me a study of furniture lexemes to corroborate impressions drawn initially and unsystematically from my acquaintance with museum collections (Goldstein, "Locational Lexemes: An Examination of Subgeneric Levels of Categories of Furniture in Eighteenth-Century Documents," unpublished report, 1989, Colonial Williamsburg Foundation).

30. John Fanning Watson began collecting oral histories from the oldest inhabitants of Philadelphia in the 1820s for his *Annals of Philadelphia and Pennsylvania,* 3 vols. (1830; reprint ed., Philadelphia, 1898), 2:527–28.

31. Daniel Defoe, *The Complete English Tradesman,* 2 vols. (1727; 1745 reprint ed., Oxford, England, 1841), 2:156.

32. See works cited in chapter 1, note 12, for bibliographies and studies of builders' manuals. There is no comparable body of work for other kinds of eighteenth-century pattern books, although some help may be found in Susan Lambert, ed., *Pattern and Design: Designs for Decorative Arts, 1480–1980* (London: Victoria and Albert Museum, 1983), 39–116.

33. Advice literature as a genre deserves the same careful study that courtesy and etiquette books received first from John E. Mason, *Gentlefolk in the Making: Studies in the History of English Courtesy Literature and Related Topics from 1531 to 1774* (Philadelphia: University of Pennsylvania Press, 1935), and Norbert Elias, *The Civilizing Process: The Development of Manners,* vol. 1, trans. Edmund Jephcott (New York: Pantheon, 1978). Renewed interest in the subject started with Anna Bryson, *From Courtesy to Civility: Changing Codes of Conduct in Early Modern England* (Oxford: Clarendon Press, 1998); Philip Carter, *Men and the Emergence of Polite Society, Britain, 1660–1800* (Harlow, Essex, England: Pearson Education, 2001); and a facsimile publication of Francois Nivelon, *The Rudiments of Genteel Behavior* (1737; facsimile ed., London: Paul Holberton, 2003). For American manners, Arthur M. Schlesinger Sr.'s *Learning How to Behave: A Historical Study of American Etiquette Books* (New York: Macmillan, 1947) has been enlarged on and given a broader context in a "courtesy-book world" in Richard L. Bushman, *The Refinement of America: Persons, Houses, Cities* (New York: Alfred A. Knopf, 1992), 30–60, and most recently and systematically in C. Dallett Hemphill, *Bowing to Necessities: A History of Manners in America, 1620–1860* (New York: Oxford University Press, 1999). Cathy N. Davidson assesses the influence of a "reading revolution" in another prescriptive genre, the novel, as it reshaped American attitudes and manners around 1800 in *Revolution and the Word: The Rise of the Novel in America* (New York: Oxford University Press, 1986).

34. The quotation is from Thomas Rawlins, *Familiar Architecture* (London, 1768). In his preface to *The Practical Builder* (London, 1774), William Pain noted a "very great Revolution (as I may say) which of late has so generally prevailed in the Stile of Architecture, especially in the decorative and ornamental department." Hence his book was intended "to furnish the Ignorant [and] the Uninstructed, with . . . a comprehensive System of Practice."

35. For American ownership of architectural treatises see Janice G. Schimmelman, *Architectural Books in Early America: Architectural Treatises and Building Handbooks Available in American Libraries and Bookstores through 1800* (New Castle, Del.: Oak Knoll Press, 1999). Schlesinger, in *Learning How to Behave,* 9, makes a start at listing etiquette books that went through multiple printings and editions, which Christina D. Hemphill extends in "Manners for Americans: Interaction, Ritual, and the Social Order, 1620–1860," PhD diss., Brandeis University, 1988, Appendix, 568–91. For pattern and betterment books as part of a bookseller's total trade, see Gregory A. Stiverson and Cynthia Z. Stiverson, "Books Both Useful and Entertaining: A Study of Book Purchases and Reading Habits of Virginians in the Mid-Eighteenth Century," unpublished report, Colonial Williamsburg Foundation, 1977, and Susan Stromei Berg, "Agent of Change or Trusted Servant: The Eighteenth-Century Williamsburg Press," master's thesis, College of William and Mary, 1993.

36. *The Writings of Benjamin Franklin,* 10 vols., ed. Albert Henry Smyth (London: Macmillian and Co., 1905–7), 3:435. Washington composed his own "Rules of Civility" in 1747 at the age of seventeen, probably by borrowing from a pirated English edition of an earlier French courtesy book. See *George Washington's Rules of Civility and Decent Behaviour in Company and Conversation,* ed. Charles Moore (Boston: Houghton Mifflin, 1926), x–xiv, 23–65. Kenneth A. Lockridge, *The Diary and Life of William Byrd II of Virginia, 1674–1744* (Chapel Hill: University of North Carolina Press, 1987), 21–26, argues that, lacking role models, Byrd learned to be a gentleman through books alone.

37. Martha R. Severens, "Jeremiah Theus of Charleston: Plagiarist or Pundit?," *Southern Quarterly* 24 (1985): 56–70.

38. *Diary and Autobiography of John Adams,* ed. L. H. Butterfield, 4 vols. (Cambridge, Mass.: Belknap Press of Harvard University Press, 1961), 1:294.

39. *South Carolina Gazette,* July 9, 1772, cited in *Arts and Crafts in Philadelphia, Maryland, and South Carolina,* 176.

40. Benjamin Henry Latrobe, *The Virginia Journals of Benjamin Henry Latrobe, 1795–1798,* ed. Edward C. Carter II (New Haven: Yale University Press, 1997), 306–7.

41. *Lower Norfolk County, Virginia, Antiquary* 5 (1906): 33–35n. The year was 1774.

42. Cited in Esther Singleton, *Social New York under the Georges, 1714–1776* (New York: D. Appleton, 1902), 380–81.

43. R[obert?] Campbell, *The London Tradesman* (London, 1747), 171–72.

44. Studies of American furniture have respected geographical boundaries since the 1930s, but only a few furniture historians have tried to explain how these regional differences occurred. About the first was Charles F. Montgomery, *American Furniture: The Federal Period* (New York: Viking Press, 1966), and subsequently his essay "Regional Preferences and Characteristics in American Decorative Arts: 1750–1800," in Charles F. Montgomery and Patricia E. Kane, eds., *American Art, 1750–1800: Towards Independence* (Boston: New York Graphic Society, 1976), 50–66. His explanation, that regional characteristics were mostly owing to craft organization and specialization, is seconded and enlarged upon by Benjamin Hewitt in Benjamin A. Hewitt, Patricia E. Kane, and Gerald W. R. Ward, eds., *The Work of Many Hands: Card Tables in Federal America, 1790–1820* (New Haven: Yale University Art Gallery, 1982), and Forman, *American Seating Furniture,* 55. Forman further demonstrates the influence of immigrant craftsmen in transmitting furniture-making practices from one place to another. As Philip D. Zimmerman explains in "Regionalism in American Furniture Studies," in Gerald W. R. Ward, ed., *Perspectives on American Furniture* (New York: W. W. Norton, 1988), 18, the buyer's preferences are almost wholly unaccounted for in research so far. Consumers played a role in shaping regional styles through purchases that cumulatively ensured the success of certain products (and their makers or sellers) over others deemed less desirable. The theory behind such a process is briefly explained by Fraser Neiman in his review of *The Work*

of Many Hands in *Vernacular Architecture Newsletter* 16 (1983): 6–11. The only works that come anywhere close to a furnishings history from the consumer's point of view are Edward S. Cooke Jr.'s highly original *Fiddlebacks and Crooked-backs: Elijah Booth and Other Joiners in Newtown and Woodbury [Connecticut], 1750–1820* (Waterbury, Conn.: Mattatuck Historical Society, 1982), his "Craftsman Client Relations in the Housatonic Valley [Connecticut], 1720–1800," *Antiques* 125 (1984): 272–80, and Wendy A. Cooper and Lisa Minardi, *Paint, Pattern, and People: Furniture of Southeastern Pennsylvania, 1725–1850* (Winterthur, Del.: A Winterthur Book, 2011), xiii–xxi, 61–115. No one yet has dealt head-on with the fundamentally different nature of regional customs in folk and polite cultures or tried to explain by what process the one may have led to the other in traditional communities that opened their doors to fashion in the eighteenth century.

45. The view used to be that folk art represented "primitive," "naive," or "amateur" misinterpretations of high-style art or was just an inept or ignorant attempt at imitation. Anthropologists disabused art historians of that notion, and most of them now understand that variations from elite models and design-book prototypes occurred all along a continuum from court to country. Artificers who were removed intellectually and geographically from the centers of metropolitan production selectively appropriated those serviceable parts of elite aesthetics that their own experience had taught them would please and satisfy their hometown patrons. Future research needs to identify which design elements were singled out for restyling and explain why. A place to start is work by Richard Bebb, *Welsh Furniture, 1250–1950: A Cultural History of Craftsmanship and Design,* 2 vols. (Kidwelly, Carmarthenshire, Wales: Saer Books, 2007), especially 2:379–419.

46. Benjamin Rush's address to the Young Ladies' Academy of Philadelphia, given in 1787 and published as *Thoughts upon Female Education Accommodated to the Present State of Society, Manners, and Government in the United States of America* (Boston, 1791), 18. David Hancock makes a similar point for colonial societies generally, that consumers "around the Atlantic Ocean rim were focused more on their own opportunities and needs than on the fashions and dictates of the mother countries' gentility," in his "Self Organized Complexity and the Emergence of an Atlantic Market, 1651–1815," in Peter Coclanis, ed., *The Atlantic Economy in the Seventeenth and Eighteenth Centuries: Organization, Operation, Practice, and Personnel* (Columbia: University of South Carolina Press, 2006), 61.

47. Alexis de Tocqueville, *Democracy in America,* trans. Henry Reeve, 2 vols. (New York: New York Public Library, 1900), 2:229.

48. Adam von Gurowski, *America and Europe* (New York, 1857), 375–76.

49. Quoted by Schlesinger, *Learning How to Behave,* 21.

50. Cummings, *Rural Household Inventories,* 237–40. Brewer's total estate was appraised at £855 16s. 7d, about £125 greater than the value of John Weld's after adjust-

ment for inflation. Brewer's household furnishings were worth £108, plus a £9 chaise and personal clothing appraised at £20; Weld's furnishings had totaled £103. I am grateful to Gloria Main for supplying the correct deflators.

51. This more-for-less paradox, so vexing to economic historians, was pondered by Carole Shammas in *The Pre-Industrial Consumer in England and America (Oxford: Clarendon Press, 1990),* 76–112, and finally put to rest by Jan de Vries, *The Industrious Revolution: Consumer Behavior and the Household Economy, 1650 to the Present* (Cambridge: Cambridge University Press, 2008); see chapter 1, note 52.

52. *Some Cursory Remarks Made by James Birket in His Voyage to North America, 1750–1751,* ed. C[harles] M. A[ndrews] (New Haven: Yale University Press, 1916), 4, 8–9, 21, 24, 27, 30–34 for information in the subsequent paragraphs.

53. James Birket was not alone in his criticism. Dr. Alexander Hamilton had a remarkably similar reaction to Malbone's fabulous house when he passed through Newport six years earlier in 1744: "It is the largest and most magnificent dwelling house I have seen in America. It is built intirely with hewn stone of a reddish colour; the sides of the windows and corner stones of the house being painted like white marble. . . . This house makes a grand show att a distance *but is not extraordinary for the architecture, being a clumsy Dutch modell"* (*Gentleman's Progress: The Itinerarium of Dr. Alexander Hamilton, 1744,* ed. Carl Bridenbaugh [Chapel Hill: University of North Carolina Press, 1948], 103, my italics). A rule was a rule was a rule!

54. London merchant Peter Collinson to John Bartram of Pennsylvania, February 17, 1737, in *William and Mary Quarterly,* 2nd ser., 6 (1926): 303–5.

55. The genteel men and women who made up the multitude of stay-at-home consumers are the real protagonists in Richard Bushman's *The Refinement of America.* He has little to say about good manners as a passport for people on the move. The teapot remark was made by *A Frenchman in England, 1784: Being the Mélanges sur l'Angleterre of François de la Rochefoucault,* ed. Jean Marchand, trans. S. C. Roberts (Cambridge: Cambridge University Press, 1933), 24.

56. Susan Kern, *The Jeffersons at Shadwell* (New Haven: Yale University Press, 2010), 183–200; Henry Timberlake, *The Memoirs of Lieutenant Henry Timberlake* (London, 1765), 49–51; Timothy J. Shannon, "Dressing for Success on the Mohawk Frontier: Hendrick, William Johnson, and the Indian Fashion," *William and Mary Quarterly*, 3rd ser., 53 (1996): 22–35.

57. Josiah Tucker, *Instructions for Travellers* (London, 1757), 3.

6. American à la Mode

1. Catharine E. Beecher, *A Treatise on Domestic Economy for the Use of Young Ladies at Home and at School* (1841; reprint ed., New York: Source Book Press, 1970), 17, 264.

2. *Gentleman's Progress: The Itinerarium of Dr. Alexander Hamilton, 1744,* ed. Carl Bridenbaugh (Chapel Hill: University of North Carolina Press, 1948), 13–14; Maria T. Daviess, *History of Mercer and Boyle Counties [Kentucky]* (Harrodsburg, Ky.: The Harrodsburg Herald, 1924), 45; Elizabeth A. Perkins, "The Consumer Frontier: Household Consumption in Early Kentucky," *Journal of American History* 78 (1991): 486–510.

3. Beecher, *Treatise on Domestic Economy,* 16–17, 267; Alexis de Tocqueville, *Democracy in America,* ed. J. P. Mayer, trans. George Lawrence (Garden City, N.Y.: Doubleday, 1969), 54.

4. William Cuninghame to Bennett Price, October 7, 1767, William Cuninghame and Co. Letter Book, 1767–73, privately owned, inquiries to National Library of Scotland.

5. Robert Southey, *Letters from England* (1807; reprint ed., London: Cresset Press, 1951), 164–65.

6. Richard Montgomery to John Montgomery, n.d. [1772], cited in Thomas H. Montgomery, "Ancestry of General Richard Montgomery," *New York Genealogical and Biographical Record* 2 (1871): 129.

7. This and the following quotations are from an 1832 diary of Ann F. Maury, a young Englishwoman widely traveled in the United States, published in *Intimate Virginia: A Century of Maury Travels by Land and Sea,* ed. Anne Fontaine Maury (Richmond, Va.: Dietz Press, 1941), 199.

8. T. H. Breen, *The Marketplace of Revolution: How Consumer Politics Shaped American Independence* (Oxford: Oxford University Press, 2004), 195–331. Breen's ambitious book introduced a wider reading public to the fact of Americans' voracious appetite for consumer goods in the eighteenth century, and parts of the book have been useful to me as noted. It is not without serious critics, notably Gordon S. Wood, "The Shopper's Revolution," *New York Review of Books,* June 10, 2004: 26–30, and John Brewer, "Ego in the Arcades: Colonials, Consumers and the Conditions of Revolt," *Times Literary Supplement,* October 22, 2004: 3–4. The "Baubles" remark was Samuel Adams's disparaging term for the imported fripperies that he complained to Virginian Arthur Lee corrupted liberty-loving Americans, in Adams to Lee, October 31, 1771, Harry Alonzo Cushing, ed., *The Writings of Samuel Adams,* 4 vols. (New York: G. Putnam, 1904–8), 2:267.

9. T. H. Breen, "Narratives of Commercial Life: Consumption, Ideology, and Community on the Eve of the American Revolution," *William and Mary Quarterly,* 3rd ser., 50 (1993): 471–501.

10. With the important exception of Ann Morgan Smart's master's thesis, "The Urban/Rural Dichotomy of Status Consumption: Tidewater Virginia, 1815" (College of William and Mary, 1986), the 1815 property tax on household furniture is virtually unknown and almost unused by social historians. Returns survive for Massachusetts, Pennsylvania, Maryland, Virginia, North Carolina, and perhaps other states. Enactment of the statute is recorded in the Records of the Ways and Means Committee, "Report on So

Much of the President's Message as Relates to the Finances of the United States," October 10, 1814 (National Archives, HR 13-A D14.4); *Annals of Congress,* 13th Congress, 3rd Session, "State of the Treasury," 1095, "Proceedings," 132, 254, "Operation of the Direct Tax," 1096–97, "Taxation of the District of Columbia," 1098; *U.S. Statutes at Large,* 13th Congress, 3rd Session, 1815, 196–98. The assessors went from house to house collecting very specific information. They organized the Virginia returns into four categories: (1) major pieces of furniture, down to chairs made of mahogany, plus carpets, window curtains, and Venetian blinds, (2) case pieces in other woods, (3) pictures, looking glasses, and musical instruments, and (4) containers for genteel beverages, fancy lighting devices, and wash basins (Tax Records, "Personal Property Tax, 1825," by county, Virginia State Library, Richmond). Taxes were also levied on expensive footwear, horse harnesses, gold and silver watches, paper, nails, and playing cards.

11. As yet only Lorena Walsh has pulled together a tentative summary view of consumption patterns in the United States in the early nineteenth century, in "Consumer Behavior, Diet, and the Standard of Living in Late Colonial and Early Antebellum America, 1770–1840," in Robert E. Gallman and John Joseph Wallis, eds., *American Economic Growth and Standards of Living before the Civil War* (Chicago: University of Chicago Press, 1992), 217–64. There is other valuable information in Bernard L. Herman, *Town House: Architecture and Material Life in the Early American City, 1780–1830* (Chapel Hill: University of North Carolina Press, 2005), and George L. Miller, "Marketing Ceramics in North America" and subsequent articles on the ceramics market nationwide in *Winterthur Portfolio* 19 (1984). See also essays in Suzanne M. Spencer-Wood, ed., *Consumer Choice in Historical Archaeology* (New York and London: Plenum Press, 1987).

12. See chapter 1, note 52. Also Amada Vickery, *The Gentleman's Daughter: Women's Lives in Georgian England* (New Haven: Yale University Press, 1998), 161–94, esp. 164–68; and John Styles and Amanda Vickery, eds., *Gender, Taste and Material Culture in Britain and North America, 1700–1830* (New Haven: Yale University Press, 2006). Lorna Weatherill asks how women's roles within the household may have altered the value they attached to materials things in "A Possession of One's Own: Women and Consumer Behaviour in England, 1660–1740," *Journal of British Studies* 25 (1986): 131–56.

13. This and much that follows are explained in Wendy A. Woloson, "The Rise of the Consumer in the Age of Jackson," in Sean Patrick Adams, ed., *A Companion to the Era of Andrew Jackson* (Chichester, West Sussex, England: Wiley-Blackwell, 2013), 489–507. See also Mary Beth Sievens, "Female Consumerism and Household Authority in Early National New England," *Early American Studies* 4 (2006): 353–71.

14. David Jaffee, "Peddlers and Progress and the Transformation of the Rural North, 1760–1860," *Journal of American History* 78 (1991): 511–35; Joseph T. Rainer, "The 'Sharper' Image: Yankee Peddlers, Southern Customers, and the Market Revolution," *Business and Economic History Review* 26 (1997): 27–44.

15. Michael Zakim, "Creating a Democracy of Common Men," in Adams, *Companion to the Era of Andrew Jackson,* 170–93.

16. Michael Zakim, *Ready-Made Democracy: A History of Men's Dress in the American Republic, 1760–1860* (Chicago: University of Chicago Press, 2003), a social history with broad political implications; and David Jaffee, *A New Nation of Goods: The Material Culture of Early America* (Philadelphia: University of Pennsylvania Press, 2010).

17. See, for example, J. Franklin Jameson, ed., "Diary of Edward Hooker, 1805–8," in *American Historical Association Reports* 1 (1896): 895, for a description of a preacher's house in the Carolina mountains; also Louis-Philippe, *Diary of My Travels in America,* trans. Stephen Becker (New York: Delacorte Press, 1977), 113–14, for a down-home bedroom scene in Knoxville in 1797 that left even the sophisticated future king of France nonplussed.

18. Besides Elizabeth Perkins's study of Kentucky in "The Consumer Frontier," other useful local histories and archaeological site reports that document the westward spread of consumer goods and habits include George L. Miller and Silas D. Hurry, "Ceramic Supply in an Economically Isolated Frontier Community: Portage County of the Ohio Western Reserve, 1800- 1825," *Historical Archaeology* 17 (1983): 81–92; Mark J. Wagner and Mary R. McCorvie, "Archaeological Investigations at the 'Old Landmark': An Early to Mid-Nineteenth-Century Tavern along the St. Louis-Vincennes Trace," unpublished report, American Resources Group, and Partners in Historic Preservation, Carbondale, Ill., c. 1989; and David L. Felton and Peter D. Schulz, *The Diaz Collection: Material Culture and Social Change in Mid-Nineteenth-Century Monterey,* California Archaeological Report 23 (Sacramento: California Department of Parks and Recreation, 1983).

19. William H. Gilman et al., eds., *The Journals and Miscellaneous Notebooks of Ralph Waldo Emerson,* 16 vols. (Cambridge, Mass.: Harvard University Press, 1960–82), 5:296–97. He made the observation in 1837.

20. Unreconstructed consensus historian Daniel Boorstin amply demonstrated for a later period in American history the price that most students of immigration pay for their neglect of this subject. Ideas that he first presented in *The Americans: The Democratic Experience* (New York: Random House, 1973), especially part 2, "Consumption Communities," were further developed in a Smithsonian Institution exhibit, "Suiting Everyone: The Democratization of Clothing in America" (1974), accompanied by an interpretive catalogue of the same title by Claudia B. Kidwell and Margaret C. Christman (Washington, D.C.: Smithsonian Institution Press, 1974).

21. More clearly inferred from the illustrations than stated in the text in Dell Upton, ed., *America's Architectural Roots: Ethnic Groups That Built America* (Washington, D.C.: The Preservation Press, 1986).

22. Don Yoder, "The Pennsylvania-Germans: Three Centuries of Identity Crisis," in Frank Trommler and Joseph McVeigh, eds., *America and the Germans: An Assessment of*

a Three-Hundred-Year History, 2 vols. (Philadelphia: University of Pennsylvania Press, 1985), 1:42–45.

23. Johann David Schoepf, *Travels in the Confederation* (1783–84), trans. and ed. Alfred J. Morrison (1788; reprint ed., New York: Burt Franklin, 1968), 125.

24. Theodore G. Tappert and John W. Doberstein, trans. and ed., *The Notebook of a Colonial Clergyman, Condensed from the Journals of Henry Melchior Muhlenberg* (Philadelphia: Muhlenberg Press, 1959), 229–30, from a journal entry dated 1783, the same year that Schoepf described German and English houses in the same locality.

25. Cynthia G. Falk, *Architecture and Artifacts of the Pennsylvania Germans: Constructing Identity in Early America* (University Park: Pennsylvania State University Press, 2008), 61–113; Klaus Wust, *The Virginia Germans* (Charlottesville: University Press of Virginia, 1969), 93–199; Henry Glassie, "Eighteenth-Century Cultural Process in Delaware Valley Folk Building," *Winterthur Portfolio* 7 (1972): 29–57; Stephanie Grauman Wolf, *Urban Village: Population, Community, and Family Structure in Germantown, Pennsylvania, 1683–1800* (Princeton: Princeton University Press, 1976), 127–53; Robert D. Mitchell, *Commercialism and Frontier: Perspectives on the Early Shenandoah Valley* (Charlottesville: University Press of Virginia, 1977), 104–9, 122–32; Lonn Taylor, "Fachwerk and Brettstuhl: The Reflection of Traditional Folk Culture," in Ian M. G. Quimby and Scott T. Swank, eds. *Perspectives on American Folk Art* (New York: Norton, 1980), 162–76; Elizabeth Augusta Kessel, "Germans on the Maryland Frontier: A Social History of Frederick County, Maryland, 1730–1800," PhD diss., Rice University, 1981, 284–342; Edward A. Chappell, "Acculturation in the Shenandoah Valley: Rhenish Houses of the Massanutten Settlement," *Proceedings of the American Philosophical Society* 124 (1980): 55–89.

26. Gottlieb Mittelberger, *Journey to Pennsylvania* [1750], ed. and trans. Oscar Handlin and John Clive (Cambridge, Mass.: Harvard University Press, 1960), 88; Theophile Cazenove, *Cazenove Journal, 1794: A Record of the Journey of Theophile Cazenove through New Jersey and Pennsylvania*, ed. Rayner Wickersham Kelsey (Haverford: Pennsylvania History Press, 1922), 84–85.

27. Chappell, "Acculturation," 61–63; Scott T. Swank et al., *Arts of the Pennsylvania Germans* (New York: Norton, 1983); Richard Henning Field, "Proxemic Patterns: Eighteenth-Century Lunenburg-German Domestic Furniture and Interiors," *Material History Bulletin* 22 (1985): 40–48; Philip Otterness, *Becoming German: The 1709 Palatine Migration to New York* (Ithaca: Cornell University Press, 2004), 1–4, 55–66; Wendy A. Cooper and Lisa Minardi, *Paint, Pattern, and People: Furniture of Southeastern Pennsylvania, 1725–1850* (Winterthur, Del.: A Winterthur Book, 2011), 1–115.

28. Cynthia Falk reaches the same conclusion in *Architecture and Artifacts of the Pennsylvania Germans,* 13–29.

29. Samuel R. Wells, *How to Behave: A Pocket Manual of Republican Etiquette . . .* (New York, 1856), 124.

30. Colin Campbell, a disbeliever, critiques the emulation arguments in *The Romantic Ethic and the Spirit of Modern Consumerism* (Oxford: Basil Blackwell, 1987), 36–57.

31. Campbell, *Romantic Ethic,* 88–95.

32. Quoted in Arthur M. Schlesinger Sr., *Learning How to Behave: A Historical Study of American Etiquette Books* (New York: Macmillan, 1947), 17.

33. *Journal of the Life of Nathanial Luff M.D., of the State of Delaware* (New York, 1848), 12–13, recalling Philadelphia in the 1770s; Sara Payson Willis [pen name Fanny Fern], *Fern Leaves from Fanny's Port-Folio* (Auburn, N.Y., 1854), 317–19; [Margaret Bayard Smith], *What Is Gentility? A Moral Tale* (Washington, D.C., 1828), 4.

34. Frances Anne Kemble, *Journal of a Residence on a Georgian Plantation in 1838–1839,* ed. John A. Scott (New York: Alfred A. Knopf, 1961), 93–94; E. D. Worthington to David Ross McCord, [1894], in Louisa McCord Smythe, *For Olde Lange Syne* (Charleston, S.C.: privately printed, 1900), 5; Shane White and Graham White, "Slave Clothing and African-American Culture in the Eighteenth and Nineteenth Centuries," *Past and Present* 148 (1995): 160–62, 176–79.

35. Kirk Swinehart, "This Wild Place: Sir William Johnson among the Mohawks, 1715–1783," PhD diss., Yale University, 2002.

36. Richard L. Bushman, *The Refinement of America: Persons, Houses, Cities* (New York: Alfred A. Knopf, 1992), part 2, explains how the line separating gentlefolk from the rest of society trended downward after 1790 to embrace more middle-class aspirants and exclude mainly workers and the poorer sort.

37. Quoted and discussed in Robert Micklus, "'The History of the Tuesday Club': A Mock-Jeremiad of the Colonial South," *William and Mary Quarterly,* 3rd ser. 40 (1983): 55–56, and Dr. Alexander Hamilton, *The History of the Ancient and Honorable Tuesday Club* (1745–56), 3 vols., ed. Robert Micklus (Chapel Hill: University of North Carolina Press, 1990), 1:240–42, 2:97–99; 2:266–70.

38. *Columbian Centinel,* December 8, 1792.

39. It was said, for example, of planter-merchants on Barbados that "they out do the Dutch in Heraldry for every man assumes what coat he pleaseth . . . and they are such unthinking Devills here that if two brothers dye the Years one after the other, they generally have different Coates [painted on the funeral hatchments] for the painter has forgott, what he Drew for the first Brother, [or] the family did not like it & makes him design another" (Capt. Thomas Waladuck to James Petiver, November 13, 1710, Sloane MSS., British Library). I am grateful to David Shields for bringing this letter to my attention.

40. Sociologist David M. Potter formulated the benign consumption thesis in *People of Plenty: Economic Abundance and the American Character* (Chicago University of Chicago Press, 1954). His critics, latter-day Veblenites and Marxists, include Stuart Ewen, *Captains of Consciousness: Advertising and the Social Roots of the Consumer Culture* (New

York: McGraw-Hill, 1976); T. J. Jackson Lears, *No Place of Grace: Antimodernism and the Transformation of American Culture, 1889–1920* (New York: Pantheon, 1981); and T. J. Jackson Lears, "The Concept of Cultural Hegemony: Problems and Possibilities," *American Historical Review* 90 (1985): 567–93. The power-struggle interpretation has drawn fire from Warren I. Susman, *Culture as History: The Transformation of American Society in the Twentieth Century* (New York: Pantheon, 1984), and Daniel Horowitz, *Morality of Spending: Attitudes toward the Consumer Society in America, 1875–1940* (Baltimore: Johns Hopkins University Press, 1985). Lears finds historical precedent and cultural significance in the debate itself in "Beyond Veblen: Rethinking Consumer Culture in America," in Simon J. Bronner, ed., *Consuming Visions: Accumulation and Display of Goods in America, 1880–1920* (New York: W. W. Norton, 1989), 73–97. All this is now adroitly capped off in Lizabeth Cohen, *A Consumers' Republic: The Politics of Mass Consumption in Postwar America* (New York: Knopf, 2003), and the key works collected in Juliet Schor and Douglas B. Holt, eds., *The Consumer Society Reader* (New York: The New Press, 2000).

41. Conveniently summarized in Bronner's introduction to *Consuming Visions*, 1–4. While Lears is not ready "to abandon my own and other historians' stress on the late nineteenth century as a period of crucial transformation," he has come round to the view that "an understanding of that transformation requires a subtler conceptual framework than simply the notion of a shift from a Protestant 'producer culture' to a secular 'consumer culture'" ("Beyond Veblen," 77n8).

7. Toward a History of Material Life

1. Adam Smith, *The Theory of Moral Sentiments* (London, 1759), 108.

2. The point of T. H. Breen's argument in "An Empire of Goods: The Anglicization of Colonial America, 1690–1776," *Journal of British Studies* 25 (1986): 467–99, and in *The Marketplace of Revolution: How Consumer Politics Shaped American Independence* (Oxford: Oxford University Press, 2004). It is also Richard L. Bushman's point of departure in "American High-Style and Vernacular Cultures," in Jack P. Greene and J. R. Pole, eds., *Colonial British America: Essays in the New History of the Early Modern Era* (Baltimore: Johns Hopkins University Press, 1984), 345–83.

3. David Hackett Fischer, *Albion's Seed: Four British Folkways in America* (New York: Oxford University Press, 1989). Fischer's argument became the subject of a forum entitled "*Albion's Seed: Four British Folkways in America*—A Symposium," *William and Mary Quarterly*, 3rd ser., 48 (1991): 223–308; see also Michael Zuckerman, "Regionalism," in Daniel Vickers, ed., *Blackwell Companion to Early American History* (Oxford: Blackwell Publishing, 2003), 317–19. Taking less extreme positions are David Grayson Allen, *In English Ways: The Movement of Societies and the Transferal of English Local Law and Cus-*

tom to Massachusetts Bay in the Seventeenth Century (Chapel Hill: University of North Carolina Press, 1981), and Edmund S. Morgan, *American Slavery, American Freedom: The Ordeal of Colonial Virginia* (New York: W. W. Norton, 1975).

4. Jack P. Greene, *Pursuits of Happiness: The Social Development of Early Modern British Colonies and the Formation of American Culture* (Chapel Hill: University of North Carolina Press, 1988); Thad W. Tate, "The Seventeenth-Century Chesapeake and Its Modern Historians," in Thad W. Tate and David L. Ammerman, eds., *The Chesapeake in the Seventeenth Century: Essays on Anglo-American Society* (Chapel Hill: University of North Carolina Press, 1979), 3–50; Sumner Chilton Powell, *Puritan Village: The Formation of a New England Town* (Middletown, Conn.: Wesleyan University Press, 1963); Cary Carson, Joanne Bowen, Willie Graham, Martha McCartney, and Lorena Walsh, "New World, Real World: Improvising English Culture in Seventeenth-Century Virginia," *Journal of Southern History* 74 (2008): 31–88, esp. 31–34, 85–88.

5. Greene, *Pursuits of Happiness,* 174–75. The historiography of this theme is discussed in Breen, "Empire of Goods," 496–99, and James A. Henretta, "Wealth and Social Structure," in Greene and Pole, *Colonial British America,* 279–81.

6. James J. F. Deetz, *In Small Things Forgotten: The Archaeology of Early American Life* (Garden City, N.Y.: Anchor Press/Doubleday, 1977), 37–40.

7. Hugh Jones, *The Present State of Virginia* (1724), ed. Richard L. Morton (Chapel Hill: University of North Carolina Press, 1956), 81, 102.

8. Greene, *Pursuits of Happiness,* 168.

9. The phrase was first used strictly in reference to the Massachusetts Bay Colony by T. H. Breen and Stephen Foster in "The Puritans' Greatest Achievement: A Study of Social Cohesion in Seventeenth-Century Massachusetts," *Journal of American History* 60 (1973): 22. For others it aptly describes the convergence of all mainland colonial societies with mainstream social and cultural developments in Great Britain.

10. William Eddis, *Letters from America,* ed. Aubrey C. Land (Cambridge, Mass.: Belknap Press of Harvard University Press, 1969), 57–58.

11. Breen, "Empire of Goods," 497–99.

12. See chapter 6, pp. 169–72.

13. My use of all these sources throughout this essay should have dispelled any suspicion that I trust them uncritically. For a further explanation of the connection I make between the use of artifacts and the meaning that users attached to them, see chapter 3, p. 79.

14. The range is represented in works cited in Kenneth L. Ames and Gerald W. R. Ward, eds., *Decorative Arts and Household Furnishings in America, 1650–1820: A Bibliography,* (Winterthur, Del.: Henry Francis du Pont Winterthur Museum , 1989).

15. Quoted in Jim Hoagland, "Reunification Qualms: From Western Shops," *Washington Post,* December 23, 1989.

16. Joanna Brenner, "Highlights of the Pew Internet Project's Research Related to Mobile Technology," *PewInternet,* June 6, 2013; Yue Wang, "More People Have Cell Phones Than Toilets, U.N. Study Shows," *Time NewsFeed*, March 25, 2013.

17. Timothy Noah, *The Great Divergence: America's Growing Inequality Crisis and What We Can Do About It* (New York: Bloomsbury Press, 2012); Joseph E. Stiglitz, *The Price of Inequality: How Today's Divided Society Endangers Our Future* (New York: W. W. Norton, 2012); Thomas Piketty, *Capital in the Twenty-First Century*, trans, Arthur Goldhammer (Cambridge. Mass.: Belknap Press/Harvard University Press, 2014).

18. Thomas Jefferson to Marquis de Lafayette, Nice, France, April 11, 1787, in Julian P. Boyd, Charles T. Cullen, John Catanzariti, Barbara B. Oberg et al., eds., *The Papers of Thomas* Jefferson, 33 vols. (Princeton: Princeton University Press, 1950–), 11: 285.

Illustration Credits

Courtesy Alexandria Archaeology: *fig. 6(g)*

Courtesy Augusta Richmond County Museum, Augusta, Ga.: *fig. 6(h)* (drawings by Nancy Kurtz)

Drawings by Jeffrey Bostetter: *fig. 9, fig. 20, fig. 21*

Courtesy Van Beuningen-de Vriese Collection, Boymans-van Beuningen Museum, Rotterdam: *fig. 6(a)* (drawings by Nancy Kurtz after David Neal)

Drawings by Cary Carson: *fig. 2, fig. 3* (based on information from Historic St. Mary's City, Maryland [*page 22*], and information from Colonial Williamsburg [*page 23*]), *fig. 9, fig. 19, fig. 20, fig. 29* (from salvaged interiors, photographs, and measured sketches in Winterthur Museum archives and from fieldwork by Edward A. Chappell)

From fieldwork by Edward A. Chappell: *fig. 29*

Courtesy of The Charleston Museum, Charleston, South Carolina: *fig. 27 (page 157, left)*

Courtesy Brooke Clagget: *fig. 8*

Courtesy of The Colonial Williamsburg Foundation: *fig. 13(e, g, h, i)* (drawings by Nancy Kurtz), *fig. 14(c)* (Knowles Collection; drawing by Nancy Kurtz), *fig. 15* (L. B. Weber Collection; drawing by Nancy Kurtz), *fig. 17* (Abby Aldrich Rockefeller Folk Art Museum, gift of

Abby Aldrich Rockefeller), *fig. 18* (Museum Purchase), *fig. 25* (Museum Purchase, The Friends of Colonial Williamsburg Collections Fund), *fig. 28* (Museum Purchase)

Photograph courtesy of The Colonial Williamsburg Foundation: *fig. 4* (with permission of Paul Steed), *fig. 8* (with permission of Bruce Clagett), *fig. 12* (reproduced by permission of/© 2017 The Society of the Cincinnati, Washington, D.C.)

Copyright Colonial Williamsburg's Digital History Center, in conjunction with The University of Virginia's Institute for Advanced Technologies in the Humanities (IATH), with funding from the Andrew W. Mellon Foundation, Institute of Museum and Library Services (IMLS), and the National Endowment for the Humanities (NEH): *fig. 1 (page 18)*

Image courtesy of the Gibbes Museum of Art/Carolina Art Association, 1915.003.0001: *fig. 27 (page 157, right)*

Drawing by William Graham: *fig. 1 (page 19)*

Drawing by Heather Harvey: *fig. 5 (page 44)* (based on examination and analysis by Joanne Bowen)

Courtesy Historic St. Mary's City: *fig. 6(e)* (drawings by Nancy Kurtz), *fig. 11(b)* (drawings by Nancy Kurtz)

Courtesy the Johns Hopkins University, John Work Garrett Library, Special Collections Department: *fig. 31*

Drawings by Nancy Kurtz: *fig. 6(a)* (after David Neal), *fig. 6(c)* (after Cathy Brann), *fig. 6(e and h), fig. 7, fig. 11(a, b, c, d, e, f, g), fig. 13(a, b, c, d, g, h, i), fig. 14(a, b, c, d), fig. 15, fig. 16*

Library of Congress, Washington, D.C.: *fig 24*

Drawings by Tricia Miller: *fig 5 (page 45), fig. 10 (page 76), fig. 10 (page 77)* (after Robert Tarule), *fig. 13(f), fig. 22*

Courtesy Mint Museum of Art, Delhom Collection: *fig. 16* (drawings by Nancy Kurtz)

Drawings by Margaret Mulrooney: *fig. 2, fig. 19, fig. 29* (from salvaged interiors, photographs, and measured sketches in Winterthur Museum archives and from fieldwork by Edward A. Chappell)

Courtesy National Park Service: *fig. 6(d), fig. 11(a, c, d, e)* (drawings by Nancy Kurtz), *fig. 13(a, b, c, d)* (drawings by Nancy Kurtz), *fig. 14(a, b, d)* (drawings by Nancy Kurtz)

Courtesy National Portrait Gallery, London: *fig. 27 (page 156, left)*

Courtesy New Brunswick Museum, Maine: *fig. 6(c)* (drawings by Nancy Kurtz after Cathy Brann)

Courtesy New York Public Library: *fig. 26(b, d)*

Courtesy North Andover Historical Society: *fig. 22* (photograph by Jonathan Owen after Samuel Dale Stevens; drawings by Tricia Miller)

Courtesy of Reynolda House Museum of American Art, Winston-Salem, North Carolina, gift of Barbara B. Millhouse, 1972.2.1: *fig. 27 (page 156, right)*

Courtesy Rochester Museum and Science Center: *fig. 13(f)* (drawings by Tricia Miller)

Courtesy of the Schwenkfelder Library and Heritage Center, Pennsburg, PA: *fig. 30*

Reproduced by permission of/© 2017 The Society of the Cincinnati, Washington, D.C.: *fig. 12*

Courtesy Virginia Historic Landmarks Commission: *fig. 6(d, e, f, g)* (drawings by Nancy Kurtz)

Courtesy, Winterthur Library: Printed Book and Periodical Collection: *fig. 26(a, c)*

Courtesy, Winterthur Museum, Garden, and Library: *fig. 7* (drawings by Nancy Kurtz), *fig. 23, fig. 29* (drawings by Cary Carson and Margaret Mulrooney)

Index

Italicized page numbers refer to illustrations.

artisans. *See* tradesmen

assemblies, 16, 187

associations, 16

backcountry, xx, 175–76. *See also* immigrants

back-stools ("chair stooles"), 100–101

Bailyn, Bernard, 52–53, 222n21, 240n61

ballrooms, 20, 131, 135, *137, 153;* en suite with card room and supper room, 135

balls, 15, 16–17, 155

Banister, Thomas, 143

Barnard (Parson) House (North Andover, Massachusetts), 249n22

baroque, *50,* 90, 143, *180*

bathhouse, gentlemen's (Warm Springs, Virginia), *20–21*

beads: worn by Indians, 164; worn by slaves, 44, 116, 241n65

bedchambers, 67, *68–69,* 92, 130, *132–33,* 135, *140–42,* 146, 160, 178

beds and bedsteads, 71–72, 173, 201–2; as basic furnishings, 10, 13, 40, 219n4; removed to separate bedchambers, *132–33,* 135, 146

Beecher, Catharine, 165–68

benches, 10, 41, 72, 100–101. *See also* stools

Berg, Maxime, xviii

Berkeley, Norborne (baron de Botetourt), 126

Beverley, Robert, 210n23

Birket, James, 161–64, 254n53

blacksmiths, 28, 159–60, 163. *See also* tradesmen

bondsmen. *See* servants; slaves and slavery

books, 88, 114, 160, 199, 252n36; advice literature, 251n33; almanacs and chapbooks, 17; courtesy and etiquette, 154,

252n36; children's, 16; cookbooks, 103, 106, 110, 229n23, 235n36; fiction, 15, 25, 155, 251n33; how-to books, 15, 17, 150–53, 155; pattern books, 150, 207n12, 250n32; polemical, 7, 31

booksellers, 16, 150, 154, 207n12, 251n35. *See also* printers

book trade, 17, 150, 207n12

Boorstin, Daniel, 204n5, 257n20

Boston, Massachusetts, 154; concerts in, 187; craftsmen in, 102, 132, 187; and fashion, xvii, 112, 138–39, 143; and furniture, 85–87, 91, 100–102, 234n23; goods from, 175; houses in, 130, 143, 245n3, 245–46n4, 249n21; merchants in, xvii, 162; travelers' observations on, 139, 162

Botetourt, Gov. (Norborne Berkeley, baron de Botetourt), 126

boycotts, 169–70, *171,* 172, 197; and Articles of Association, 170; and Stamp Act, 170; as symbols of resistance, 172; and Tea Act, 170, *171;* and Townshend duties, 170

Boyleston, Nicholas, 154

Braudel, Fernand, 213n31, 237n53

Breen, T. H., xvii, xviii, 169–70, 172, 197, 225n5, 255n8, 260n2, 261n5, 261n9

Brewer, John, xvii, 255n8

Brewer, Stephen, 159–60, 163, 253–54n50

Brewton (Miles) House (Charleston, South Carolina), *136–37*

Bridges, Charles, 90

broadsides, *151,* 174

Brush, John, 244n90; drinking vessel, *97*

buffets, 139, 143. *See also* cupboards

buildings, dwellings: evolution of "Modern Architecture," 9–10, 81, *144,* 161,

178–80, 181; hierarchy of architectural ornament, *134,* 135, *136–37,* 247n10; Palladian, *136–37;* privacy, 9, *45,* 73, 130–31, *132–34;* public entertainment spaces, 130–31, *132–34,* 138, *140–41, 149,* 177, *189;* rooms/chambers by name (*see* ballrooms; bedchambers; card/game rooms; cellars/storerooms; closets; dining rooms; drawing/ withdrawing rooms; dressing rooms; en suite: suites of rooms; entertaining rooms; galleries; garrets; halls; kitchens; parlors; passages; "studies"); rooms, personalized, 62; rooms identified by color, 102, *132,* 135, 248n15; vernacular, 7, 66, *68–69,* 130–31, *132–34,* 135, 161, *178–80,* 207n12, 215n44, 224n35, 247n11, 252–53n44. *See also* windows

buildings, farm, *22,* 40, 60, 66–67, 68, *70*

buildings, public. *See* taverns and ordinaries; theatergoing; *and specific buildings by name*

buildings, service: dairies; 68, *70;* kitchens, separate, 66, *140–41;* quarters, 29, 66, 117, 119, 127, *140–41,* 174

Bushman, Richard L., xvii, 231n41, 254n55, 259n36, 260n2

Byrd, William, II, 252n36

cabinetmakers, 150, 155, 157; work by, *144–45. See also* carpenters; joiners; tradesmen

Campbell, Colin, 259n30

card/game rooms, 135, *142*

card/game tables, 15, 147

card parties, 16, 187

carpenters, 129, 135, 143. *See also* joiners; tradesmen

Carter, Robert, 95

case furniture, 73–74, *144–45,* 255–56n10. *See also specific case furniture forms by name*

cellars/storerooms, *68–69, 132–33, 140,* 230n30

ceramics revolution, 219n4

chairmakers and -sellers, 102, 155. *See also* tradesmen

chairs, 8, 10, 13, 40, 73, 146, 256n10; absence of, 10, 100, 175; armchairs ("elbow"), 42, 62, 78, 100, 147; cane, 101–2, 125; carved ("wrought"), 72–73; "chair stools," 100; corner, 147; easy, 146–47; export of, 102; highbacked, 101–2; leather-covered, 101, *134,* 210n23; lolling, 147; matched sets of, for dining, 14, 72, 87, 100; in passage or entry, 159; smoking, 147; "Spanish," 101; of state, 74, 189; upholstered/upholstery, 72–73, 87, 100–101; wainscot, 100; "wicker," 72; in withdrawing room, 160. *See also* benches; stools

chandeliers, 173

Chappell, Edward, 247n10

Charles City County, Virginia, artifacts from, *48, 84*

Charleston, South Carolina: African Americans in, 117–18, 185; architecture in, 247n10; goods sold in, 155; hospitality in, *148;* houses in, *136–37;* theater in, 18; travelers' observations on, 118, 185; work of portrait painter in, *156–57*

Chesapeake region: labor in, 29; plantation housing in, 66; rebuilding delayed in, 9; slavery in, 28–29; stores in, 118. *See also* Maryland; Virginia

chests, 10, 40–41, *76–77,* 86, 100, 159,
175, 230n30; chests of drawers, 86–87,
91, 114, *144–45,* 226n9, 229n26,
230n32; chests-on-frame, 85, 114–15;
with locks, 62, 224n36; with mannerist
ornament, 73, 78; for seating, 100, 175

Chippendale, Thomas, *Gentleman and
Cabinet-maker's Director,* 150

cities and towns: citified blacks, 185;
city vs. country, 13, 75, 158, *181,*
239n56; housing in, *136–37,* 139,
144, 148, 149, 161; lifestyles in, 58, 86,
113, 139, 172–74, 186–87, *188–89,*
215n49, 229n26, 239n58; migration
into, 51–52, 238n55; Parisian town
house model, 130; trendsetters in,
15, 112–14, 123, 143, 172–73. *See
also* Annapolis, Maryland; Boston,
Massachusetts; Charleston, South Carolina; Jamestown, Virginia; London,
England; New London, Connecticut;
New York City, New York; Philadelphia, Pennsylvania; Roxbury, Massachusetts; St. Mary's City, Maryland;
Salem, Massachusetts; Williamsburg,
Virginia

civility, arts of, 15, 33–34, 57, 99, 108,
148, 150, *152, 188–89,* 252n36. *See
also* etiquette; politeness

closets, 97, 130, 131, 146

clothespresses, 86, 173

clothing, 11–12, 41, 59, 85–86, 90, 159,
183, 223n24, 253–54n50; buttons,
87, 118–19; fashionable, 58, 113, 147,
163, *188–89;* in France, 215n49; hats,
58–60, 118, 131, 164; livery, 116,
122, 148; and patriotism, xviii; rich
vs. poor, 211n26; seasonable, 86; for
slaves, 116–18, 151; and status, 58–59,

159, 242n75; storage of, 86, 160, 173,
229–30n29; worn by blacks, 116–19,
120, 185, 240n64; worn by Indians,
121, *122,* 164, 242n78. *See also* dress
and dressing; sumptuary laws; wigs

clubs and clubbing 15, *148,* 163; Tuesday
Club, 186, *188–89,* 214n40

coats of arms. *See* heraldry

Cobbett, William, 8, 99, 208n16

cockfighting, 17, *22–23, 24,* 170

comfort, 9–10, 13–14, 92, 130, 138,
168–69, 175; for slaves, 117. *See also*
luxury/luxuries

concerts, 16–17, 187

consumer goods: as clues to use, xxii, 14;
demand for, 4, 25–36; democratizing influence of, 6, 173–76, 201, 204n5; depreciated and replaced, 27; import/export
of, xviii, 13, 80, 88, *97,* 101–2, 234n27;
intrinsic vs. notional value of, 47, 62,
74; newly invented, 81–92, 93–112;
portable, 113, 119, *120,* 121; symbolic
value of, xxii; traditional, 10–12, 38–57;
as visual communicators, xvii, 5, 57, 172.
See also dress and dressing; furniture;
tablewares; toilet preparations

consumer revolution: beginnings of, 36,
57, 71–74, 125–28; consumption prior
to, 9–10, 40–47, *48–50,* 57–59; and
Industrial Revolution, 1–5, 191–93;
preconditions for, 7–8, 25–36; sources
on, xvii–xviii, 205n6, 205–6n7,
211–12n27; study of, 192–93. *See
also* material life, history of; summary
propositions

consumption: and acculturation, 176–77,
178–81; by African Americans, 115–21,
185; and American Revolution, 169–70,
171, 172, 193–97; different from

England: as fashion exporter, 100–102, 125–26, 175; industrialization in, 1–5; living standards and styles in, 11–14, 67, 99, 192–94; migrations at home and abroad, 53–54; preconditions for growth in, 25–28, 169. *See also* London, England

England, late medieval and early modern: craft practices in, 74–75; furnishings in, 40–42, 85, 218–19n4; folk beliefs in, 59; measure of worth in, 41; mobility within, 38–39, 52; rebuilding in, 9, 67; social order in, 42. *See also* animism

en suite, 14, 67, 100, 150, 229n26; dressing furniture, 87, 91; introduced by French, 130; meaning of, 102; suites of rooms, 14, 102, 130, *132–33,* 135, *136–37,* 150, 246n4, 248n15. *See also* furniture; tablewares; tea and tea drinking

entertaining rooms, 130–31, 132, 138, *140,* 146, 246n7

entries. *See* passages

epergnes, 173

etiquette, 7, 126, 155, 158, 176; instruction in, 150, 154–55, 184, 251n35; rules of, 33, 36, 184; at table, 95; at tea, 121, *149,* 155, 249–50n28. *See also* gentility

Everard (Thomas) House and kitchen (Brush-Everard House, Williamsburg, Virginia), *45, 97*

fashion/fashionable, 5, 8, 32–36, 91, *140–42,* 169, 191–93, 196; colonies deriving from England/London, 13, 139, 154, 177, 195, 196, 248n18; defined, 13–14; and emulation, 65, 182–84; English influence on, 154, *156–57,* 177, 253n46; exclusionary, 73; —, but also accessible, 109, 176, 182; and fashion setters, 29, 34, 112–13; French, 197, 245n1; —, and French "perfect ease," 99; and gentility, 57–59; and goods, 15, 26–28, 81, 86–88, *89, 97,* 98–106, *107,* 138, *144–45,* 146, *151,* 155, 174, 210n23, 229n26, 236n41, 249–50n28; and houses, 143, 225n6; as instrument of social control, 183, 186–87, *188–89;* and lifestyle, 14, 57, 78, 129–31, *149;* new vs. old-fashioned, 147, 157, 161–63; onset and timing of, 10, 28, 39, 55, 71, 94, 135; as portable, 112–13, 119, *120,* 121; and slavery, 29, 185; spread of, 26, 28–30, 98, 112–14, 126–27, 158–59, 248n18; and sumptuary laws, 57–59; and travel, 160–65

fiction. *See under* books

Fielding, Henry, 2, 3, 32

Fischer, David Hackett, 194–97, 260n3

fish feasts, 17

Fitzhugh, William, 95, 98, 104, 108, 232n9

folkways: become formalities, 127, 158, 177, *178–81,* 182, 194–97, 213n32; folk art, 253n45; persist, 16–17. *See also* animism; talismans

food and drink, 51–52, 117, 127; French cuisine, 234n29, 235n36; multiple courses of, 15, 98, 103; new, 9, 11, 103–4, 106, 108, 126; —, containers for, *96–97;* traditional, 41, 94–95, 102, 104, 127, 221n13. *See also* books: cookbooks; tablewares; tea and tea drinking

Forman, Benno M., 226n10, 227n14

Fraktur, *House with Six-Bed Garden, 181*

Franklin, Benjamin, 154

Fredericksburg, Virginia, clubs in, 214n40

furniture: design of, 75, *76–77,* 78; ebonized, 73, 91, 101, 102, *144–45,* 229n26; exported, 101–2, 234n27; in medieval England, 40–42, 85, 218–19n4; ornamentation of, 73–74; paintwork on, 73–74; personalized, 60, 62; placement of, 147, *149,* 250n29; suites/sets of, 14, 67, 87, 91, 100–102, 135, 150. *See also* case furniture; mannerism; seat furniture; *and specific furniture forms by name*

furniture makers. *See* tradesmen

galleries, 131, *140–41,* 245–46n4

garrets, *134, 140,* 230n30

gentility, xviii; beginnings and spread of, 67, 123, *132–34;* as coercer, 176–77, *181,* 185–86; as lingua franca, 5, 57, 163–64, 168, 196–97; and leisure, *50,* 146; as performance, 92, 108, 128, 146; regional adaptations of, 135, 155–58, 177; and rules of etiquette, 7, 33, 128; and slavery, 29, 216n58; supersedes precedence, 42. *See also* civility, arts of; instruction: in gentility and politeness; politeness

gentlemen. *See* ladies and gentlemen

gentlemen's bathhouse (Warm Springs, Virginia), *20–21*

gourmets, 103, *107,* 126; imitators of, 118–19, 121, *122,* 164, 184, 186, 222n20; lifestyle of, 10, 82, 86–87, 91, 100–101, 113, 135, *136–37, 148,* 246n8; observed, 13, 66, 103, 139, 155, 159, 161, 195, 244n90; at play, *22–23,* 46, 110, *111,* 146, *188–89;* as trendsetters, 93, 100, 126; at work, *50*

gentry: "by acquisition or descent," 63; "dark gentry" of Charleston, 185; international culture of, xvi, 194–95;

lifestyles of, 101, 103, 108, 131, *132, 140;* their manners, 95, 195

Georgianization, 194

glass cases, 72–73, 94

glassware. *See under* tablewares

goblets, 41, *82,* 108

Godlington Manor (Kent County, Maryland), *44*

Goeree, Willem, *An Introduction to the General Art of Drawing,* 152

"great rebuilding": in American colonies, 9, 173; in Britain, 9

Greene, Jack, 194–97

grooming. *See* dress and dressing; toilet preparations

Gunn, John, *The Theory and Practice of Fingering the Violoncello,* 152

hairstyles, 229n25; worn by blacks, 115–16, *120,* 121, 185

halls, 37, 42, *68–69, 72–73, 107,* 131, *132–34, 136–37, 140–41;* become entertaining/dining rooms, 131, 146, 246n7; furnishings in, 41, 87, 99, 135, 210n23; "summer halls," 131

Hamilton, Dr. Alexander, 186, 188, 214n40, 254n53; *History of the [Ancient and Honorable] Tuesday Club,* 186, *188–89,* 214n40; on luxury, 32–33, 104

Hamilton, Dutchess of, *156*

Harwood, Henry, wares from house site, *105*

Harwood, William, 58, 105

Haulman, Kate, xviii

Hehn-Kershner House (Heidelberg Township, Berks County, Pennsylvania), *178–80*

heraldry, 62, 89, 98, 259n39

Hesselius, Gustavus, 90

Heubner, David, *House with Six-Bed Garden* (Fraktur, attrib.), *181*

Holly Hill (Samuel Harrison House, Anne Arundel County, Maryland), *61,* 143

Holmes, Susannah, *157*

home industries, 28

homesteading, 11–12, 123, 125, 175, 194, 211n25

Horne Point plantation (Dorchester County, Maryland), 238n54

horse races, 15, 17, 170

Hoskins, W. G., 9

house tours, 154

Hunter, Phyllis Whitman, xviii

immigrants, xix, 22, 48, 66, 76, 87, 102, 114, 154, 169, 176; acculturation of, 176, 196, 238n55, 240n61; from Africa, 115; from British Isles, 53–54; from Germany, 176–77, *178–80;* out-migration of, 123–24; psychology of, 125; volume and timing of, 55–56, 243n80. *See also* homesteading

indentured servants. *See under* servants

Indians. *See* Native American(s)

individualism, 60, 62, 224n33

Industrial Revolution, xvi, 1, 205–6n7; origins and preconditions, 2, 5, 8, 11, 27, 192, 204n1; timing, 3–4

industrious revolution, xvii, 26–27. *See also* economic growth

instruction: for cooks and hostesses, 103; at dancing schools, 16; by example, 155; in gentility and politeness, 109–10, *111,* 128, *148, 149,* 155, 251n33; for leisure activities, *152–53;* at singing schools, 17; for tradesmen, 150. *See also* books

inventory studies, probate, xx, 10, 41–41, 63, 104, 126, 138, 198; Bermuda, 140; England and Europe, 11, 211–12n27, 218–19n4, 237n53; and newfangled consumer goods, 85, 87–88, 91, 98, 101, 108, 147; and living standards, 209–10n22; New England, xx, 10, 71, 85, 91, 98, 125, 159–60, 253–54n50; Pennsylvania, 10; room names in, 250n29; southern colonies, 10, 81, 87, 98, 108, 143, 224n35, 229n25, 246n6, 249–50n28; and status symbols, 81; under-representation in, 14, 27, 210n22; wealth groups, 13, 101, 173. *See also* amenities index

Jacksonian era, 173–75

Jaffee, David, xviii

Jamestown, Virginia, 49, 80, 106, 108, 139, 228n18; artifacts from, *82–84, 96, 105;* and fashion, 112, 139. *See also* Virginia

Jefferson, Thomas, 25, 118, 201. *See also* Monticello plantation

jewelry, 41, 59, 87, 90, *156–57,* 174. *See also* beads

Johnson, William, 121, 164, 185

joiners, 73, 75, 86–87, 101, 132, 157; work by, *76–77. See also* cabinetmakers; tradesmen

journeymen, 54

kasten, 230n29

Kentucky, 168

Kershner, Conrad. *See* Hehn-Kershner House

kitchens, *45,* 66, *68–69,* 119, *132–33, 140–41,* 160, *178–79;* utensils in, 15, 40, *107,* 173–74, 219n4, 226n9 labor and labor market: in colonies, 29, 53; in England, 38, 51–52; wages for, 11, 26–27, 51

ladies and gentlemen, xix, 39, 57, 67, 195; cosmopolitan, 12, 94, 159

Lafayette, Marquis de (Gilbert du Motier), 201–2

leisure, 7; commercial, *18–19, 20–21,* 25; informal, 15–16, 72, *148, 149, 152–53;* leisured class, 33, 114, 146, 177, 191; traditional, *22–23, 24. See also* assemblies; balls; card parties; clubs and clubbing; cockfighting; concerts; fish feasts; horse races; house tours; public baths; punch/wine parties; tea and tea drinking; theater-going; visiting

Lely, Sir Peter (or school of), Wetenhall portraits, *89*

libraries, 16, 154

lithography, 174

livery, 116, *122, 148*

London, England: migration into, 26, 39, 52; population of, 52; as tastemaker, 36, 53, *97, 99–*101, 103, *107,* 112, 139, *156;* tradesmen in or trained in, 101–2, 132, 139

looking glasses/mirrors, 85, 87–88, 91, 102, 136, 159–60, 229n25, 256n10. *See also* toilet preparations

Lowndes, Sarah Park, *157*

luxury/luxuries, xviii, 1–7, 10, 28–29, 65, 169–70, 193; "beneficial luxury," 26; debate, 31–33, 190; and household goods, 71, 104, 135; and social structure, 26, 186; spread of, 175; in towns, 113, 244n92; and U.S. 1815 property tax, 173, 255–56n10

Lynch, Elizabeth Allston, *156*

Maine, 124; artifact from, *48*

Malbone Hall (Capt. Godfrey Malbone House, Newport vicinity, Rhode Island), 162, 254n53

Manigault, Peter, *148,* 155

mannerism, 74–75, 78, 226–27n11, 227n13; art theory of, 88; theatricality of, 227n15

manners and polite behavior: American-style, 158–59, 187; boorish, *24,* 95; etiquette's paradox, 155, 158; Fielding on, 2–3; paragons of, 154–55, 186, *188–89;* at table, 95, 99, 104, 109–10, *111, 148. See also* books; etiquette; instruction: in gentility and politeness

maps, 113, 240n59

markets and marketplace, 1–2, 4–7, 38, 95, 190; and American Revolution, 169–72; export market, 5, 29, *48,* 101–2, 234n27; growth of, 30, 59–60, 75, 106, 108, 173–75, 183; home market, 2, 5, 7; market production, 27–29, 54, 101–2; and social structure, 26, 244n92; viable size, 17; and women, 27, *171,* 173–74. *See also* book trade; labor and labor market; shopping and shoppers

Markham, Francis, 63

Maryland: artifacts from, *44, 49, 82;* economy, 28; inventory studies of, xx, 87, 113–14, 240n59; living standards in, 10, 209–10n22; migration from Virginia, 124. *See also* Annapolis, Maryland; Cornwaleys, Thomas; Godlington Manor; Holly Hill; Horne Point plantation; portraits: of Sir Thomas and Lady Elizabeth Wetenhall; St. Mary's City, Maryland; U.S. 1815 property tax

Massachusetts: inventory studies of, 71, 125; living standards in, 217n59; settlement and economy, 114; sumptuary laws in, 58. *See also* Barnard (Parson) House; Boston, Massachusetts; Brewer, Stephen; Cushing (Daniel, Sr.) House and farmstead; Searle/Dennis workshop; Turner (John, Sr.) House; U.S. 1815 property tax; Weld, John

mass production, xix, 2, 75, 94, 101, 183, 190–92

material life, history of, xxii–xxiii, 5; author's working assumptions, 79, 198–99, 227n16, 252–53n44, 253n45; evidence for, 197–99, 261n13; as narrative, 197–202; relevance of, 199–202; study of, 192–93. *See also* summary propositions

Mathews Manor (Samuel Mathews House, Denbigh vicinity, Warwick County, Virginia), *107*

Mayr, Christian, painting by, *24*

McKendrick, Neil, xvii, 30

mechanics. *See* tradesmen

merchants, xviii; and American Revolution, 169; charlatans (Barbados), 259n39; in Chesapeake, 28; as fashion setters, 85, 99–100, 114, 162, 186, 229n26; as town dwellers, 114; as travelers, 113, 163. *See also* Birket, James

middle class, xix, 7, 13, 15–16, 86, 101, 124, 138, 173, 177, 259n36

Middle Colonies, 29, 247n11

miniaturists. *See* painters and portraitists

mirrors. *See* looking glasses/mirrors; toilet preparations

modernization model, 16, 34, 218n70

Mohawk Valley trade route, 121, 164

monteiths and wine coolers. *See under* tablewares

Montgomery, Richard, 169

Monticello plantation (Albemarle County, Virginia), 118

Moseley, William, 155

Mount Vernon plantation (Fairfax County, Virginia), 119

Mulberry Row. *See* Monticello plantation

music and music-making: hybrid American folk music, 16–17; instruction books, *152–53*; musical instruments, 16, *120*, 143, 256n10; music rooms, *141–42*; sheet music, 15–16

Native American(s), xix; artifacts by or traded to, *49, 97*; assimilation, 121, 185–86; body paint, 164; clothing, 121, *122*, 164, 242n78; mobility, 123, 165

Navigation Acts, 113

New England, 102, 131, 217n59; and consumption, 175, 217n59; farms in, 66, *68–70*; inventory studies of, xx, 85–87, 146; settlement and economy, 9, 29, 53, 114, 123–24, 185–86; travelers' observations on, 32–33, 161–63. *See also* Boston, Massachusetts; Maine; Massachusetts; New Hampshire; Vermont

New Hampshire, 175

New London, Connecticut, traveler's observations on, 163

newspapers, 15, 16, 32, 116, 125, 154, 174, 187, 250n29

New York, colony of: and furniture trade, 102; migration into, 176, 178; and Mohawk Valley trade route, 121, 122, 164; traveler's observations on, 32–33

New York City, New York, as tastemaker, 112

non-importation. *See* boycotts

North America: immigration to, xix, 43, 53–55, 66, 75, 196; living standard and styles, 9, 11, 17, 26, 57, 125, 170, 184, 187, 192–93; movement within, 123–25, 168

North Andover, Massachusetts, Parson Barnard House, 249n22

North Carolina: patriotic women of Edenton, *171;* population of, 123; settlement of, 54, 176; traveler's observations on, 54. *See also* backcountry

novels. *See* books: fiction

Pain, William, 154

painters and portraitists, 61, 154, 187, 259n39. *See also* Bridges, Charles; Hesselius, Gustavus; Lely, Sir Peter (or school of); Mayr, Christian; Pelham, Peter; Smibert, John; Theüs, Jeremiah

paintings, *7, 24, 61, 78,* 95, 199; art of painting, *152. See also* furniture: ebonized; portraits

parlors, 14, 61, *68–69,* 92, 130, *140–42,* 143, 146, *149,* 150, 178, 184, 246n4; for dining, 94, 100–101, 146; formal, 131–35, *136–37,* 139–43; furnishings in, 71–74, 87, 102, 135, 160, 210n23, 226n7, 229n26, 233n16; parlor chambers, 88, 130, *132–34,* 143; and privacy, 73, 78; as sleeping rooms, 71–74

passages, 9, 131, *136–37, 140–42,* 159, *188–89,* 246n6; become saloons, 131

pastimes. *See* leisure

patent medicines, 174

pattern books. *See under* books

pearlware, 119

Peck, Linda Levy, xviii, 219n5

peddlers, 174–75

Pelham, Peter, 90

Pennsylvania: homesteading in, 211n25; houses in, *178–80, 181;* inventory studies of, 10; population of, 124; settlement and economy, 53–54, 124, 176; traveler's observations on, 176–77. *See also* immigrants; Philadelphia, Pennsylvania

performance: as contests, 94, 187; defined, 94; and mannerist theatricality, 227n15; as theater, 91–92, 102, 127–28, 143

Pettus, Thomas, 106, 236n40

pewter, 33, 62, 80, 106, 159; and living standards, 104, 108, 236n41

Philadelphia, Pennsylvania: and American taste, 158; craftsmen in, 102, 138; houses in, 138, 143, *149,* 247n10; trendsetters in, 85, 112, 147

Plumb, J. H., xvii, 15, 28, 31

politeness, 33, 159, 163, 185. *See also* civility, arts of

poor, 13, 38, 52, 168, 259n36; "best poor man's country," xxii, 125, 169; compared to rich, 10, 33, 51, 147, 211n26; lifestyle of, 10, 14, 33, 36, 40, 41, 126–27; and luxury, 32, 218n69

porcelain, 80, *96–97,* 119, 235–36n40, 237n49, 249–50n28; fireplace tiles, 139. *See also under* tablewares

portraits, 15, 88; of Charleston gentlewomen, *156–57;* conventions, 88, *89,* 90; of estates/houses, *61, 144–45, 181;* group portrait of slaves, *120;* of King Hendrick (Hendrick Theyanoguin), *122;* and mannerism, 88; print sources, *156–57;* of public figures, 230–31n38; of Sir Thomas and Lady Elizabeth Wetenhall, *89. See also* painters and portraitists posset pots, 106, 250n28. *See also* tablewares: beverage containers

potters, 75, 106, 108–9, 127, 221n13; vessels by, *48–49*

precedence, 98–100; and clothing, 59; versus rank, 42; superseded by gentility, 42, 51, *73–74*, 79–80

printers, 16, 75, 103, 150, 174. *See also* booksellers; tradesmen

prints, 95, *156*

privacy. *See under* buildings, dwellings

public baths, 16, 20–21

punch/wine parties, 96, 171

Rameau, Pierre, *The Dancing Master; or, The Art of Dancing Explained,* 153

rank. *See* precedence

Rawlins, Thomas, 154

reading, 15; "reading revolution," 251n33. *See also* books

reception rooms. *See* passages

recreation. *See* leisure

recreational travel, 15

regionalism and local styles, 12–13, 30, *76,* 115, 129, 135, 155, 158–59, 177, 182, 204n5, 247n11, 252–53n44. *See also* folkways; immigrants: from Germany

reputation: abroad, 55–56, 63, 78, 110, 114, 124–25, 146, 160–65, 191; among blacks, 115–19, 121; and furnishings, 40–42; local, 25, 38–40, 47, 114

revolution in manners. *See* manners and polite behavior

Rose, John, *The Old Plantation,* 120

Roupell, George, *Mr. Peter Manigault and His Friends,* 148

Roxbury, Massachusetts, 71–74, 85, 94, 159–61,163

Rush, Benjamin, 158

St. Mary's City, Maryland, *22,* 80, 235n40; artifacts from, *49, 82;* and fashion, 112, 139

Salem, Massachusetts, xviii, 130–31; John Turner House, *132–34*

salvers, 98, 159, 232n8

sash windows, *132–33,* 139, *142, 143, 144,* 249n21

Sayle (William) House, Smith's Parish, Bermuda, *140*

schools: "American and republican school of politeness," 159; dancing, 16; singing, 17. *See also* instruction

Searle/Dennis workshop (Ipswich, Massachusetts), work by, *76–77*

seat furniture, 42, 68, 72, 74, 94, 100, 113, 146. *See also specific seating furniture forms by name*

servants: as consumers, 59; and household economy, 27; house slaves, 116, *171;* indentured, 29, 54, 66, 224n36; livery for, 116, *122, 148;* lodging for, 66, *134, 140;* as migrants, 38, 124, 240n61

settees, 173

Seven Years' War, 170

Sewell, Samuel, 88

Shammas, Carole, xvii, 239n57

Shippen (William) House (Philadelphia, Pennsylvania), *149*

shopping and shoppers, 172–74, 183. *See also* markets and marketplace

sideboards, 174

sign painters. *See* painters and portraitists

silver, 80, 106; and clothing, 58; investment in plate, 10, 40–41, 62, 74, 95, 98; personalized, 62; skillets, *107;* and sumptuary laws, 58; tinned to look like, *84;* tipped with, 80, 228n19. *See also* clothing: buttons; tablewares: Fitzhugh's silver service

slave, as metaphor, 27, 170, *171*

slaves and slavery, xix, 5, 27, 28, 29, 43, 54, 66, 115, 116, 117, 118, 119, *120,* 121, 123, 127, 173, 174, 185, 216n58, 224n36, 241n65. *See also under* African American(s); Chesapeake region; consumption; fashion/fashionable; gentility; servants

slipcovers, 87

Smibert, John, 90

Smith, Adam, *The Wealth of Nations,* 26, 191–92

Smith, Woodruff, xvii

social order, 7, 14, 34, 93, 98, 186–87, 192; in America, "best poor man's country," xxii, 46–47, 50, 71, 114, 125, 168–73, 182, 225n5; in England, 26, 33–34, 38–40, 57, 169; traditional, 14, 38, 46–47, 50, 98

South Carolina, xx, 29, 118, *120;* artifact from, *49. See also* Charleston, South Carolina

sports, 15–17. *See also* leisure

Stamp Act, 170

standards of living: in American colonies, 9–14, 25, 71, 104, 127, 192, 200–201, 217n59; Black Death, effects on, 11; in England and northern Europe, 11–12, 25, 71, 127, 199, 211–12n27, 213n31, 218–19n4, 242n79; living standards vs. lifestyles vs. fashions/modes, 12–13. *See also* economic growth; homesteading; inventory studies, probate

stands, 87

stocking knitting industry, 60

stools, 10, 40–42, 72–73, 100–101, 146, 220n12

stores and storekeepers, 16, 28, 160, 163, 168–70; advice to storekeepers, 168; African American customers, 118, 127, 185; city vs. country stores, 239n56; stock-in-trade, 28, *151,* 238n56; women shoppers in Jacksonian era, 174–75

Stubbes, Phillip, 58, 60

"studies," 131

summary propositions, xxi–xxii, 8–9; 1st, 12; 2nd, 25; 3rd, 31; 4th, 34; 5th, 35 36; corollaries, 176, 187

sumptuary laws, 57–59, 183, 193, 211n26. *See also* clothing; dress and dressing

tables: coverings, 98; dining, 98–110; dressing, 85–86, 102; gaming, 15, 113, 147; known by location, 147, 250n29; and manners, 95; seating at, 100–101, 232–33n11; setting of, 103, *111;* as social venues, 94–95, 98–102, 109–10, *111;* tabletop shapes, 99–100, 159; tea, 126, 135, 147, *149,* 155, 159, 173

tablewares: beverage containers, 41, *48–49, 50, 82–83,* 94–95, *96–97,* 104, 108, 146, 249–50n28, 256n10; cutlery, 14, 81, *84,* 98, 104, 108–9, 126, 237n53; dish rings, 106; Fitzhugh's silver service, 95, 98, 108, 232n9; flatware (also plates, platters, and serving dishes), 80–81, 98, 104, *105,* 106, 108–10, *111,* 127, 159, 244n90; fruit plates, *111,* 106; glassware, 14, 80–81, *82,* 94–95, *96,* 98, 108, 159, 232nn3–4; hollowware (also bowls, dishes, and trenchers), 104, 106, 127, 168; individual place settings, 14, 98, 106; leather (also horn

66, 118, 131, 155, 159, 162; and social communications, 35, 91, 113, 129, 163–65, 168, 176–77, 185, 196. *See also* Birket, James; Hamilton, Dr. Alexander; Jefferson, Thomas; Lafayette, Marquis de; Tocqueville, Alexis de

Turner (John, Sr.) House (Salem, Massachusetts), *132–34*

upholstery and upholsterers, 41, 87, 100–102, 135, 146, 150, 234n23. *See also under* chairs

U.S. 1815 property tax, 173, 255–56n10

Vaughan, William, 59
Veblen, Thorstein, 182
Verdmont (Smith's Parish, Bermuda), *140–42*
Vermont, 175
Virginia: artifacts from, *45, 48–49, 82–84, 96–97, 105, 107;* blacks in, 66, 116, 119, 127; economy of, 28–29, 112; inventory studies of, xx, 62, 81, 87–88, 99–100, 108; living standards in, 10, 13, 58, 113; observations on, 10, 66, 95, 103, 119, 131, 143, 162. *See also* Berkeley, Norborne; buildings, dwellings; Douglass (David) Theater; Fitzhugh, William; Jamestown, Virginia; Jefferson, Thomas; Mathews Manor; Native American(s); Warm Springs, Virginia; Washington, George; Williamsburg, Virginia
visiting, 155
visual literacy, xvii, 5, 57, 172
Vries, Jan de, xvi–xvii, xix, 26–27, 31

wainscoting. *See under* architectural finishes
wall hangings ("pentyt clothes"), 41

wallpaper. *See under* architectural finishes
Warm Springs, Virginia, bathhouse, *20–21*
Washington, George, 13, 119, 252n36. *See also* Mount Vernon plantation
Watson, John Fanning, 147, 150
Weatherill, Lorna, xvii, 239n58, 244n92, 256n12
weavers, 75. *See also* tradesmen
Wedgwood, Josiah, 60
Weems, Parson Mason, 25
Weld, John, 71–74, 78, 85, 94, 98, 160, 226n9, 253 54n50
Westerwald stoneware, *83*
Westwood Manor (Charles County, Maryland), 228n20
Wetenhall, Thomas and Elizabeth. *See under* portraits
wigs, *171*
Williamsburg, Virginia: blood sports in, *23;* Cherokee delegation to, 164; clubs in, 214n40; foreign-born residents in, 238n55; stores in, *151,* 239n56; theater in, *18–19;* trendsetters in, *96–97*
windows, 162, *180,* 254n53; casements to sash, *132–33, 142,* 143, *144–45*
women, xviii; and African American dress, 116–18, *120,* 185; and African American matriarchs, 119, 174; as consumers, 78–79, 85, 127, 192, 256n12; in the economy, 26–27, 51–52, 125; and emulation, 32–33; and gentility, 33, 42, 72, 88, *89,* 158, 162–63; indentured, 114; and leisure activities, 15–17, 20; politicized, 170, *171;* as shoppers, 174–75; at table, 103, 110, 233n11. *See also* Americans; consumption; dress and dressing; economic growth; industrious revolution; ladies and gentlemen; markets and marketplace; portraits